The Captain

THE CAPTAIN

The Life and Times of Simon Raven

Michael Barber

Duckworth

For Susanna

First published in 1996 by
Gerald Duckworth & Co. Ltd.
The Old Piano Factory
48 Hoxton Square, London N1 6PB
Tel: 0171 729 5986
Fax: 0171 729 0015

A catalogue record for this book is available from the British Library

ISBN 0 7156 2707 4

Typeset by Ray Davies
Printed in Great Britain by
Redwood Books Ltd, Trowbridge

PREFACE

Many people have helped me with *The Captain*, but I am particularly grateful to Lord Annan, who read, and where necessary, amended the King's chapters; Mrs Ruth Paysant, Simon's aunt, whose recollections of her father and of her sister and brother-in-law were invaluable; and Lt. Col. J.D. Whitamore, late of the KSLI, who very generously put 30 years' worth of letters and postcards from Simon at my disposal.

I am also indebted to the following for their time and trouble:

Anthony Blond, Desmond Briggs, Bruce Broker, Alan Caiger-Smith, Conrad Dehn, Robin Espley, Jack Hands, Francis Haskell, Andrew McCall, the late Dickie Muir, Lord Prior, Lord Rees-Mogg, Norman Routledge, Martin Shuttleworth, Michael Strevens, Michael Webb.

The late Sir Kingsley Amis, John Barton, Diana Baring, Peter Budden, Nina Bawden, Leo Cooper, Peter Dickinson, Peter Dixon, David Evers, Laurence Harbottle, Kenneth Harrison, Lady Kilmarnock, Tim Lewis, Nickie Lund, Ivan Lynch, Christopher Moorsom, Joanna Murray, John Ogden, Peter Parker, Frances Partridge, Lennox Phillips, Sir Oliver Popplewell, Philippa Pullar, Frederic Raphael, Brian Rees, Stella Richman, John Selby, Julian Slade, Charles Sprawson, Julian Spurrier, Elizabeth de Stroumillo, Dyker Thew, Lord Thomas, Margaret Viner, Michael Walters, Sydney Wilkinson, Patricia Woods.

The Rev. H.C. Alexander, Grace Arrowsmith, J.G. Ballard, Martin Blake, May Buckingham, John Budden, John Calder, John Carson, Anne-Marie Casey, Isobel Colegate, Major-General Simon Cooper, Bruce Critchley, the late Rodney Dennys, John Drewett, Sir George Engle, Nick Furbank, Philip Gaskell, Peter Green, Tom Hartman, Eric Hobsbawm, Francis King, Angus Mackay, Jeremy Paxman, George Plimpton, Anthony Powell, Dr David Saunders, John Raven, Susan Raven, Alan Ross, George Rylands, Paul Spurrier, Dick Taverne, Gore Vidal, Katharine Whitehorn.

My research involved visits to King's College, Cambridge, where I received every assistance from the Modern Archivist, Ms Jackie Cox; and to Charterhouse, where Dame Shirley Corke was equally obliging. I must also thank the Charterhouse Librarian, Mrs Ann Wheeler, who lent a sympathetic ear to my telephone enquiries; and her colleague, Mr Brian Souter, who reproduced for me a photograph of the 1945 school Cricket XI.

Until he moved on, Giles Gordon was my agent; my thanks to him and his successor at Shiel Land, Robert Kirby, for their enthusiasm. In this context I must also pay tribute to Alan Watkins, at whose suggestion Giles offered *The Captain* to Colin Haycraft. One lunch with Colin was enough to convince me that my book would be in safe hands at Duckworth, and I am sad indeed that he never had a chance to read it all. Luckily his successor, Robin Baird-Smith, can see the point of Simon as well; and he and my meticulous editor, Deborah Blake, have been every bit as supportive as I could have hoped.

It was through writing for radio that I developed a style, and I now offer long overdue thanks to Gordon Hutchings and Alastair Wallace-Norton, late of Radio 4 and the BBC World Service respectively, for the many broadcasting opportunities they afforded me. My neighbour David Elliott also deserves a mention for his patient instruction in the mysteries of Microsoft Word.

Finally, there are two people without whom I could never have begun *The Captain*, let alone finished it. One is Simon himself, whose candour and cooperation ought, I believe, to make me the envy of biographers everywhere. The other is my beloved wife Susanna, to whom I dedicate this book.

M.B.

Acknowledgements

For permission to reproduce excerpts from their publications I am grateful to the editors and publishers of the *Spectator*, the *Times Literary Supplement* and the *London Magazine*. I am also grateful to BBC Magazines for permission to quote from the *Listener*; to Major J.H.H. Yorke MBE, Regimental County Secretary, for permission to quote from the KSLI *Regimental Journal*, and to the Governors of Charterhouse for permission to quote from the *Carthusian* and from the minutes of the Charterhouse Shakespeare Society. Permission to include part of a review first published in the *Observer* was granted on payment of a fee.

I should also like to thank the following: Frances Partridge, for permission to reproduce an unedited diary extract; Peter Porter and Oxford University Press for permission to reproduce *The World of Simon Raven*; Richard Hoggart and Chatto & Windus for permission to reproduce a short extract from *An Imagined Life*; Francis King and King's College, Cambridge, for permission to quote from a letter of J.R. Ackerley to E.M. Forster; Peters, Fraser and Dunlop and the estate of Evelyn Waugh for permission to quote from *Put Out More Flags*; Rogers, Coleridge and White and the estate of Cyril Connolly for permission to quote from *The Fate of an Elizabethan* and from Connolly's tribute to Maurice Bowra; Jonathan Clowes Ltd and the Kingsley Amis Estate for permission to reproduce, on payment of a fee, 6 lines from *An Ever-Fixed Mark* and 7 lines from *Ode to Me*, © 1963, 1979 Kingsley Amis.

INTRODUCTION

Among Simon Raven's contemporaries at Charterhouse was the writer and broadcaster Gerald Priestland. On learning about this book, Priestland commented,

> So Simon has a biographer already? I wouldn't have thought it possible until he – and a good many people he knew – were safely underground with clay in their mouths ... What are you going to call it? 'Brimstone and Treacle'?

Regrettably, I was never to meet Priestland, who died very shortly afterwards. But his reaction testifies to the Luciferian aura surrounding Simon since he was a schoolboy, and which also hovers over his books. In metropolitan circles his name is synonymous with delinquency in high places. For instance when Alan Clark's *Diaries* were published, Craig Brown wrote,

> This blissfully unpleasant book should do much to restore the reputation of Simon Raven; indeed it is almost as if Alan Clark were once Raven's earthly representative at Westminster ...

And at about the same time I recall reading an article on the City fraudster, Raymond Posgate, in which the writer compared him to 'a rather naughty character from an early Simon Raven novel'.

Simon has always encouraged people to think of him as a sinner for whom literature was the only possible salvation:

> For in a literary career there was one unfailing advantage: no degree whatever of moral or social disgrace could disqualify one from practice – and indeed a bad character, if suitably tricked out for presentation, might win one helpful publicity. It wouldn't even matter if one went to prison. The abdication was final; by becoming a writer one bade farewell at once to ethical restraint and to any kind of conventional status in society. (*The English Gentleman*)

Long before he became a writer Simon had 'bade farewell to ethical restraint'. Paradoxically, however, his literary achievements have conferred on him a status that society might otherwise have withheld. If he has never become respectable (a 'dreary middle-class' aspiration), he has certainly earned respect, not least for his protean industry. In 36 years he has written 34 books,[1] over a dozen radio and television plays, innumerable essays and reviews, and television serials of the calibre of *Edward and Mrs Simpson*, *Love in a Cold Climate* and *The Pallisers*. Add to these the many dramatisations that came to nought and you have a formidable body of work.

To what end? The short answer is, personal survival. 'Art for art's sake, money for God's sake' he used to say, particularly in the early days. But if Simon wrote to live – and, if possible, live rather well – he was never in any danger of becoming too popular. 'I've always written for a small audience consisting of people like myself who are well-educated, worldly, sceptical and snobbish (meaning that they rank good taste over bad). And who believe that nobody and nothing is special.'

The sort of reader Simon had in mind would appreciate an anecdote like this:

> Some years ago I had the rather bizarre experience of dining with three newly married friends, all of whom were homosexual, and their three wives. Two of my friends had married to procure social or professional respectability; one, our host, because he wanted an heir. Throughout dinner there was a great deal of billing and cooing from the first two, and after the women had left us they started a smug discussion about the unequalled benefits and virtues of the married state. None of this was pleasing to our host, a forthright character who had preserved his honesty; and eventually, when the conversation reached a crescendo of hypocrisy and silliness, he leaned across the table and said, 'Well now, you chaps. What are you doing these days about *boys*?' I never saw two men more utterly put out. (*Spectator*, 9.9.66)

I have often wondered whether it was really Simon, and not the host, who so discomfited the other two. It would have been typical of a 'private nuisance', which is how he once described himself. When, for instance, a 'vehement anti-monarchist' friend of his went to Buckingham Palace to receive the CBE, Simon said he supposed she would 'manage a curtsey on *this* occasion'. And when a don's wife told him she suspected an undergraduate of taking an unhealthy interest in her thirteen-year-old son, he said, 'Don't worry, dear. With legs like his he has nothing to fear.' ('And he didn't!')

Simon's relish for 'the unacceptable truth' is one of the things I have

[1] I am indebted to the late Sir Kingsley Amis for alerting me to the 'infernal bloody cheek' of one reviewer – not himself a novelist – who in 1991 wrote that Simon had 'managed to turn out' some two dozen novels.

always liked about him. But it was his style that grabbed me in the first place. From the moment, some 34 years ago, that I opened *The Feathers of Death*, I was hooked. Here, I remember thinking, is a writer I shall never tire of. Nor have I. Indeed one of the pleasures of writing this book has been the amount of Simon's work that I have had to re-read, particularly his essays and reviews. 'What a pity Simon no longer reviews,' said a number of his friends. I agree. But knowing what a chore it became – and an ill-paid chore, at that – I am also pleased that he is long since quit of it.

I first met Simon in 1971, and discovered immediately that the style was the man. Like Evelyn Waugh he had the gift of thinking in perfect sentences, so that when he spoke you could almost hear the semi-colons. At the time I took this for granted; it was only after I had interviewed several other writers that I realised how rare such facility with words was.

The key to Simon's style, and thus to Simon himself, lies in his education. He was a Classical scholar at a time when proficiency in the Classics was still, just, regarded as the pinnacle of sixth-form achievement. As his old friend, Noel Annan, has noted,

> The verbal dexterity required, the accuracy of mind, and the response to words was prodigious .... At the age of twelve a boy would be expected to recognise zeugma, hendiadys, litotes, oxymoron and hysteronproteron, and to distinguish iambics from alcaics and alexandrines from hexameters or hendecasyllabic couplets. (*London Review of Books*, 4.3.82)

Thus equipped, he could grapple with what Simon called 'the essence of the thing: translating this way and that, from Latin and Greek into English, and from English into Latin and Greek.' Some idea of what this might entail is given by the Classical historian, Peter Green, three years senior to Simon at Charterhouse. A future winner of the blue-riband Craven scholarship, Green had been 'precociously elevated' to the Classical Sixth shortly after his sixteenth birthday. Even so he took a very deep breath when, during his first week there,

> [the form-master] produced Duff's text of Juvenal's third and tenth *Satires*, accompanied by cyclostyled copies of Samuel Johnson's imitations, *London* and *The Vanity of Human Wishes*, and set us to translate the Latin at sight while committing the English to memory by way of what he termed 'a little prep'. (*Juvenal Revisited*)

Green denounced this imposition as 'cruel and unusual punishment', but Simon thought the constant translation Classicists did was 'very worthwhile, if only because you had to be certain what the English meant before you could hope to find the nearest equivalent in Greek or Latin, and vice-versa. So you learnt to be precise, and if necessary, flexible, in your use of language.'

You also, if you were curious as well as clever, learnt a few things that were *not* in the syllabus. 'Take the question of pleasure. This, one was taught, was not exactly wrong but was certainly not quite right. Discomfort, self-denial, tedious forms of duty – these were what counted, particularly in time of war, which was when I was at school. But most Latin and Greek poets, it soon became apparent, relished pleasure, and wrote of it as something, possibly the only thing, of undoubted value by and for itself. I remember how excited I was by these verses of Catullus:

Vivamus, mea Lesbia, atque amemus,
Rumoresque senum severiorum
Omnes unius aestimemus assis.
Soles occidere et redire possunt:
Nobis cum semel occidit brevis lux
Nox est perpetua una dormienda.

Come, Lesbia, let us live and love
And at a farthing's worth we'll prove
The sour talk of crabbed old men.
The suns which set can rise again:
But we, once set is our brief light,
Must sleep an everlasting night.

'In other words, "We aren't here for long, and when we do go, that's that. Finish. So for God's sake, enjoy yourself *now* – and sod anyone who tries to stop you." A robust pagan philosophy which I have followed, where possible, these past fifty years.'

Simon did, however, allow that in certain circumstances it is better to give pleasure than to receive: 'For a writer, this is a condition of earning his bread.' In one of his earliest reviews he rebuked Rex Warner for 'carefully advertising' his new novel 'as an entertainment pure and simple, written for no serious reason'.

> What more essential reason one could have for writing than a wish to entertain I have no idea.

In fact there was usually a moral message to Simon's work as well, if only the notion that we should all walk carefully under the gods. Having ignored this himself, and suffered accordingly, he never let his readers forget that nemesis follows hubris as surely as night follows day.

*

After my first meeting with him in 1971 I kept a watching brief on Simon, reviewing his books and twice interviewing him for radio. But it was not until I wrote and presented a radio profile of him in 1987 that the idea for this book first surfaced, though I was careful to keep it under my hat until an opportune moment arose. This did not occur for another four years, and a further two were to elapse before I could set to work. Throughout, Simon could not have been more helpful. From time to time we would meet for a long chat; otherwise communication was by telephone or, preferably, post-card (the pile at my side is 4" high).

Simon has a theory that practically nobody, however renowned or accomplished, is content with what he is; and that given half a chance, most people will promote a private vision of themselves which does not accord with the facts. He is not free from this vanity himself; but being Simon, he has made a joke of it. Hence 'Captain' Raven, as he is listed in the King's College Register, and as he was known, until quite recently, to the hoteliers, taxi-drivers and tradespeople of Deal.[2]

'Technically speaking' (a phrase that will recur in this narrative) Simon is entitled to call himself Captain Raven. But by doing so he invites comparison with Captain Grimes, Evelyn Waugh's discredited 'public school man'. That this is deliberate I have no doubt. Even today his friends sometimes refer to him as 'the Captain'.

Which brings me to my title. Had it not been used before[3] I would have chosen 'The Captain's Innings'. I rejected 'Dirty Story' for the same reason. Leo Cooper, at whose urging I first picked up my pen, said why not simply 'The Captain'? To begin with I thought this rather terse. Then, in a second-hand bookshop, I chanced upon an Edwardian annual 'for boys and old boys'. It was called *The Captain*, an epiphany I have gratefully accepted.

[2] In much the same spirit he added MA after his name and rank in captions to regimental photos.

[3] By Godfrey Smith, in his profile of Simon in the *Sunday Times* colour magazine.

CHAPTER ONE

My background was middle-class, for which read respectable, prying, puritanical, penny-pinching, joyless.

Simon Raven, in conversation with his biographer

Simon Arthur Noel Raven was born on December 28 1927. He was named Arthur after his father and Noel because his mother had been a Miss Christmas. It is tempting to speculate on what they might have called him had he been born three days earlier. As it was, his mother hung in Simon's night nursery 'a soppy picture of gentle Jesus blessing and caressing a bevy of wet little children'. This disturbed him, not because it was in such bad taste, but because there was something about the shroud Christ wore that gave him the horrors. Later he would formulate more cogent arguments against Christianity, but the seeds of his scepticism were sown in the night nursery.

Rather more auspiciously, Simon's birth coincided with news from Johannesburg of England's ten wicket victory over South Africa. This was due in large part to a career-best performance by the Leicestershire all-rounder, George Geary, who took seven for 70 in the first innings and five for 60 in the second. Geary later became coach at Charterhouse, for whose First XI Simon played in 1945 with Peter May, Oliver Popplewell and James Prior.

Arthur Raven styled himself 'Gentleman' in *Kelly's Directory*. Insofar as he had been educated at Repton and Cambridge, held a temporary commission during the Great War, and did not need to earn his living, this was a plausible conceit. But 'Rentier' would have been more accurate, for Arthur lived off his share of the fortune his father, William Raven, had amassed in making socks. Since Simon owed his privileged upbringing to this enterprising Victorian and may also have inherited from him his capacity for hard work, we ought to consider what is known of his life and achievements.

At his death in 1914 aged 82 William Raven was hailed by the Leicester press as one of a select band who had grown up with the city and seized the opportunities it presented to make their way in the world. He began his working life as a humble 'stockinger' operating a primitive knitting frame and rose to become owner of one of the largest hosiery works in the country, employing over a thousand hands. Then, as now, self-made men were not noted for their compassion. But his obituarists recorded that in addition to being a considerate employer and a generous contributor to local charities, William Raven took the workers' side in politics and was a convinced Radical. Appointed to the local Bench without his knowledge he refused to sit on the grounds that having been 'one of the people', he would not be a party to sending anyone to gaol. It was also rumoured in the family that he had turned down a knighthood. If true, this underlines his integrity, since at that time wealthy men were so eager for titles that both political parties operated a discreet but thriving traffic in honours.

William Raven married twice. Nothing is known of his first wife except that she died without issue. In 1882, aged 50, he married 20-year-old Annie Pole, one of his millhands. She bore him five children (not ten, as Simon thought), the youngest of whom by several years was Arthur, born 1898. By now the Ravens were firmly established 'at the Top', to borrow John Braine's phrase. Portland House, Knighton, where Arthur grew up, was a large suburban mansion set in ample grounds which subsequently became Leicester High School for Girls. The retinue of servants included a nursemaid, in whose charge Arthur, like all well-to-do little Edwardians, spent most of his time. Prep school must have come as a nasty shock, particularly to a boy with no aptitude for team games. Not that this deterred his mother – 'she knew no better, poor dear' observed Simon – from insisting that he be tried for the First XI – 'imagine the horror!'

Of course it ended in tears. Arthur made 0, was hit all over the ground, and dropped a sitter. 'Perhaps,' Simon concluded, 'this explains everything.'

At thirteen Arthur followed his two elder brothers to Repton, in those days second to none as a cricket school. Simon thought his father must have been bullied, so rarely did he mention the place. But in view of the fact that he returned to teach at Repton for a couple of terms before going up to Cambridge I think this is unlikely. A more probable reason is that in his four-and-a-half years there he achieved absolutely nothing: no prizes, no colours, no offices – not even the rank of Lance-Corporal in the OTC. When he left in December 1916 all the *Reptonian* recorded beside his name in its Valete column was the term he arrived. Small wonder that his sons never forgave him for belittling their achievements, which in Simon's case were considerable.

Arthur was commissioned into the Royal Naval Air Service in May 1917. Why he chose to become a pilot is a mystery. Perhaps he saw flying as a way of achieving the distinction that had eluded him at school. Alternatively he may have reasoned that piloting a seaplane, although undoubtedly perilous, was less likely to consign him to the Repton Roll of Honour than serving as a subaltern on the Western Front. In the event he had at least one close shave when the crane that was hoisting his seaplane out over the water dropped it, whereupon Arthur and his machine rapidly sank. But as Simon commented, 'He was not easy to kill, my father, and after a time he bobbed up.'

(Shortly after this book went into proof I was introduced to a golfing acquaintance of Arther Raven who gave a different account of his ordeal. Arthur, he claimed, was shot down – at any rate forced to ditch. As the sea rose to meet him he thought, 'This is a nuisance. This is the end,' a formula so appealing to my informant and his family that in moments of crisis they used it themselves.)

Late in life Arthur boasted to a young neighbour of his in Hunstanton that he had inherited three fortunes. Where two of them came from is unclear, if indeed they ever existed. But inherit one fortune he certainly did, thanks to his family's reluctance to go on making socks. In November 1919 the business was sold, though it continued to trade as W. Raven & Co until 1971. According to Simon, Arthur's share of the proceeds was £100,000, approximately £2,500,000 in today's money. This enabled him to do pretty much as he pleased for the next 49 years, to the detriment of his character and the discomfiture of his wife and children – or so Simon would maintain.

Arthur decided to complete his education at Cambridge, whose entrance requirements for ex-servicemen were minimal. Arthur, who had reached the Lower Sixth at Repton, was no dunce, but he evidently lacked *savoir-faire*. His first letter of application was addressed to the admissions tutor at 'Keys College'. He had better luck with Queens', and was admitted there in 1920. His arrival was noted in the *Cambridge Old Reptonian Letter*:

> At Queens' Raven, late of the Repton staff, and proportionately dignified, is to be seen in the labs finding the thickness of glass plate.

Which is where we shall leave him for the time being and proceed north to No. 9 Green Street, now occupied by a pub called, appropriately, 'The Volunteer', but in those days the site of Christmas and Son, bakers.

*

In *Before the Cock Crow*, Simon's alter ego, the 'unwholesome' novelist Fielding Gray, gets carried away describing the exploits of his maternal grandfather, 'the Grand Grinder': how he broke the record (and also his arm) winning the East Anglian Cross-Country Championship, 'The Grand Huntingdonshire Grind'; and how during the Boer War he was commissioned in the field – 'like being made a knight in the old days'. In general Fielding is a better guide to Simon's character and motives than his past, but there is just enough truth in what he says here for it to serve as an introduction to Esther Raven's father, Fred Christmas.

While William Raven rose and rose, Fred Christmas marked time: a baker he commenced and a baker he remained. Yet his was certainly the more varied life and ultimately, perhaps, the more fulfilling. He served honourably in three wars, was a notable athlete, an ardent race-goer and the father of two daughters who ran for England and married well.

Fred was born in 1876 and on leaving school joined the family bakery, which supplied many of the University colleges from its premises in Green Street. In his spare time he soldiered with the Suffolk Yeomanry, speed-skated on the fens when they froze and ran cross-country and middle-distance events. A photograph shows him breasting the tape at Fenners with no other runners in sight. This could well have been one of his victories in the 'Ranji' cup, named after its donor, the great cricketer Prince Ranjitsinhji, who had rooms in Cambridge and took a keen interest in local sport. So regularly did Fred win the three mile open handicap race for which the 'Ranji' cup was awarded that he was allowed to keep the trophy. Subsequently it came to rest on the sideboard of his younger daughter, Ruth, who in the early Thirties was the second fastest woman in Britain over three miles.

In 1900 Fred saddled his horse and sailed to South Africa as a Trooper with the Suffolk contingent of the Imperial Yeomanry. Since this eccentric Corps served as mounted infantry, like Martock's Foot in Simon's first novel, *The Feathers of Death*, I think they merit a small digression. They were raised in the wake of 'Black Week', during which the Army's inflexible parade-ground tactics had exposed it to three humiliating defeats at the hands of the free-ranging Boer commandos. Very belatedly the commander-in-chief, General Sir Redvers Buller, recognised the need for mobility. He sent back a telegram requesting 'eight thousand irregulars [who could] shoot as well as possible and ride decently'.

Irregular the Imperial Yeomanry certainly were. For a start, more than half the volunteers were middle-class, with a fair sprinkling of gentry in the ranks. Such was their patriotism that many of these 'gentleman-troopers' kitted themselves out at their own expense, and a few not only found the cost of their passage to South Africa but also donated their pay to charity. Their appearance was unorthodox too, with more than a touch of the Wild West about it. They wore slouch hats in preference to helmets, were armed with rifles rather than sabres, and carried three bandoliers, one slung across each shoulder, the third round the waist.

To begin with the Yeomanry took their orders from the committee of 'influential and patriotic gentlemen' responsible for raising them. But then it was found that private armies could not legally embark on the high seas under the British flag, so not without misgivings – what place did raw amateurs have in a professional Army? – the War Office took them over.

After a farewell dinner at the local Liberal Club presided over by 'Ranji' himself, Fred galloped off to war. Almost exactly a year later, in February 1901, he was back, his soldiering cut short by injury. He described what had happened to the *Cambridge Daily News*:

The Suffolks were acting as bodyguard to Lord Methuen in the

> Zeerust district when we were turned out all in a hurry to act against Commandant Limner. Just as we went round a bend at a gallop the Boers opened fire on us and my horse rolled on me. I was a bit stunned for a moment but another fellow caught my horse and I rejoined the troop. (19.2.01)

But not for long. The fall had burst his left eardrum which became abscessed and after 'two or three operations' he was invalided home with his hearing in that ear permanently impaired. Two months later Fred and the other Cambridge volunteers were made Freemen of the Borough, which honour, he used to say, allowed you to be drunk in the streets as long as you stayed in the gutter. In August he married the girl he left behind, Maude Mary Moden. The following year their elder daughter Esther, Simon's mother, was born.

Despite his injury Fred remained on the roll of the Suffolk Yeomanry, who in common with the rest of the Militia became part of the new Territorial Army in 1907. In August 1914, aged 38, he was mobilised, and the following year was commissioned into the Fife and Forfar Yeomanry. In 1916 he was unlucky enough to be sent to Macedonia, where a forgotten army with neither the resources nor the incentive to do more than stay put, endured the unhealthiest of all climates for campaigning. In summer there was baking heat, dust and swarms of flies; autumn brought the malarial mosquito, and the winters were bitterly cold and damp. Like another Yeomanry officer of mature years, the novelist Dornford Yates, Fred became very ill. He was sent home suffering from dysentery, malaria and colitis. Restored to health, he saw the war out at the Curragh in Ireland and was demobbed as a Captain.

At this point Fred must have thought that he would soldier no more. But twenty years later the bugle sounded and Captain Christmas answered the call. He was promoted to Major and given command of a company of the local Home Guard. Simon, who spent some of his wartime holidays at his grandparents' house, recalled how cross his grandfather had been that on the one occasion his company was called out, Esther's dog bit him so badly he couldn't accompany them. 'We never heard the end of it.'

By now Fred had sold the bakery and retired with Maude to his father's old house, 9 Chesterton Hall Crescent, right opposite Dr and Mrs F.R. Leavis. It's possible the two families knew each other already since Leavis's father had been a Cambridge tradesman and a keen fen skater, while Leavis himself loved cross-country running. At any rate when Simon was thirteen Leavis did him a good turn, as we shall see.

Simon owed his height to the Christmas family and he shared his grandfather's love of the Turf. Otherwise they were very much town and gown. Fred, who died in 1951, would not have been surprised to learn that his 'snobby, funky' grandson kept quiet about him at King's. 'Later I became very proud of him, but in those days I thought he was really rather common. Shame! Shame!'

*

In 1919 a contributor to the *Cambridge Review* who signed himself '*Festina Lente*' smugly observed that thanks to their proctors, 'from the point of view of morality, our two great universities are the cleanest in the world'. Presumably *Festina Lente* thought the proctors deterred tarts, since only in May Week did undergraduates have prolonged contact with women of their own age and class. Nor did they appear to resent this.

> Keep away. You are not wanted here. We are all friends, men content together. We want no female to trouble us,

wrote Rosamund Lehmann of Cambridge then in *Dusty Answer*. No wonder, as Lord Annan has noted, 'a growing number of young upper-middle class Englishmen ... seemed to regard heterosexual relations as a choice between bores and whores'.

But not all undergraduates were hostile to women; Esther admitted as much to Simon. 'She told me she'd known a lot of undergraduates before she met my father, and even hinted that she'd had it off with a few of them.'

An old photo album confirms that Esther was a popular girl. It contains several snaps of her punting and picnicking with young men in College blazers. She can also be seen in a couple of May Ball photos, one of them taken in Trinity Great Court. Not bad for the daughter of the college baker, but then Esther was no dowdy Miss Bun. With her bobbed ash-blonde curls, boyish figure and shapely legs she looked every inch a 'flapper'. Nor did she ever quite lose her Jazz Age gloss. Years later, on meeting her in Cambridge, a friend of Simon's thought that 'although rather tarnished, she belonged to that era like a chromium-plated cocktail shaker'.

Mad about dancing, Esther had originally hoped to take it up professionally; when this fell through she decided to become a children's dancing teacher and spent a year at the Italia Conti School in London before returning to teach in Cambridge. This would have been in about 1923. Two years later, on August 25th 1925, she and Arthur were quietly married at a registry office in Cambridge by special licence. What brought them together?

To try to answer this we must rescue Arthur from the Science labs and consider what is known of his career at Cambridge. Despite being a few years older and immeasurably wealthier than most of his contemporaries, he seems to have made no more of a mark on Queens' than on Repton. *Dial*, the College magazine, records that he ran for the Queens' cross-country team in 1921; but this is his only mention.

It is possible, of course, that like others who had served in the war he felt cut off from those who hadn't. The Reverend H.C. Alexander, who entered Queens' straight from school a year after Arthur, recalled a group of young naval officers, 'survivors of the horrors of war', who didn't mix and who held 'noisy parties occasionally marked by a heavy splash in the river flowing just beneath our windows'. That doesn't sound like Arthur's form at all: 'too timorous', in Simon's words. A more likely explanation for his obscurity is that he had discovered his life's passion, golf, and spent all his spare time perfecting his swing on one of the local courses.

Simon maintained that his father nursed serious ambitions to become a physicist and work under Rutherford at the Cavendish. If true, this was about as far-fetched as Simon's hopes of being selected to play for the Southern Schools at Lord's with a batting average of fifteen. Throughout the Twenties competition for post-graduate entry to the Cavendish was intense. To have stood a chance of getting there Arthur would have needed at least a Second in Mathematics Part 1, followed by Firsts in Natural Sciences Parts 1 and 2. What he got was a Second in Natural Sciences Part 1, which in those gentlemanly days earned you an Honours degree. He could have stayed up for a fourth year to do Part 2, but according to Simon his tutor advised against this.

'He said, "You're a rich young man, Raven. Why waste another year of your life studying when you can afford to look round for something that suits you?" Well my father was a sucker for bad advice, so naturally he took it and lived unhappily ever after. He wasn't cut out for a life of idleness, you see. Too puritanical. So he never really enjoyed not working, poor fellow. Now if only he'd found a job and stuck to it he wouldn't have been so discontented. But because he wasn't compelled to stick to something, he stuck to nothing. For instance he thought he might become a doctor and, so the story goes, the day after registering as a medical student played in the annual doctors' golf tournament and won the cup. So his career in medicine had started rather well, whereupon he decided he didn't really like the idea very much – playing around with corpses was different from being a scientist – so he gave up a few days after hooking the cup.'

Arthur's experience of medicine must have been so brief that he was never officially enrolled because I could find no record of his having been accepted by any of the London teaching hospitals and no evidence of the cup he was supposed to have won. On leaving Cambridge he did however distinguish himself by buying a Bentley, which he drove back and forth between Leicester and Old Hunstanton, where the family had built a large house called Portland Lodge[1] on the le Strange estate, a short walk away from the golf links. Hunstanton Golf Club, which he joined in 1921, eventually became his second home when he and Esther settled nearby after the war. In the words of Dyker Thew, the club's historian, 'Arthur

[1] Not to be confused with Portland House, Leicester.

spent most of his long retirement at the club bar and was always wanting someone to play with him.'

It was the sight of Arthur behind the wheel of his Bentley – 'he seemed rather young to be driving a car like that' – that first encouraged Mr Thew, then an impressionable sixteen-year-old, to take an interest in him. And when, a year or two later, Arthur was joined in the car by a petite blonde, Mr Thew's curiosity was shared by many other golfers.

> There was a lot of talk. She was said to have been passed on to him by a Cambridge friend with whom she was very much in love. Why he got rid of her I don't know. Perhaps it was something to do with class, which was so important in those days. Anyhow, I assume that not wanting to be poor again she settled for Arthur. He was rather naive ... There was a story in the golf club that Arthur took her for a walk on the beach beside the golf links up to Gore Point – and came back engaged! Older members actually joked with me about which girls in the club I would like to go round the Point with!

I think there's something rather Arcadian about this story. It's just the sort of thing that happens in P.G. Wodehouse's books. Curiously enough Wodehouse often played at Hunstanton: he knew the le Strange family who named Wodehouse Road, where Portland Lodge was, in his honour. But if Mr Thew's scenario is correct – and we shall never know for certain – this still doesn't explain why Arthur and Esther were in such a hurry to marry that they obtained a special licence.

Could Esther have been pregnant, as Simon's wife-to-be Susan was 26 years later? And if so, who was responsible? – Arthur? or his friend? Again, we shall never know. But Esther told Simon she'd had two miscarriages before he arrived, and the arithmetic suggests that the first of them took place in the early months of her marriage. Assuming Arthur was naive, as Dyker Thew asserts, he might well have been persuaded that it was his baby Esther was carrying, not his friend's. At any rate, both parties seem to have been satisfied with what they got. In Arthur's case, a pretty girl to sit beside him in the Bentley and applaud his prowess off the tee. For Esther, the sort of well-upholstered lifestyle which in that pre-expense account era only inherited wealth could provide.

Perhaps, on reflection, this is too harsh. Love must have come into it as well. For although it seemed to young Simon that his parents quarrelled incessantly about nothing at all – 'I used to hear these angry words coming up the staircase and thought, "No marriage for me" ' – they were still together at Esther's death 36 years later.

*

Although they had surrendered control of W. Raven & Co in 1919, Arthur and his brothers remained on the board until 1927 when the company was sold again. Arthur was also on the board of another hosiery firm called Toone and Wells which collapsed in 1934. Otherwise his occupation was golf, with a bit of squash on the side. He played so much that a few years later, when Esther was beginning to make a name for herself as a runner, a piece about her in the *Leicester Mercury* referred to Arthur as 'her husband, the golfer'.

Simon dismissed this as a mere courtesy title – 'whereas Mama really did deserve to be called a runner'. Predisposed towards élitism ever since he realised, aged thirteen, that mastering Greek grammar made you 'special', he saw his father's passion for a sport at which he would never excel as proof of his 'futility'.

'Had he been playing alpha-class amateur golf there'd have been some point to the thing, particularly before the war when amateur golf was much more important than it is now, but his best possible handicap was four. So all he could really aspire to was good gamma-class.'

A more polite way of putting it would be to say that Arthur was a good club golfer at a time when amateur golf was at its zenith. For instance a tournament like the Halford Hewitt, for public school old boys, received the same sort of coverage in the *The Times* as an event like the Ryder Cup. Arthur, whose handicap usually see-sawed between five and eight, played for the Old Reptonians' fifth pair from 1930 to 1933. They never progressed beyond the third round.

*

It seemed to Simon as a boy that one of the few tastes his parents shared was for foreign travel. Usually they indulged this during term-time, but on at least one occasion they went abroad during the school holidays. On learning that he and his younger brother Myles were to be boarded out at a children's home in Bexhill, Simon asked Esther why she was leaving them behind. This produced an unexpectedly dusty answer: 'Because there are times when one neither needs nor wants children.'

Oddly enough Arthur and Esther did not go abroad for their honeymoon. After spending their wedding night at the Lamb Hotel, Ely, they went to stay with Annie Raven at Portland Lodge. If, as I have proposed, Esther was pregnant, this might explain why they chose to remain at home. But it is also worth noting that in September 1925 the Hunstanton Golf Club celebrated the extension of its links by several hundred yards with a series of top-class amateur and professional events. Such was Arthur's devotion to golf in general and Hunstanton GC in particular that he may well have insisted on being present.

Arthur's golf meant that wherever he and Esther settled there would need to be good courses near at hand, but to begin with they lived in London. Simon thought this was a rare instance of unselfishness on his father's part. 'He didn't like London at all. Too many people. Not enough fresh air. Whereas Mama rather enjoyed the hustle and bustle. She didn't want it all the time, mind. But London did excite her.'

Exactly how long the Ravens were in London is unclear. Simon doubted whether his father would have stuck it for much longer than a year, an assessment supported by the London telephone directory, from which they had disappeared by October 1927. Their first few months in the capital were spent at a flat in Museum Street, Bloomsbury. Esther often said how happy she'd been here because it was round the corner from the British Museum, one of her favourite places. They then moved to Chelsea, taking a short lease on a flat in Sloane Gardens.

At this point the trail goes cold for two years, by which time Simon had been born and the family were living in Sunningdale. The only clue to their whereabouts after leaving London is Esther's claim to Simon that he was conceived on the banks of the Danube at Budapest. This would have been in the Spring of 1927. Given Esther's two miscarriages it is reasonable to assume that her pregnancy was passed quietly in Leicester and Hunstanton. Not that she cared for the resort in winter: it was too bracing and made her feel out of sorts. Arthur's decision to settle there after the war must have seemed like a slap in the face, though by then she would have known him well enough to realise that his own interests always came first.

CHAPTER TWO

This is the land of lost content,
I see it shining plain,
The happy highways where I went
And cannot come again.
A.E. Housman, *A Shropshire Lad*

Simon's earliest memory was of being squirted with a hose in the garden of 'Callaly', a large Edwardian house about a mile from Sunningdale station. This would have been in the summer of 1930, shortly before his brother Myles was born. Simon's other memory of Callaly was that they had a 'Buttons' there. This sounds incongruous. Sunningdale then was smart, even a bit raffish, rather than grand. Its *genius loci* was the Prince of Wales, whose week-end retreat, Fort Belvedere, was only a short drive away from the Golf Club, which in 1930 he captained. Arthur played there too. And it was, no doubt, the proximity of well-appointed courses like Sunningdale and Wentworth, of which he was also a member, that brought him back from Leicester to this sleek corner of the Stockbroker Belt in 1932.

The Ravens removed to Leicester in 1931 at the urging of Arthur's elder brother, William, who had sunk most of his capital in Toone and Wells and was apprehensive – justifiably, as it turned out – about the firm's ability to weather the Slump. He persuaded Arthur to join him in a managerial role, and for several months the brothers went in almost every day, the nearest Arthur ever came in peacetime to working for his living. There is no reason to doubt his resolve: after all, he had bought a large house in Knighton Rise, not far from Portland House, and installed his family there. But for one reason or another the experiment failed and by the autumn of 1932 he was teeing off at Sunningdale again.

Simon's only memory of Leicester was of being taken on a very long walk and complaining so vociferously that he was eventually allowed to ride in Myles's pram. Thirty years later, when he was just beginning to make his mark as a television dramatist, his brief sojourn in Leicester encouraged the local press to announce that he had spent his childhood there. Had he done so his upbringing would have been quite different, with incalculable effects upon his subsequent development. For while he might still have gone to Charterhouse, he would certainly not have attended Cordwalles School, Camberley, where at the age of nine he was 'deftly and very agreeably seduced' by the games-master, a formative experience if ever there was one, as we shall see.

Esther meanwhile had unexpectedly transformed herself from a grass widow into an 'athletic mother', to quote the *News of the World*. In March 1932, barely eighteen months after Myles was born, she ran for England against France in a two mile cross-country race, finishing sixth, two places behind her sister Ruth. Over the next four years, representing London Olympiades, she competed at the highest level in cross-country and road-relay races; and with a best time of 20′18″ succeded Ruth as the second fastest female in the country over three miles. Simon always maintained that she also held the unofficial record for the women's mile, but I have been unable to confirm this.

What we can be sure of is that had women runners then enjoyed the same level of attention as they do today, Esther would have been quite a celebrity. For a start she didn't fit the bill. Here was a well-to-do mother of two in her thirties showing a clean pair of heels to the young typists and shopgirls who typically took to the track. Furthermore she looked very appetising in her running shorts. Add to this a younger sister who also ran for England and a father who had won races over the same distance thirty years before and you have a story worth telling. But apart from the comment noted above in the *News of the World*, the only national newspaper to take women's athletics seriously before the war, and an earlier reference in the same journal to 'the splendid sisters Christmas', Esther's achievements went unsung.

So why did she do it? Why spend hours flogging over places like Wimbledon Common, where the Olympiades trained, with the prospect of a long and sweaty journey home afterwards because there were no baths or showers to be had in the Windmill where they changed?

Simon's Aunt Ruth, 91 years old at the time of writing, told me that to begin with her example spurred Esther on. She and their mother had gone to the 1928 Olympic Games in Amsterdam, the first in which women competed, and Ruth had returned home to find Fred Christmas in a lather. 'He said, "Look here. You used to run well at school. Why aren't you running now? You're good enough to win lots of races. All you need to do is train properly and I'll help you with that. You'll be running for England in no time." And I was. I ran for England in the Women's World Games in 1930 and came fifth in the final of the 800 metres. Next year I was in the cross-country team too.'

When Ruth went to stay with Arthur and Esther in Sunningdale, as she did quite often, Esther would join her for a training run round Virginia Water. Then she became pregnant with Myles, but because she was fit and healthy she was able to start running again within a few months of his birth. By now they had moved to Leicester and there was another incentive: Esther was bored. She admitted as much to Simon years later.

'She had nothing to do, you see. There was a nurse to look after Myles and me, a cook-general to prepare the meals and a daily to do the housework. My father was out all day, either at Toone and Wells or the golf course, and she didn't know anybody in Leicester except Granny Raven, who used to swan about in a chauffeur-driven Rolls and sip sherry on the sly – she was diabetic. If my mother had been a ball-player she could have taken up tennis or even golf, but she wasn't. None of the Christmases were. So running kept her off the gin – for the time being, anyway.'

Although never tempted to follow in her footsteps – he took as little strenuous physical exercise as possible after his first year at Cambridge – Simon was proud of his mother's achievements. 'She had several roses, you know,' he used to say, a reference to her international vests. Then he would add that of course his father had been bitterly envious, 'as he was of anyone in the family who succeeded at anything'.

I think this must have come after the war when recriminations filled the air. At the time Arthur was too preoccupied with his golf to lose any sleep over Esther's brilliant running career. For instance on the day she made her England début he was playing in the Halford Hewitt. Had he wanted to stop her running he would certainly have tried. He was that sort of man. But when she retired in 1936 it was because, at 34, she no longer felt like training hard, particularly since the departure of Ruth, who had married a French petrochemist and gone to live in Nice the year before.

*

The Ravens left Leicester for a house in Virginia Water called 'Warren', which they leased. Although smaller than Callaly it was, in Simon's phrase, 'well-found'. Here, aged about five, he had his first confrontation with Arthur. 'He forbad me to have my favourite pudding, apple suet. I thought it was going to be ginger, which I hated, and said I didn't want any pudding. Then when I saw it was apple suet I of course did want it, but my father said No: I'd said I didn't want pudding, so no pudding would I have. I never forgave him.'

Simon's indignation was still apparent almost sixty years later, and it is a measure of the distemper his father's memory could arouse in him that he seemed unaware that Arthur had behaved quite correctly – if not by modern 'progressive' standards then demonstrably by those of Simon's beloved 'Old Gang' (q.v.). In view of this lapse, now would seem the right time to examine his abiding hostility to his father.

In his third year at Cambridge Simon wrote an autobiographical novel called *An Inch of Fortune* which, although rejected as libellous at the time, survived to be published thirty years later. It contains this description of the hero's father.

> His father was a futile and embittered man who had spent all his life pretending to look for a suitable occupation. Since he had £2,000 a

year of his own it had to be exactly suitable – which, after the first month, no occupation ever was. So he developed a grudge about the difficulty of life on £2,000 a year and the general lack of suitability, for a man of his type, of every known occupation, and settled down to play golf in order to preserve his appetite – which was quite unnecessary, as he was in any case an inordinately greedy man. After he was forty-five he could neither play so well nor so often (age and the war having taken their toll of himself and his companions), with the result that, while his appetite was unimpaired, he became more embittered than ever. In after years Esmé would measure his own transition from childhood through adolescence and to man's estate not so much by time or by incident as by the increasing disagreeableness of his father ('that was the year when he thought he had an ulcer').

In conversation he could be even blunter about his father's shortcomings. 'He was a man without qualities except one or two rather nasty ones. First meanness. He wouldn't pay for Myles to go to Cambridge, yet he willingly handed over £2,000 to some rotter who said he could make him a fortune at roulette by doubling up on even numbers. He was naive about money as well as mean. Secondly envy. He had that with knobs on. When one got one's cricket colours he said it must be because all the good men are away at the war. And when one got a commission he said anyone can get a commission these days: it was different in 1917. He simply had to shit on other people's successes. He was also selfish. If he wanted to do something then the rest of us had to do it too, regardless of whether we liked it or not. He used to make me go on long walks in the Lake District with him, which I hated. And he once dragged my poor mother up a mountain in North Africa on a donkey despite the fact that she'd just had my sister Robin and anyway didn't like heights. And he was a bully. Myles and I used to dread Sunday lunch before the war because if he'd lost his golf match or something else had happened to annoy him he'd take it out on us. He was a very disagreeable little man. Deep self-dissatisfaction, you see. Now if only he'd got off his bum and done something instead of worrying about whether or not his money was going to last the course he might have been more amiable.'

How much truth is there in this? Hard to say, since there is practically no one left alive in a position to comment. That Arthur could be selfish and inconsiderate was confirmed to me by his sister-in-law, Ruth, who added that 'although he was a good golfer, he was not a particularly good sport'. Another witness, Dyker Thew of Hunstanton Golf Club, thought Arthur 'a shy, morose fellow who was not much fun to be with'. On the other hand we have the testimony of James Prior, one of the few friends of Simon actually to have met Arthur:

Simon was uncompromisingly rude about his father the whole time, so one was surprised to find that he was not the 'lazy, ogre, skinflint' that Simon made him out to be. He seemed quite a reasonable man, even if one didn't exactly warm to him as one did to his mother. Mind you, she did once say to me, 'Does your father treat your mother as badly as Simon's father treats me?' I was flabbergasted. It was simply not the thing you expected anybody's parent to say in those days.

Shortly after this Simon was expelled from Charterhouse, the first of several misdemeanours that tried Arthur's patience and sometimes his pocket. Stingy he may have been, but when it mattered he bailed Simon out. Simon was grateful to him for this, but mistrusted his motives. He compared him to Sir Maurice Bowra, 'who poked £100 notes through the bars when you were in prison, but when you came out and wrote a bestseller about your prison experiences got cross and jealous and upset'.

By the time Simon was in his early twenties, which is when he produced that unflattering cameo in *An Inch of Fortune*, he and Arthur were barely on speaking terms. Clearly it was in both their interests to see as little of each other as possible, but two things prevented this. One was Simon's capacity for getting into scrapes, after which he had no option but to return home to lick his wounds. The other was Esther's possessiveness, which I shall return to later. Some idea of what would happen when father and son did meet is provided by David Evers, a fellow Kingsman:

> Simon and I were going to spend the night at Hunstanton. His mother was away and his father hadn't returned from his golf. 'Time for a gin,' said Simon and found a bottle. 'Oughtn't we to wait for your father?' I said. 'He won't know,' said Simon. 'We'll water it.' He then poured two enormous gins and topped the bottle up with water. Soon afterwards his father returned and immediately poured himself a gin. He took one sip and said, 'Simon, you've watered this.' He was pretty cross so we gulped down our drinks and went to the pub instead.

Was this deliberate on Simon's part? If it wasn't, it was certainly convenient to have a friend present when Arthur lost his rag. 'Long before he began to write his father was his best invention,' said another Cambridge friend, adding that since Mr Raven never appeared, Simon was free to represent him as 'an utter failure who played golf, drank too much and quarrelled with his family'.

But it was *what* Arthur drank, rather than how much, that Simon despised as an undergraduate. Like most of his generation Arthur was a beer and spirits man whereas at Cambridge Simon had swiftly formed a serious attachment to wine. Hence his snobbish complaint that although his father could perfectly well have afforded 'proper French wine' with his meals, all he ever served, and that rarely, was 'trumped-up colonial muck like South African burgundy'.

Simon looked down on Arthur in more ways than one. He grew to be a good six inches taller, which added piquancy to stories like this:

> Simon said his father had returned from a visit to Australia after the war with a passion for wearing shorts. When he tried to get Simon to wear them, Simon said, 'No, father, you know how red my knees get.'

No wonder Arthur was gob-smacked when Simon got a commission!

Before picking up the thread again I think it is worth emphasising that both Myles and Simon's sister Robin shared his low opinion of their father, indeed Myles was if anything more hostile. Once, towards the end of Arthur's life, Simon instinctively caught the old man when he tripped coming down the stairs of the Royal Cinque Ports Golf Club at Deal. Myles was furious and Simon spent the rest of the day apologising to him.

*

In *The Feathers of Death* Simon offers a rather dispiriting glimpse of growing up in pre-war stockbroking country. He pictures young Alastair Lynch, his hero, 'loitering dully through the hours in a grey shirt and grey shorts, taken to his mother's drawing room at five, removed at six, scrupulously bathed and made to say his prayers before hot milk and bed'. No doubt this did correspond to Simon's experience in some respects. He certainly wore a grey shirt and grey shorts, and with no television to distract him there must have been times when he was bored, particularly in the days before Myles was old enough to hold a cricket bat. Then in June 1934, when Simon was six, Arthur bought a house on the Wentworth estate called 'Lismore'. At once new vistas opened up.

Lismore was a Tarrant house, Tarrant being the builder who bought the Wentworth estate in 1924 and then developed it according to the same successful blueprint he had drawn up for St George's Hill, Weybridge. What Tarrant offered his wealthy suburban clients was made-to-measure homes and gardens in a lush, upper-middle-class enclave with a country club nearby where they could ride, swim, play tennis and golf. It was on the ladies' course at Wentworth that Simon and Myles played their first few rounds of golf. They were also taught to swim and box at the club by an ex-RSMI. But according to Simon the best thing about living at Lismore was the large meadow which in those days ran from their back garden right to the top of Gorse Hill. It was here that the boys would spend hours in the 'intensely pleasurable pastime' of flying model planes and gliders.

Another good thing about Lismore was that it was only a few hundred yards up the hill from Virginia Water Kindergarten, which had been founded the year before by two dedicated young teachers, Miss McKinnon and Miss Fish. Here, in a large house beside a playing field where sports were held, children were taught the three Rs, plus the rudiments of History and Science and a little French. Despite never having had any formal teaching before – he thought Esther must have helped him learn to read – Simon soon made his mark. 'I think what impressed them was my attitude as much as my ability. They could see that I wanted to learn, and believed, quite rightly, that I ought to be encouraged.'

Consequently Miss McKinnon proposed that instead of going home for the day at lunch time, Simon should attend afternoon classes as well. To everyone's surprise this was 'bitterly, even viciously' resisted by Esther. 'Her official excuse was that in the afternoon children should be out and about getting fresh air. But what I now realise, though it wasn't immediately apparent at the time, was that she smelt – what she was to smell much stronger, much later, with both myself and Myles – some new and more attractive influences and/or interests appearing to take me away from her. Luckily my father stepped in and said, "No, of course he must go to school if he's any good at it." And so to school in the afternoon I went.

'This was the first hint I got of my mother's terrible possessiveness which cropped up subsequently and frequently during one's school years *and after that*. Even when one was a regular soldier one was expected to spend all one's leaves at home. If one didn't, and she found out, things could get very nasty indeed. I remember once when I was on leave – it must have been prior to sailing for Kenya – arranging with Myles that we would go down to Hunstanton for a few days and take her to Newmarket. And at the end of the meeting Myles remarked, "Well, we've just had three days of pure pleasure" – and it was known we were leaving the next day – and on the way back from Newmarket there was the most venomous, spiteful row you can imagine, all because the pleasure was over and we were going. It may be that she'd had one gin too many. That was rather liable to happen from 1946 onwards. One too many gins on an empty stomach. Nothing like that for turning somebody sour. But these rows would crop up independent of drink. And Myles and I were very miffed because we'd gone out of our way to give her a good time – the fact that it was also our idea of a good time made it rather less virtuous, I agree. Still, to have done that and then to have this terrible termagant woman, this harridan, screeching in the back of the car.'

Interestingly enough Esther seems to have been quite happy to share her sons with their nannies, the longest serving of whom was a chief petty officer's daughter called Margaret Newman. Always dressed in a blue nursemaid's uniform (though Simon thought her only training had been at Esther's hands) and with a slight resemblance to the actress, Anna Massey, she crops up time and again in photos from those years. 'She drew the line pretty low on the paper,' recalled Simon, 'but where she drew it, she drew it.' Later he and Myles would invoke her at opportune moments: 'What *would* Nanny say!' But she cannot have rebuked them, as Bessie does Hugo in *Close of Play*, for not washing properly 'underneath there', since in the words of a fellow cricketer who observed them in the showers, both Simon and Myles were 'radically circumcised'.

CHAPTER THREE

Alas, regardless of their doom,
The little victims play!
No sense have they of ills to come,
Nor care beyond today:
Keats, *Ode on a Distant Prospect of Eton College*

In May 1936, aged eight, Simon was sent as a boarder to Cordwalles School, Camberley. His parents chose Cordwalles because it had a good reputation in the area and was close at hand. But although the school was only a few miles from Virginia Water it might just as well have been off the map as far as Simon was concerned; for in those days boys were not allowed home every few weeks as they are now: they were there for the duration and would be lucky to see their parents more than once a term.

This prospect pleased Simon. Unlike most children he had no qualms about leaving home. In fact he insisted on arriving at Cordwalles ninety minutes earlier than everyone else, at 4.30 rather than 6.00. His explanation, which I see no reason to disbelieve, was that for more than a year he had been under the spell of that potent mythmaker, Frank Richards, creator of Greyfriars and St Jim's, and could not wait to savour boarding school for himself. Given how appalling many prep schools were then it says much for Cordwalles that he was not disappointed. Indeed he once described the school to me as 'a paradise', admittedly in the course of a conversation about an 'Extra' that was certainly not in the prospectus.

Situated about a mile out of Camberley on the corner of London Road and what was then Bracknell Road (now Ballard Road), Cordwalles in the Thirties was a modern, purpose-built prep school for between 50 and 60 boys, with two large playing fields – one for soccer and rugby, the other for cricket – a tennis court and a swimming pool. Despite its proximity to Wellington, Sandhurst and the Staff College, it was not an 'Army' school. This may have been because, at £63 a term,[1] it was too expensive. Possibly it was also considered a bit soft – that was Simon's theory, anyway. He recalled being packed off to bed by Mrs Loly, the headmaster's wife, simply because she thought he looked tired – 'she was always doing that'. He also accused her of having 'dietary fads', but according to John Selby, who was there at about the same time,

[1] More than Charterhouse and most other leading public schools.

all this really amounted to was having grapefruit rather than cereal or porridge for breakfast, pilchards for tea and every now and then cheese instead of meat for lunch. I think she picked these ideas up in Switzerland, where she'd been treated for TB. She certainly wasn't a vegetarian or anything like that. We had a joint two or three times a week.

Selby, the son of an Indian Army officer, had no complaints about Cordwalles, which he considered a well-run school.

They were keen on games, made you work hard but didn't cram you, and kept you generally up to the mark. Everybody had to box and they marched you about a bit.

Although two years older than Simon, Selby remembered him well. 'He was red-haired, freckled and angular, with a wicked sense of humour.' – Wicked? – 'Sharp. He saw the funny side of things, which was a good way of coming to terms with life at a pre-war prep school.'

Cordwalles was owned and run by Gerard Loly, a Cambridge graduate of about 40 whom Simon described as 'tall and willowy, like Aldous Huxley, but with a round-owl face and round spectacles'. John Selby praised Mr Loly for his ability 'to get the most out of boys with the minimum of physical coercion. He very seldom beat us and was the only master permitted to do so.' Loly's deputy head was another Cambridge man, C.H. Ledward, a very able mathematician who also ran the Scouts. Scouting took place once a week and was compulsory. Simon disliked it at the time but subsequently came to realise 'how sensible it was to be taught about things like signalling, cooking, and fire-making'. Twenty years later, as officer commanding the training company at his regimental depot, he 'even tried to get up a movement to recruit Boy Scouts rather than Army cadets'.

Simon was a connoisseur of schoolmasters and the man who impressed him most at Cordwalles was Lieutenant-Colonel Killock,[2] the games master, 'a trim, balding figure in his early forties, about 5′10″ tall, with a clipped moustache, slightly aggressive jaw and unemphatic Roman nose'. Happily married with two sons, one of whom was at Cordwalles, 'Colonel K' had retired from the Gurkhas a few years before. As well as running the soccer and rugby he taught English, and it was thanks to him that Simon first began to take an interest in literature – 'He gave me Buchan[3] and Conan Doyle to read and I was hooked. I was a proper little philistine up to then.'

[2] Simon's pseudonym, which I have retained.

[3] Simon said memorably of Buchan that he wrote 'the kind of books in which women don't go to the lavatory.' You could not say the same about his books (see pp. 214-5).

But reading was not the only pleasurable pastime Simon discovered at the hands of Colonel K:

> He liked playing with little boys' penises, and he did it so deftly that we positively queued up for him. He also liked letting us play with his own, an object of gratifying size, agreeable texture and startling capacity. One of his particular favourites had a tent which he put up in a remote part of the pine woods which surrounded the cricket ground; and as soon as cricket for the day was over .... I would hurry through the warm pines to 'The Tent' (as it was known), inside which several boys, ranging in age from nine to thirteen, would already be lolling about with their shorts round their ankles, exploring one another's anatomy and waiting for the arrival of Colonel K. It was a scene of great erotic fascination, vividly memorable to this day, of Petronian power and indecency. (*Shadows on the Grass*)

This sounded too good to be true and I put it to Simon that, at the very least, he was remembering with advantages. 'You mean, Am I hiding something nasty, like buggery? The answer is No. Colonel K was a great one for fellatio but our arses didn't interest him at all. Occasionally he would place his erection between our innocent little thighs. Nothing more.'

Very well. But wasn't it highly unusual for small boys to be sexually aroused before puberty, let alone experience the dry orgasms he said Colonel K was able to induce? Again, Simon was adamant. 'I'm not making it up. Byron said the same thing happened to him when he was seduced at the age of nine by his nurse. After all, if pre-pubescent boys can have erections, what's to stop them coming – even if they can only manage to jerk and judder?'

Where Simon does employ novelist's licence is in his account of how the scandal broke, and its consequences. In *Shadows* he says that he and a boy called Crawford, another of the 'Tentites', were taken to the 'timeless' Oval Test of 1938 by Crawford's father. As Len Hutton grafted towards his record-breaking 364, Mr Crawford began to berate his son for failing to get his First XI Colours the previous term. Finally the boy could take no more and offered this excuse: 'It wasn't my fault ... I was worried about Colonel Killock.' Whereupon all was revealed.

This, as Simon admitted, was pure conjecture. 'I've no idea who shopped him, or why. We used to talk about it among ourselves, but we kept mum because it was so enjoyable. So my guess is that whoever spilled the beans was either goaded into it for some entirely outside reason, or else wanted to create a big red herring. With this in mind I invented the scene at the Oval, where I did sit through several very tedious days of the timeless Test. But in fact it wasn't until the following year that the storm clouds began to gather – as indeed they did everywhere – only the ones over Colonel K never actually broke. When we came back in September 1939 we were told that he'd been recalled to his regiment because of the war. End of story.'

Nor were there any consequences. 'We were not hauled in and told the facts of life. We were not told to keep our mouths shut, or else. Nothing was said at all. We resumed our activities, sadly without Colonel K, and that was that. This now makes me think that he probably got away with it.'

While acknowledging that paedophilia was 'not on' because it enraged so many people, 'particularly proles', Simon always maintained that far from suffering any grievous psychological damage as a result of Colonel K's attentions, he had in fact learnt 'several valuable and lasting lessons'. These he listed in the 'My Obituary' column of the short-lived *Sunday Correspondent*:

> Firstly, that sex (of whatever kind), although matchless as an occasional diversion, is too ridiculous to be taken seriously; secondly, that it is too trivial to be allowed to interfere with more stable and satisfying preoccupations, such as cricket and the flicks, or (later) horse-racing and books; and thirdly, that sex is best spiced with a degree of shamelessness which love or serious affection would probably inhibit.

Exactly when Simon reached these conclusions I cannot say, but he was guided by them for most of his adult life. It would have been interesting to compare his conduct with that of the other Tentites, but sadly I was unable to track any of them down. As for Colonel K, he returned from the war to found a pre-prep school for boys aged between six and ten, earning this pithy valediction from Simon:

> He must have died (which he did suddenly some fifteen years later) a very happy man.

*

In his famous article 'Boys' Weeklies' George Orwell concluded his send-up of Greyfriars like this: 'Everything is safe, solid and unquestionable. Everything will be the same for ever and ever.' Even Orwell, writing shortly before the fall of France, could not have realised the import of this. And yet oddly enough Simon's early addiction to Frank Richards' school stories was in some sense vindicated by his experiences as a schoolboy after Munich. For while he could never be sure from one holiday to the next where he would find himself, school remained 'safe, solid and unquestionable'.

This pattern was established in December 1938 when Simon and Myles, who had just started at Cordwalles, returned home for the Christmas holidays to find that Lismore had been sold, the domestics let go, and the family, including their baby sister Robin, aged six months, installed in a residential hotel nearby. Although the boys had been warned that this might happen on one of their Sundays out, Simon said it had still come as rather a shock.

'Of course one had heard of Hitler. He was *bad*. So was Mussolini pretty bad, but somehow one couldn't take him that seriously because he was only a floppy wop. Still, it was clear that all was not well. Then along came Chamberlain saying "Peace in Our Time" and everyone heaved a great sigh of relief because it meant we'd squared those nasty foreigners and would live happily ever after. Now give him his due, my father wasn't taken in by this. He thought Appeasement wouldn't work and that there was bound to be a war, in which case a large house like Lismore would be a liability. And although he was 40 by now he went straight to the Air Ministry after Munich and offered his services as a pilot. In the event all he ever flew was a desk, which peeved him no end. But it was good behaviour all the same.'

Although he had happy memories of Lismore, Simon did not repine at its loss. He had had enough experience of hotels to know that there were definite advantages to being a 'hotel child'. Away from the nursery discipline was 'incalculably' relaxed. There was also more to see and do and ample opportunity to escape parental supervision. Esther probably felt the loss of Lismore most keenly. 'For Mama it was downhill all the way from now on.'

Throughout the Thirties the Ravens had spent several weeks each summer at Hunstanton, basing themselves at a comfortable private hotel called 'The Lodge'. This is where they were when war was declared. It came, said Simon, as a relief. 'Here was an end to uncertainty. Now one knew where one stood.' But relief soon gave way to resentment, a common phenomenon during the phoney war when people felt they were being bullied for no good reason. At Cordwalles Mrs Loly immediately insisted that the boys 'do their bit'. First she decreed that at tea they must choose between jam and butter with their bread; then she took jam and butter off the menu altogether and substituted watercress. Even worse, she refused to replace the school boot-black when he was called up. Henceforth shifts of senior boys would devote at least one evening a week to cleaning all the school's shoes.

> When someone inquired how we were to do our prep on our shoe-cleaning evenings, he was told we would be excused. When he pointed out that his parents were paying for him to learn the normal school subjects and not the tasks of servants, he was called a nasty and unpatriotic little boy who wouldn't even clean his own shoes to help the war effort. When he said he was perfectly prepared to clean his

own shoes but didn't see why he should clean anybody else's, he had his ears boxed. (*The Old School*)

'And serve me jolly well right!' commented Simon, who was, nevertheless, unrepentant. 'It was a question of priorities. One was at school to learn. And what I really resented was people saying things like, "Instead of doing Latin today we shall all go out and sell poppies." This was a nightmare to me.'

But if the war robbed Simon of a few hours' Latin, it gave him Greek in return. What happened was that in the summer of 1940 his parents learnt that Cordwalles, being in a military area, would have to be evacuated – though where to, and when, no one knew. In the face of such uncertainty, and with the prospect of German bombs raining down before the evacuation was accomplished, they decided to move the boys to a less vulnerable school. By now Arthur was stationed at an aerodrome in Somerset, and since it looked as if he might be there for a while, a school nearby was sought. As luck would have it there were vacancies at St Dunstan's, Burnham-on-Sea, which at £38 a term was cheap compared with Cordwalles. This, thought Simon, was probably why they chose it.

'But what they didn't know, and what I was to discover, was that the staff were extremely good, war or no war, and in particular there was an old man called Potts who had a genius for teaching Greek which of course changed one's whole life. Starting from scratch, because they didn't do it at Cordwalles, he taught me enough Greek between September 1940 and May 1941 for me to win the top scholarship to Charterhouse. I might have got one anyway, but without Greek I certainly wouldn't have come top. Greek was still taken very seriously at Charterhouse in those days, so they were impressed when one came top of the grammar paper with 100% (or so the story goes) and also did well in translation.'

The Headmaster of St Dunstan's was a 'jolly and worldly' survivor of the Great War called Captain Evan Stokes, who had played soccer for the Corinthians and England. When he and his capable wife, a 'Girton bluestocking', took the school over in 1919 it had 24 boys; by 1940 there were 70 plus, of whom three or four a year were expected to win scholarships. Although Captain and Mrs Stokes died several years before this book was conceived I was lucky enough to learn about their methods from Mr Bruce Broker, who arrived at St Dunstan's as a young master in 1939 and remained there for the next forty years (as a diabetic he was not called up).

Captain Stokes lived for sport, in other words, team games. Individual games were all right, but he cut you down to size! He was a businessman, not an academic (Mrs Stokes was everything that he was not). His became the leading prep school in Somerset by virtue of its low fees and excellent results. The boys ate enough to keep them alive but had few luxuries. They were expected to work hard and play hard. Fathers loved it – mothers weren't so sure. The school was right on the beach, and unless it was raining it was obligatory to go down onto the beach at mid-morning break and from 12.30 to 1.00. The boys looked healthy!

Captain Stokes did not of course ignore the war but he was determined that games should continue regardless. One summer when petrol ran out we kept the games field playable for a month with four hand-mowers. School matches never stopped. If our opponents could not get to us, Mr Stokes sent a couple of big taxis to fetch them. He was Chairman of the local Magistrates, but he knew a crooked garage owner who preferred to bend the law and keep on the right side of the Chairman! (Similarly he regularly fined heavily a farmhouse which served cream teas illegally throughout the war, but sent parents there when they asked where to take the boys out on a Sunday afternoon.)

Although he taught Myles for much longer than Simon, Mr Broker said that it was Simon who left a more vivid impression.

> He was an altogether more calculating boy [than Myles]. He had one of the five best brains that I came across in my teaching career, but he had a lazy streak. If he could not see the advantage to himself, he did not bother. Thus he worked hard at Greek because he could see the advantages of winning a scholarship, and with the aid of Mr Potts, who was a dedicated Classicist, achieved his goal. He was a good all-round cricketer, but I always felt that he only really wanted to do well at it to prevent Myles from overtaking him and also because it might open doors to him in the future.

I think Mr Broker was right about Simon's Greek, but wrong about his cricket. Greek, he very soon realised, was the way on and up, which was where he intended to go. But cricket he did genuinely love for its own sake, and the notion that there was rivalry between him and Myles is absurd: he was far too protective. Bruce Broker also told me how Simon had fitted in at St Dunstan's:

> Among the boys Simon had the attraction of being a clever rebel. He had moved in a much wider circle than the largely Somerset farming community from which most of them came. He knew a higher class of dirty jokes. When 'on duty' I expected to find him gossiping with two or three cronies (not always the same ones) and looking faintly guilty, as if I might have caught them out if I had been two minutes earlier, or later. The staff, especially the young staff like me, were wary of him, almost as if we felt he was capable of engineering our downfall. I am thankful that I never had any inclinations towards

anything that might have led to blackmail. Simon might well have known how to exercise any power he had. Myles, I think, would not.

That Simon deserved to be treated with caution was confirmed by John Drewett, who was a year behind him at St Dunstan's.

He must have been rather a thorn in the flesh of the authorities because he was a nimble nonconformist who knew exactly how far he could go. He was scruffy, but not scruffy enough to disqualify him from being a prefect – though in this, as in other duties, he was not very diligent. He was obviously an academic phenomenon, and knew it. He was a bit cocky, a bit aloof. We could see that he ran on a higher octane petrol than the rest of us and this, I suppose, enabled him to keep two jumps ahead of us. Consequently he was able to anticipate trouble and change direction accordingly. Simon was one of two very good cricketers in the First XI that year, but he was no good at sports like rugger that involved physical contact. He was the sort of boy who hated getting his knees dirty.[4]

To illustrate Simon's precocity, Drewett told this story.

At the end of term there was a division between car boys, who lived locally, and train boys. Those whose parents were picking them up by car, the vast majority, went home a day earlier than those going home by train. As a train boy I found myself spending the night in a dormitory with Simon and one other boy. He soon went off to sleep and I was dozing off myself when I heard Simon talking to our matron, who was very pretty. I didn't let on that I was awake and so heard Simon making her a very plausible proposal of marriage. I think this is indicative not just of the man, but of how mature he was for his years.

Simon could not recall this, but conceded that in those days he must have seemed 'rather a devious number'. On the other hand, he was never a true rebel: 'I only quarrelled with the Government when it had temporarily spited me. But I wasn't at all concerned to remove it – oh dear me No! I wanted a firm Government that would work to my advantage.' Nor did he 'get up to anything' at St Dunstan's: 'I never really had a chance to case the joint. What with working hard for a scholarship and helping with the war effort and playing games one had very little time to call one's own. I seem to recall that on the rare occasions when something might have happened, one's companions were not so much hostile, as bewildered.'

[4] On the other hand, he held his own at boxing, particularly in his teens, when his height and reach made him an awkward opponent.

CHAPTER THREE

None of Simon's school reports have survived. But thanks to Bruce Broker, who found it at the bottom of his desk when he retired, there does exist Simon's last English exercise book at St Dunstan's. This is a fascinating document for all sorts of reasons. To begin with there are rather more spelling mistakes than one might expect from a budding scholar: 'indefinently', 'scolarship', 'writen', 'castrophe', 'wiped' (whipped), 'incidently'. Some of these are the sort of phonetic mistakes associated with dyslexia, from which Simon said that Myles probably suffered. It may be that he had it mildly too.

Then there are some early pointers to style including a scattering of Latin tags and Classical references and a taste for witty imagery. True, he can be ponderous and is overfond of commas, but in these two short pieces one can clearly distinguish the emergence of a point of view.

> Malvolio
> Malvolio strikes me at once as being a clown at a circus who has suddenly turned Puritan; he goes about with a face like a graven image and a voice like the last Trump in diminuendo, looking and feeling (perhaps we had better omit the former) as though he was mighty Jupiter and the Emperor omnipotent of the World (and only a steward at that).
>
> But he is an obvious fool, and deceives himself that the Lady Olivia has seen something in him, which she hasn't in that worthy follower of Bacchus, Sir Toby, or any other dashing young courtier who comes her way. If you have not yet worked out his character, it was all conceit and self-esteem, with a touch of the Pharisee thrown in.
>
> Sir Andrew Aguecheck [*sic*]
> Sir Andrew Aguecheck would seem to be a mixture of Bernard Shaw[5] and a London playboy. For the one (I won't say which, but it might possibly be in order of literary success) he is highly conceited and [addicted to] making learned remarks, rather spoiled by the influence of the other, which incidently makes him a fop and – *horresco referens* – an owl who watches for his prey – and his drink – by night. Notwithstanding, he is rather comical that [*sic*] otherwise, and, may it stands [*sic*] eternally to his credit, as soon as some one mentioned an idiotic knight, knew it for himself.

In addition to Shakespeare, Simon was evidently having to read a good deal of Dickens. There are pieces on Mr Jingle – 'a bad hat', Mr Winkle – 'rather unfortunate in his choice of a father' and an essay on 'The Interest of Dickens in Social Reform and Institutions' which concludes by noting that a century after *Oliver Twist* and *Nicholas Nickleby*, 'the lower classes

[5] 'Beware of libel' wrote Mr Broker, an admonition Simon chose to ignore fifty years on.

are beginning to come [in] to their own'. Because it would be 'something to fall back on', Simon includes 'The Holy Bible' in his list of desert island books, the others being *Greenmantle*, *The Count of Monte Cristo* and *Thank you, Jeeves*. Another favourite was *Ivanhoe*, which even as an adult he would dip into from time to time. Here began his preoccupation with Medieval Romance, the motif for some of his later novels, notably *The Roses of Picardie* and *September Castle*. Nor did he ever lose his love of the feudal system – 'It was so neat.'

Of the longer essays he wrote, I think one about U-boats is worth reproducing in full. First, because it shows that he was learning how to argue a case, one of the hallmarks of his journalism for the *Spectator* in the Sixties. Secondly, on historical grounds: here is an intelligent schoolboy coolly appraising the U-boat threat at a time – February 1941 – when the Battle of the Atlantic was entering a critical phase.

'England can only be beaten by the U-boat'

Only the passing of time can show how much truth there is in the above statement, but a few arguments at once spring to light [mind].

A famous general once said, 'An army marches on its stomach'. In the past few months the German U-boats have been doing valuable work – from the point of view of Germany – sinking merchant vessels. If this was to continue indefinently, on a larger scale, the food problem would be much more serious than it already is.

Another point, if merchant ships were to be destroyed on a still larger scale, is that, besides foodstuffs, munitions and raw materials, vital to our cause, would also become scarcer. A well-conducted U-boat campaign might wreck the splendid work of General Wavell by stopping supplies being sent to the [Middle] East.[6] This would mean that all ideas of sweeping through Italy and into Germany from the Northern shore of Africa would have to be abandoned.

On the other hand ways and means could soon be found to supplant [destroy] the U-boats. The British Navy is definently superior to the German; it will be remembered that, earlier in the war, very many U-boats were destroyed in a short while by its unceasing efforts. Why should this not happen again?

In addition to this there are many more potent ways of winning the war than by a submarine campaign. Invasion in the coming summer, although we are well prepared, might possibly, if favoured by the gods, be fatal. Surely the entry into the war, on the side of Germany, by Japan, or even the inefficient Russia, would be as demoralising as a blockade? Again, it will be as an unhappy day for England when Petain turns the French fleet over to Hitler, as when

[6] Wavell had just routed the Italians in East and North Africa.

the latter, in a furious hate-storm, proclaims the construction of an entirely new fleet of U-boats.

Weighing up the arguments for both sides, it seems to me that, even if the U-boat can beat England, it is by no means the only thing that can.

'Pessimist' was Mr Broker's reaction to this gloomy scenario. Fifty years later Simon was at pains to set the record straight. 'Everybody, myself included, assumed we'd win the war. It never occurred to me, even at the worst moments, that we could conceivably lose it. And one of the reasons for this was that a lot of people, from Churchill downwards, did their level best to keep things as normal as they could possibly be kept. Birley[7] was tremendously good at that. So was Captain Stokes. The war was a tedious interlude which would sooner or later come to an end, and meanwhile, "let's get on with work and play". We had to "dig for victory" of course, but otherwise it was "business as usual" – and pleasure as usual, too. The day I first understood what it was to love one's country was when I saw, in a daily paper, a list of the probable runners at Newmarket adjacent to an account of a hideous defeat.'

This I think proves, if nothing else, in what sheltered circumstances Simon spent most of the war. But since it is bound up with his experience of Charterhouse I shall deal with it in context. His parents, meanwhile, were exposed to the buffeting of adversity for the first time in their married lives.

Predictably, given that he had spent twenty self-indulgent years in Civvy Street, Arthur soon regretted his quixotic decision to volunteer. Whether he had really expected to fly again at 40 plus I cannot say, but he evidently hoped for something more exalted than the humbling administrative tasks he was given as an elderly Flying Officer. While he was in Somerset he could at least moan about this to Esther, who was living near the aerodrome. But in late 1940 he was transferred to North Africa and it was there, according to Simon, that matters came to a head. Buttressed by his wealth, which was still considerable, he took to haranguing his superiors about the misuse of his talents. When that fell on deaf ears he announced that he couldn't do his job properly because he was missing his wife, whereupon he was told that there was a brothel over the next sandhill and 'for God's sake stop being so silly'. But he continued to be such a nuisance that finally they just put him on a troopship home. His last posting was as billeting officer in Blackpool, from which he was allowed to resign, being over-age, at the beginning of 1942.

Whereas Arthur was his own worst enemy, Esther had real problems to contend with on the domestic front. Having brought up two boys in

[7] Sir Robert Birley (1903-82), Headmaster of Charterhouse 1935-47, subsequently Headmaster of Eton.

comfortable surroundings and with ample help, she now found herself servantless, of no fixed abode and with a toddler to look after in addition to Arthur, Simon and Myles. For the first three years of the war she was peripatetic, dividing her time between her parents' small house in Cambridge and a variety of digs. The strain of living like this left its mark, as Bruce Broker recalled:

> It was my job to escort the boys from Highbridge [in Somerset] to Cambridge at the end of every term. Mrs Raven met us at the station and we exchanged a little small talk. She had no doubt been a striking blonde, but in the early 1940s she had aged. She looked careworn and unhappy. I assumed the boys were happy to be with her. Now I am not so sure. I never met the father, nor do I remember him ever being discussed.

Captain and Mrs Christmas were not best pleased at having Esther and her brood, plus a boisterous dog, descend upon them. Consequently Simon in particular was encouraged to spend as much time as possible out of the house during the holidays, which he was only too ready to do. Tall enough by now to con his way into 'A' films , he saw 'anything from Abbott and Costello to *The Corsican Brothers*, from Cagney to Raft to Gable.' Moreover, as he later recalled in the *Spectator*, there was something 'curiously cosy' about Cambridge in wartime.

> As a child living there during the early Forties I found it more attractive than at any time since. The great thing was that one had the whole marvellous place to oneself. One could spend an entire morning in Heffer's basement with elegantly bound classical texts and arcane dissertation on series and matrices as one's only (very soothing) company. One could walk the length and breadth of King's and meet nobody – except possibly Donald Beves, on his way out to a black-market lunch. (Of course he wasn't a secret agent:[8] he was far too good-natured – he once lent me fifty pounds – and far too lazy.) Although the wartime scaffolding, erected round the chapel as an air-raid precaution, was depressing and unsightly, it was almost infinitely less depressing and unsightly than peacetime students. (23.7.77)

Now that seaside holidays were out of the question Esther bought a caravan which she parked at Waterbeach, a few miles to the north. Here in the fens Simon discovered the contrasting delights of fishing. 'It was peaceful, and yet also extremely exciting. When your float suddenly

[8] Before the exposure of Anthony Blunt, *The Times* had identified Beves as the 'Fourth Man'.

dipped it was an orgasmic moment.' Later, to his great annoyance, Esther moved the caravan to a site outside Barnet. 'She had the hots for London again. I think she fancied her chances with all those men in uniform. There was certainly a Yank on the scene at one point when my father was away.'

*

Simon was due to take the Charterhouse scholarship at the end of May 1941. During the previous term Captain Stokes wrote to Esther and suggested that in order to be certain of reaching the required standard in Greek grammar, Simon ought to have some coaching in the Easter holidays. Neither Esther nor her parents were competent to arrange this, so Mrs Christmas decided to consult her neighbour, Dr Frank Leavis, who she knew was a don. Leavis, who had a daughter about the same age as Robin, was sympathetic. He recommended a young undergraduate at his own college, Downing. Simon forgot his tutor's name, but not his achievement, which was 'to convince me that there was something very special about Greek grammar and those who could do it. It was as esoteric as the Caballa. This appealed to my vanity, with the result that I did so well in the exam.'

In fact Simon won the top scholarship to Charterhouse, the first of several glittering prizes he carried off during the next ten years. Nor did he only shine in the classroom. He enjoyed great success at cricket as well, averaging 20.7 with the bat, high by prep school standards, and topping the bowling averages with 35 wickets at an average of 4.9. His most distinguished victim, in a match against the Sherborne Mini-Colts, was the future Captain of England and Bishop of Liverpool, D.S. Sheppard, whom he bowled for 15. What made these triumphs all the sweeter was that they were not followed by swingeing peripeteia. This was to be the pattern later on, but in the Summer of '41 the Gods stayed their hand.

CHAPTER FOUR

What matters is getting popular and winning colours, tasting the joys of power for the first time, acquiring knowledge and avoiding punishment; in fact, growing up.

Cyril Connolly, *The Fate of an Elizabethan*

Recalling the privations he endured at Lancing during the Great War, Evelyn Waugh pronounced it 'the most dismal period of history for an English schoolboy'. Those in authority were either too young or too old. There were interminable Corps parades. The food was execrable. Expediency ruled. 'We were cold, shabby and hungry in the ethos, not of free Sparta, but of some beleaguered, enervated and forgotten garrison.'[1]

Like Lancing, Charterhouse is perched in splendid isolation on a windswept spur, and superficially conditions there in 1941 were not dissimilar to those at Lancing in 1917. There was stringent food rationing, Corps twice a week, compulsory war work,[2] a virtual ban on all inter-school fixtures except at the highest level and, every Saturday morning in chapel, the melancholy roll of last week's Old Carthusian casualties. An additional burden was the black-out, requiring six miles of black-out cloth; of necessity this meant that the boys were largely confined to their houses after dusk, increasing the sense of isolation. Yet for Simon, Charterhouse in wartime was no 'beleaguered garrison' but 'a little enclave of civilisation, pleasure and learning' in a country that had seemingly abandoned these desiderata for the duration. Far from begging his parents to remove him, as Waugh had done, Simon was always very sorry when the end of the quarter[3] came, 'and home one went to quarrelsome Mummy and Daddy, to austerity, to scowling, unshaven proletarian faces, soldiers in those terrible boots and sidecaps, gasmasks, the whole ghastly paraphernalia. So I was only too glad to come back at the beginning of every quarter, I can tell you.'

One man in particular was responsible for creating and maintaining this enlightened environment, the headmaster, Robert Birley, who as Simon put it, 'spent the war protecting us against the war'. Of Sir Robert's personal dealings with Simon I shall have more to say in its place. Now is the moment to consider his achievements as Headmaster in wartime.

[1] *A Little Learning*, Chapman & Hall 1964.
[2] Known as 'National Service'.
[3] Carthusian for term.

Birley had become headmaster in 1935 when he was only 32. He inherited a school that for 25 years had been run according to the stern, late-Victorian principles of his formidable predecessor, [Sir] Frank Fletcher, a man whom it was easier to respect than to love. Fletcher had rescued the school from mediocrity and made it a byword for Classical scholarship and conventional character-building. Birley, who had a strong social conscience and who later became one of the architects of the Fleming Report,[4] recognised that such a conservative formula would need modifying if Charterhouse were to flourish in a changing world. He chose to effect this by persuasion and example rather than edict, and by the beginning of the war, when the school was made up entirely of boys who had come during his time, the atmosphere was markedly more liberal than before, particular emphasis being placed upon the need to think first and conform afterwards where social attitudes were concerned.

The war came as no surprise to Birley. A lifelong opponent of tyranny, he had returned home from a visit to Berlin in 1934 convinced that unless Hitler were removed from power, another European war was inevitable. In 1935 he wrote to Fletcher, 'You guided the school through the last war. I shall have to guide it through the next.' One of the first steps he took had the incidental effect of increasing his intimacy with Simon. Believing that as Headmaster he ought to be in the thick of things, he vacated his official residence, which was some distance away from the centre of the school, and in January 1940 took over Saunderites, a boarding house in the main block. So when Simon entered Saunderites in September 1941 he found that Birley was his housemaster as well as his headmaster.

As a boy at Rugby during the Great War Birley had been cold and hungry, so he threw his weight behind activities like market gardening and log cutting which greatly supplemented the school's rations of food and fuel. And in order to avoid another bane of public school life in the Great War, incompetent temporary masters, he persuaded key members of his staff to stay on past retirement age and brought back others who had recently retired. One of those who stayed on was the Head of Classics, A.L. 'Uncle' Irvine, in Simon's opinion 'the best and most affable teacher I ever sat under'.

Birley knew that in wartime it was not only Nazis who reached for their revolvers when they heard the word culture. To pre-empt the philistinism that might otherwise have dominated he saw to it that the Arts received their due. Recalling the attention paid to Music and Painting, Gerald Priestland, a year senior to Simon, said that by the time he left, 'the Arts had become almost respectable'. Simon never forgot how, in the midst of all his other duties, Birley had taught him how to read an orchestral score.

'That's why he was a great man. There we were in the middle of a

[4] Wartime report on the relationship between public schools and the State educational system.

full-scale war. He was headmaster and housemaster, a member of this committee and that, *and* writing a book on American documents, yet he still found time to take four or five of us through Beethoven symphonies with orchestral scores. It just goes to show how polymath the best schoolmasters were then. Uncle Irvine was the same. He was a Classical scholar, but it didn't end there. He was a great *appreciator* and marvellous at suggesting things to read, look at, learn. Every time I enter a gallery I'm grateful to him for the wonderful weekly Art lectures he used to give. He and Birley and one or two of the others like Bob Arrowsmith (q.v.) were determined to *civilise* us, which, when you consider what was going on elsewhere at that time, was extraordinary.'

On October 25th 1940 Birley narrowly escaped the fate which had just befallen his colleague, Robert 'Bobbie' Longden, the Headmaster of Wellington, who was killed in an air-raid. One of a stick of four bombs that fell across Charterhouse landed within fourteen yards of where he was sitting in his study; fortunately the ground was soft after prolonged heavy rain and as a result the blast was directed harmlessly upwards. The other bombs proved equally innocuous, but as a precaution the boys all slept downstairs for the next two years, in what had been day rooms whose ceilings were strengthened by cross beams and timber supports.

In fact it was Whitehall, not the Luftwaffe, which posed the greatest threat to Charterhouse at this time. Shortly before the bombs fell Birley received a visit from representatives of the Admiralty who said that they intended to commandeer the school for their administrative staff. He must tell no one, they said. Realising how difficult it would be for the school to find a suitable alternative site at such short notice, Birley insisted that he be allowed to inform the Chairman of the Governors, 'the real Head of the School'. And who might he be? they asked. 'The Archbishop of Canterbury.' Very grudgingly, permission was granted, whereupon Birley dashed up to Lambeth Palace the same afternoon. 'This is out of the question,' said the Primate, Cosmo Lang, 'I shall see Anthony Eden at once.' He did, and the Admiralty's plans were torpedoed forthwith.

This shows what a canny operator of the Old Boy network Birley could be. Remote as he sometimes appeared to boys who were overawed by his great stooping presence,[5] lack of small talk and antiquarian tastes, he never struck anyone as ineffectual. One other story of his string-pulling is worth repeating, first, because it sheds a humane light on 'the Old School Tie', and secondly, because the punchline could have come from one of Simon's books.

In January 1938 Otto Fisher, the son of a prominent Viennese diamond merchant, entered the school. Shortly afterwards came the *Anschluss*, resulting in the arrest of Fisher's parents. Birley realised that the immediate offer of a British visa might save them. Luckily, the British

[5] He was 6′6″ tall.

Consul-General in Vienna was an Old Carthusian. Birley sent a letter to him via the diplomatic bag. 'You cannot,' he wrote, 'let the parents of a Carthusian smart in Hitler's prison.' The Consul-General concurred. Visas were issued and Fisher's parents were able to make their way to England.

*

Birley's predecessor at Saunderites had been an old-style housemaster whose wife stayed firmly behind the green baize door and who gave his Monitors carte blanche. Under Birley and his wife Elinor the green baize door was flung open and the atmosphere became markedly less monastic. But the hierarchy remained intact. Consequently, although Birley played a very considerable part in the moral and intellectual development of all the boys in Saunderites, he exercised practically no control or influence over the ethos of the House, which was a good deal more Spartan than he would probably have wished.

Saunderites was a 'keen' House: keen on games, keener still on Corps, which because of the war had to be taken far more seriously than in the piping days of peace. Luckily for Simon – 'the idlest and scruffiest cadet I can remember', according to a friend – there existed a soft option in the shape of the Air Training Corps. As soon as he had completed his basic training Simon joined this 'sloppy outfit' which did little foot drill and was in any case easy to cut. But meanwhile he had fallen foul of a Saunderites' procedure known as 'Showing Up'.

Many years later Simon exposed this insidious practice in *Sneak House*, his contribution to a *Spectator* series called 'John Bull's Schooldays'. In his second term, he explained, he had remarked to a friend that the Chinese had once been a civilised people with a low opinion of military activities. This was overheard by a third boy, who reported Simon to the Head Monitor, from whom Simon received a severe wigging for his 'unsatisfactory' attitude. When Simon confronted his delator and accused him of sneaking, he was put right immediately.

> 'We don't use the word "sneaking",' Cave-Watkins said, 'we talk about "showing up".'
>
> Showing up, he said, was a permissible practice, much encouraged by masters and older boys, when there was any question at all of it being one's duty or responsibility to speak out. In the bad old days, nothing short of murder would have elicited a word from anyone. And just look at all the bullying and immorality and slacking there had been. But nowadays everyone knew better. Anything said or done that raised a moral issue, however piddling or remote, or that touched upon the tone or efficiency of the House, was suitable material for retailing to the authorities .... If I myself, for example, was to get anywhere in the local hierarchy, I must soon start taking in my

own reports. I need not wait to be summoned. I should just go along and knock on the Head Monitor's door and announce that I would like 'to talk to him' for a while. (3.10.58)

This Head Monitor was known as 'Keyhole Kate', for the very good reason that as Second Monitor he had reported seeing the then Head Monitor and some colleagues enter a pub, with the result that they were de-Monitored and he became Head of House. This put Simon's nose out of joint too because he lost his cushy job as study fag to the disgraced Head of House, and reverted to being a lowly running fag, at every Monitor's beck and call. When Simon consistently failed to comply – even then he bitterly resented anything that impinged upon his own personal freedom or wishes – Keyhole Kate was urged to beat him. Although opposed to corporal punishment he made an exception in Simon's case. Next day this graffito appeared in the House lavatories:

KEYHOLE KATE GAVE RAVEN EIGHT

Simon also came to oppose beating, but on the perverse grounds that it was too feeble a punishment. 'Yes, it hurts – but not for long,' he used to say. 'Whereas having to spend the whole afternoon doing some frightful chore like vegetable digging, that really was not to be borne.'

Simon's rather subversive views, which he was never slow to air, meant that he was always being shown up, particularly during his second and third years. 'Of course it was a good way of paying off old scores, particularly by boys who were just a little bit senior to one. You know, "It's in the interests of the House that I show you up, Raven." In brackets, "That'll teach you, you little sod." But guilt played its part, too. Every week, as the roll of honour got longer so tempers became shorter, because people disparaged themselves for enjoying a first-class education while their protectors were being killed. It made the atmosphere very oppressive at times, particularly for slackers like me who thought they had better things to do than dreary war work.'

Simon was also punished for being 'festive', meaning bumptious or cheeky. On one occasion Matron sent a fag to tell him that he must get his hair cut. 'Tell Matron that I like it long and she can bloody well mind her own business,' responded Simon. This the boy did, verbatim. 'So of course I was beaten. Normally the fag would have been blamed for being such a fool, but not then – guilt and puritanism made everyone very literal-minded.'

Although it frequently got him into trouble Simon's irreverence made him as many friends as enemies, some of them in high places. Lacking in 'character' he may have been, but he made up for it by a winning combination of intelligence, acumen and effrontery, qualities that bachelor schoolmasters in particular have always found hard to resist. Nor could there be any complaint at this stage about his work. Already marked down in the academic form book as 'one to follow', he rewarded the tipsters by swiftly opening up a wide gap between himself and his fellow yearlings. One of those he left behind was William Rees-Mogg:

> We arrived the same term. He was the top scholar and I was the bottom scholar, but because our names started 'Ra' and 'Re' we were placed next to each other in Mr Lake's form. He impressed me right away because he was so clever – streets ahead of the rest of us, particularly in Classics. As scholars we were given 30 lines of Latin verse to construe every night. Most of us found this a fearful slog but Simon took it in his stride. He also had an extraordinarily quick and keen mind, and a very well trained one. I think he was moved up a year at the end of his second term.

Rees-Mogg owed his scholarship to a brilliant History paper that in Birley's eyes more than compensated for his poor showing in Classics and Maths. Although Simon outpaced him to begin with, he had surprising staying power for a boy whose sickly appearance convinced the authorities that he should be excused all games, Corps parades and war work. In the long run he repaid Birley's faith in him by winning the coveted Brackenbury History Scholarship to Balliol; his other great achievement was to become only the second Carthusian to be appointed Head of School but not Head of House (the first was William Beveridge).

Intensely ambitious, prodigiously erudite, deeply reactionary (at the age of fifteen he was seriously advocating slavery as a cure for unemployment), Rees-Mogg also had a sly wit, as Simon discovered towards the end of his second quarter. In order to test people's credulity and, if possible, discourage them from the 'mortal sin' of onanism, he put it about that masturbation caused syphilis. Simon was among those taken in, and, until a friend disabused him, desisted from a practice he had repeated almost daily since his first, joyous emission the previous October.

This shows how ill-informed about sex schoolboys could then be. As I said earlier, Simon was not told the facts of life at Cordwalles, or, for that matter, at St Dunstan's. His parents ignored the subject as well. The only official pronouncement on puberty and its consequences he received was from Tommy Garnett,[6] House Tutor of Saunderites in his first quarter. 'He said we shouldn't worry if we sometimes got "a nasty feeling down there". He made it sound as if we were going to have periods – not that I knew what they were then.'

Simon got his revenge on Rees-Mogg in his *Alms for Oblivion* sequence by saddling Somerset Lloyd-James, Rees-Mogg reinvented, with his own rather puerile sexual fantasies about nannies and matrons. (' "Naughty

[6] Later Master of Marlborough and Headmaster of Geelong Grammar School.

Somerset," said Maisie resignedly. "Nanny saw him playing with it. Nanny will have to smack." ') For the most part, though, he was entertained by 'Mogg', finding him 'absurd – his name alone is enough to make you fall about laughing – and yet in a curious way rather impressive. We never saw eye to eye about sex, of course, and Mogg would give one minatory lectures about how Hell was a bad tooth that went on getting worse and worse for Eternity. But then, as now, he was a figure of probity.' (Shortly after writing this I read in the papers that the Broadcasting Standards Council, chaired by Lord Rees-Mogg, had censured Central Television for broadcasting a raunchy sex scene immediately after the 9 p.m. watershed, when children could still have been watching. The scene occurred at the start of *The Blackheath Poisonings*, scripted by Simon.)

*

Saunderites may have been a keen House, but thanks to Robert Birley it had a lively intellectual side as well consisting of clubs and societies devoted to literature, drama, politics and so on. As the top scholar of his year Simon was automatically a celebrity; even quite senior boys would give him the time of day. 'Compared to someone like me he had a lot of respect in the bank from the word Go,' said his friend Ivan Lynch, who was not a scholar. 'He handled this pretty well. I dare say a few older boys resented him but he was popular with his contemporaries. He'd always help you out with a bit of Latin or whatever, and of course he was quite good at games, which certainly earned him points in our house.'

Simon's favourite game at Charterhouse was cricket; soccer held no more appeal for him there than it had at Cordwalles and St Dunstan's. In days gone by this would have been unfortunate: soccer was *the* major sport and cricket merely 'a device for keeping footballers in training during the summer'. But from 1939 onwards, following the appointment of George Geary as coach, Charterhouse cricket came good and Simon was lucky enough to coincide with some outstanding performers, notably the future captain of Cambridge, Surrey and England, Peter May.

What Simon would have liked to have played during the winter was rackets. In *The English Gentleman* he complained that the courts had been closed for the duration because this 'costly and aristocratic game' was pronounced out of tune with the egalitarian spirit of the times. The real reason was circumstantial. In 1940 the rackets pro left to take up another post, and as the supply of balls was becoming erratic it was decided not to replace him until the status quo was restored. Soon afterwards the supply of balls dried up completely and the courts became storerooms for emergency rations.

In fact Simon learnt the equally esoteric, if less patrician, game of Eton fives, a Saunderites' speciality. Although he never excelled at this Simon retained a fondness for it that finds its best expression in an egregious passage at the end of his novel, *The Troubadour*. While a stately home is burning down, four appetising young persons, all stark naked, serenely knock up against one of its wings:

> Theodosia was the first to throw the ball up, and was immediately swinged down by Eurydice, who cut elegantly but viciously at the ball while it hovered at the top of its bounce.
>
> 'Well played,' said tumescent Marius.
>
> 'Such a pretty sight,' the Corporal Major was saying to the Chamberlain and Geddes and Glastonbury. 'The great thing about you upper-class lot, sir, is that we never know what you're going to do next.'
>
> Fielding Gray and Doctor La Soeur joined the military group .... 'Christ, [said Fielding] those girls ... Tessa's little gold bush and Eurydice's little silver bush and Thea's great rambling bush – '
>
> ' – If that horny little Marius isn't careful,' said La Soeur, 'he'll do himself an injury on that buttress.'
>
> 'One of them young ladies would soon kiss it better,' said the Corporal Major.

*

In Simon's second year he began to sit under Messrs Irvine and Arrowsmith, two of the three Charterhouse masters he was most indebted to, the other being Robert Birley. Uncle Irvine, as we have heard, was a man of parts who combined Classical scholarship of a high order with an infectious enthusiasm for literature, art and music. In Simon's eyes he could do no wrong; but since it was the old man's laughter – 'deep, kindly, unquenchable' – rather than his 'humane and nourishing teaching' to which he awarded the palm in his valedictory notice in the *Carthusian*, I think it is worth quoting this tribute from another former pupil of the Uncle, L.P. (Patrick) Wilkinson, later a key figure in Simon's career at King's:

> [H]e insisted that when translating in school we should not go on to the next sentence until we had found exactly the right word, which was an invaluable linguistic and critical training.

Here is one explanation for the clarity and precision of Simon's prose.

Bob Arrowsmith was also taught by Uncle Irvine and in 1938, after nine years at Lancing, he returned to Charterhouse as master-in-charge of the Classical Fifth and the Under 16 Cricket XI. Again, Simon was lucky to encounter him: had he not been disqualified from military service by severe arthritis he would certainly have spent the war in uniform. A tall, stern, conventional Edwardian bachelor who was rumoured to wear Old Carthusian pyjamas, 'The Arrow' put a premium on effort and good form.

'Come on, you're supposed to be a *professional*,' he would chide a negligent scholar; while any breach of sporting etiquette would invite summary retribution. But this old school pedagogue had one chink in his armour: he liked personable, intelligent games-players. Oliver Popplewell was one of his favourites, Simon was another and Myles, as we shall see, became something like the son he never had.

Simon praised Bob Arrowsmith for his 'brisk and accurate' teaching of the Classics, particularly Horace and Demosthenes, and for introducing him to Pope, Sterne and Tennyson (his favourite English poet). But he was chiefly grateful to his old teacher for these two reasons.

'First, he was an unrivalled arbiter of correct behaviour, whether on the cricket field or in the drawing room. One learnt to say, "Will you have a drink?" not, "Will you have another drink?" That sort of thing. And one was left in no doubt that unpunctuality, for instance, was a breach of good manners. Secondly, he did all he could to mitigate the most irritating consequence of my expulsion. Officially, I was not an Old Carthusian; *ergo*, I could not play for The Friars [the old boys' touring side] which I very much wanted to do. But Bob was secretary of The Friars, and he saw to it that I played for them long before I was finally admitted to the Old Carthusian Club.'

One of Arrowsmith's obituarists identified him as the model for the reactionary old 'Senior Usher' in *Fielding Gray*, Simon's autobiographical novel of school life. But they differ in one crucial respect: unlike Arrowsmith, whose code was that of a Christian gentleman, the Senior Usher is a master of expediency. This is very apparent from the moment that Fielding defends the pagan view of life.

> 'It's not ... compulsory ... to accept the Christian ethic, sir. Lots of prominent men in the last two thousand years have rejected it.'
>
> 'But this school, Gray' – dryly and not unkindly – 'does accept it. Christianity has the official sanction here. Individuals may have their own ideas, but they must nevertheless conform with the official ones. It is a condition of belonging.'
>
> 'And if this condition is based on what is doubtful or untrue, sir?'
>
> 'You are only asked to conform. Not to believe.'
>
> The Sixth Form stirred, scenting heresy in high places.
>
> 'But why conform,' I insisted, 'if one does not believe?'
>
> 'It is convenient to run this institution, any institution, for that matter, on certain assumptions. One assumption here, as enjoined by our founder, is that Christ was the Son of God and that the morality which he preached is therefore binding. This is the basis of our rule. We cannot compel you to believe in it, indeed many of us would not wish to, but we can and must compel you to act by it. Otherwise our whole careful structure will fall apart ...'

As an adult Simon enjoyed poking fun at Christianity, particularly Pauline Christianity. But at Charterhouse in his day Christianity was no laughing matter. After all, the Chairman of the Governing Body – 'the real Head of the School' – was the Archbishop of Canterbury; and the one building of any real merit on the campus was Sir Gilbert Scott's War Memorial Chapel. Then there was Robert Birley, a liberal, yes, but also an exacting Christian moralist who, as Ivan Lynch recalled, 'could put the fear of God in you with one glowering look if he spied you messing about in Chapel'.

It was during a debate about compulsory chapel that Simon's subversive views on religion first came to the attention of the authorities. In support of a motion before the Junior Discussion Society that compulsory chapel was 'a bad thing', Simon made what the *Carthusian* described as 'a highly irrelevant and somewhat improper speech and was justly reprimanded by the Chairman'. What gave cause for concern was his intemperate attack on God. Fourteen-year-old boys could be forgiven for finding chapel boring (in fact Simon quite enjoyed both the services and the setting). But a public endorsement of atheism could not go unchallenged and Simon was summoned by Birley and catechised about his lack of faith.

To be fair, this probing had as much to do with morality as with Christian fervour. As Simon conceded in *The English Gentleman*, most people need 'a firm frame of moral reference .... Christianity has its faults, but at least it keeps people out of trouble and encourages them to behave decently and often courageously.' Birley was no zealot, but according to Conrad Dehn, another Saunderite with atheistic tendencies,

> It was *staggering* the way in which he regarded the moral development of the boys in his house as of prime importance. As his biographer[7] relates, when he was worried that my lack of religious beliefs might lead me to think that there was no such thing as morality he went to very great pains to persuade me that morality was not dependent on religion and I was made to think that my views on questions of morality were of very great importance. Here was this enormously busy and very important Headmaster devoting a lot of his time to the views of this adolescent boy on these matters. It very much drove home the importance of one's opinions and that one ought to be very responsible about holding them if it could cause so much concern to people older and wiser than oneself.

Dehn was a scholar, but unlike Simon, who had played for the Under 16 Cricket XI while still only fourteen, he had no pretensions to becoming

[7] Arthur Hearnden, author of *Red Robert*.

a major blood[8] as well. It was because Simon was on course for this academic and sporting double, the achievement of which would confer 'enormous power and prestige', that he presented such a challenge once his moral character came into question.

> I really do believe [insisted Conrad Dehn] that members of the Staff like Robert Birley and Bob Arrowsmith felt, 'This is a boy whose soul I should try to save, and whose soul I ought to be able to save being the skilful teacher that I am.' Birley in particular went to tremendous lengths with Simon and I think his failure to reform him was a significant blow. There was a rumour, which I've never been able to verify, that over the sacking of Simon and related incidents his hair went grey.

This may sound melodramatic to modern ears but schoolmastering then was still a calling. 'We are teaching them habits for life,' Bob Arrowsmith used to say, and he was not just referring to deportment. Why Simon proved obdurate I shall consider in due course. But it is worth re-emphasising here that although he certainly found aspects of Charterhouse tiresome and even oppressive, in general it was very much to his taste. First, there was the sheer *excitement* of living in a closed community for up to twelve weeks on end. A great deal could happen in twelve weeks, 'particularly in twelve week-ends'. And if the drama was tremendous, it was also most instructive: an unrivalled education for the world which day-school boys were denied.

> There is no milieu [he argued in the *Spectator*] in which the workings of ambition can be seen more true and naked than in an English public school. As Cyril Connolly has remarked in *Enemies of Promise*, the boy who is head of his house often wields more power than the housemaster himself. Small wonder, then, with such a prize at stake, that even good men will delate, bribe and betray, will perjure and prostitute themselves to get it; and all this is to be observed, not as the distant and speculative affair of unfamiliar men in Westminster Palace, but as an actual and blow-by-blow contest which is being carried on in the next block, the next room, the next bed .... Lust, envy, guilt and spleen; treachery, imbroglio, humiliation; the forlorn hope, the last-ditch stand; cold, loneliness, misery and hunger; the arrogance of victory and the snivelling of defeat; even, on occasion, honour, loyalty and love: here is God's plenty, and [the public school boy] can see and know it all .... So naturally enough, when he goes

[8] A member of the First XI at football or cricket.

into the world, he scoops the kitty from under the nose of less experienced competitors from other kinds of school. (30.6.67)

*

At the end of his second Summer quarter Simon scooped another kitty himself, winning a Senior Scholarship worth £30 in addition to the Foundation Scholarship he already held. So all Arthur now had to find for Simon's education was £40 a year, a bargain by any standards – 'though naturally this didn't stop him complaining that our school fees were beggaring him'.

Arthur had at last found a niche. He was gainfully, usefully and contentedly employed as part of a ballistics team testing tank armour on a range outside Sheffield. Home was a bungalow in Worral, a mining village on the edge of the moors. There was a golf course nearby and plenty of scope for long walks. Simon liked to play golf – 'one of the few treats left in wartime' – but resented having to go hiking as well. His abiding memories of Worral were of gazing out across 'the bloody moors' and wishing the nearest cinema wasn't so far away – 'one didn't know when one was well off'. But it was Esther who found the isolation hardest to bear.

She was now 40, beginning to fray a bit at the edges but still attractive enough for Simon to fancy her in his teens ('Doing it with Mummy' is approvingly alluded to more than once in his books). With her sons away at school and Arthur out of the house all day, she had plenty of time to brood. What she missed most of all was the sort of attention she had received in the locust years before the war. She rediscovered it as a convert to the Roman Catholic church.

'It came about because my mother thought Robin ought to be learning something – she must have been five or six – but not at the local school, which was full of miners' children. So what she did was to walk her over to a Carmelite convent about three miles away where there were a couple of nuns whose vows weren't so strict. These nuns agreed to teach Robin the three Rs. And did so quite well. But they also took advantage of a rather lonely, slightly silly woman who was upset because the war had spoilt everything she enjoyed. And the next we knew she was a Catholic.'

Like all converts Esther began by being very zealous. She would try to drag her children along to services and was quite hurt when Simon objected on aesthetic grounds – 'I told her I was put off by all that red brick and sealing wax.' A more serious consequence was that she refused to allow Arthur to wear a french letter and would not use a contraceptive herself. 'So of course she got pregnant. Had she been a healthy woman, then despite her age I think she could have had another healthy child. But she'd started drinking and the result was two messy miscarriages followed by an operation to have her works out. This didn't improve her state of mind and from then on she was never far from a bottle.

'So is it any wonder,' concluded Simon, 'that I've come to believe that God has a lot to answer for?'

CHAPTER FIVE

On the rugger field, in the gym,
Buck marked down at his leisure
The likeliest bits of stuff;
The notion, familiar enough,
Of 'using somebody for pleasure'
Seemed handy and harmless to him.
Kingsley Amis, *An Ever-Fixed Mark*

At the beginning of Simon's third year he entered the Classical Sixth, which meant, among other things, that he swapped the hurly-burly of Saunderites' Longroom, where the junior boys lived, for the comparative privacy of his own study. This was a great boon since he was about to make some surprising discoveries about Classical authors, and in particular Roman poets, that would require peace and quiet to digest.

Hitherto Classics had been rather like Algebra, an exercise in problem-solving with grammar and syntax taking the place of mathematical symbols. But having reached a level of proficiency where he could read for enjoyment rather than as a chore, he embarked on a voyage of discovery that left him breathless with amazement and excitement at the sheer subversity of what he found.

'Here was Horace, openly boasting of how he ran away from a battle. Tacitus, quietly equating enthusiasm with stupidity. Thucydides, grimly announcing that the only law of human affairs was "Necessity". Lucretius, recommending regular one-night-stands as a way of securing immunity from passion, which was simply the unwholesome and ridiculous product of suppressed or thwarted lust. Catullus, advocating sex with women or sex with boys, whichever you fancy at the time, because there is no such thing as right or wrong in this context .... *All* of them insistent that you take what pleasure you can from this world because only superstitious fools believe in the existence of the next.'

And yet, as Simon well knew, neither the Uncle nor Bob Arrowsmith were superstitious fools. This was what was so puzzling. How could an intelligent man revere the Classics and still be a practising Christian? It really would not do to argue that Catullus and Co were 'yearning unconsciously for Christ before his birth'. Simon never forgot how discomfited the Uncle became when they arrived at this sentence in his favourite passage of Lucretius: *Tantum religio potuit suadere malorum* (Such horrible ills religion has been the cause of). 'His explanation was that *religio* didn't mean religion as we understood it, but superstition. However, since Lucretius devoted the whole book to putting religion down, one wasn't really convinced. Nor, to be fair, do I think he thought we would be.'

Meanwhile there was a war on, with all that entailed in the way of extra responsibilities for masters and boys alike. This was why, Simon thought, his scepticism went unchallenged except when it became too blatant to be ignored. A case in point was this poem, which he submitted to *The Sagger-Magger*, the Saunderites' house magazine.

'The Efficacy of Prayer'

Archetype of the bureaucrat
Stiff the recording angel sat,
Noted the prayers of high and low,
Of the whole undaunted band who *know*;
And then, it being half-past seven –
Routine is strictly observed in Heaven –
Brought the Book before Jehovah
And read the day's petitions over.

'Dives, it would seem, has bought
The latest thing in wheeled transport;
Like all that's futile in every way
It's coming from the U.S.A.
Without a scratch, he prays to Thee,
His car may cross th'Atlantic Sea …
Lazarus, you'll be grieved to hear,
For seven days has fed off air;
His wife coughs blood increasingly,
His children whine unceasingly;
To find some bread I heard him ask,
To find some dull (but honest) task.'

Said God: 'Not even a scratch shall mar
The resplendent veneer of Dives' car;
But as for Lazarus – let him rot,
And his rickety brats, the whole damn'd lot.
'Tis a pleasure unhoped for that rich men should pray,
T'other sort bother me every day.'

Conrad Dehn, the editor, accepted Simon's offering, but Birley overruled him. Instead, Dehn ran an article by Simon on National Service, in which he equated those who were keen on this 'degrading manual labour' with the sort of people who talk about 'Discipline in Lent' and 'Taking the Plunge'.

*

Simon was not the first clever schoolboy to discover that if you cast your net wider than Aristotle, Plato and Cicero, all pronounced 'sound' by Dr Arnold, Classics could be improper as well as improving. A generation before, Cyril Connolly had reached the same conclusion and been labelled 'cynical and irreverent' for his pains. But though he knew full well that 'homosexuality formed an ingredient in this ancient wisdom', 'Ugly' Connolly kept his hands to himself (if you can say that of someone who swore he never even masturbated at Eton). Simon, by contrast, let his hands wander at will; and more often than not they found what they were looking for. 'I was a tall, healthy, handsome sort of boy,' he explained. 'There were always plenty of takers.'

For what exactly? an inquisitive modern reader might ask. 'Stroking-off together', for the most part; otherwise, a bit of 'fumble-wumble'. Practically no fellatio. And never, then or later, any buggery, 'because I've always been mindful of Juvenal's complaint about meeting last night's supper'. (50 years later, writing in the Spring edition of *ad familiares*,[1] Simon 'gave thanks for a number of experiences far more erotic (and poetic) than the perfunctory grabbing and snatching and jerking depicted on Greek vases'. He thought 'those poor Greek laddies' missed out because, unlike him, they never got to grips with boys their own age.)

The fact that Simon lusted after other boys was not in itself very remarkable. As James Prior notes in his autobiography, *A Balance of Power*, 'Drinking, smoking and homosexuality were optional extras.' But what did strike Lord Prior as unusual was how frank Simon could be about his proclivities. 'He would say how beautiful so-and-so was and how satisfying it would be to seduce him. And if he did seduce him, he would tell you. In graphic detail!'

All of which delighted the scandal-mongers who were, said Conrad Dehn, especially active in Saunderites. 'We were a very gossipy House, always speculating about what other boys were up to. Having said that, and speaking for myself, I wouldn't have thought there was that much active sexuality. There was a lot of rumour, a lot of innuendo .... So the fact that Simon apparently put into practice what other boys just talked about made him different.'

Quite how different was brought home to them all when he arrived back at school in September 1944 and announced that on his way back from farm camp during the summer holidays he had had a woman. 'His exact words were, "I went to London and took a prostitute",' recalled Ivan Lynch.

[1] The journal of the Friends of the Classics.

And how had he picked her up? they wanted to know. 'You flip the end of your tie over your shoulder,' replied Simon. 'It's the universal signal.'

It cost Simon one pound to lose his virginity. The experience was 'quite pleasant, but not very pleasant. She was a bit thin for my taste, and of course one was rather nervous. Far pleasanter was returning to my hotel room, washing thoroughly – although she had made me wear a French letter – and suddenly remembering how exciting it was and having an enormous wank over the basin. Then home I went to Sheffield the next day, in the course of which I shoplifted something for the first and last time in my life. It was a copy of Maugham's new novel, *The Razor's Edge*, which I whipped from the station bookstall. I remember sitting in the train sweating with fear until it departed. This taught me that stealing simply isn't worthwhile because the agony far outweighs any possible benefit.'

Within a week or so of his return to school Simon was horrified to discover 'a pimple on my winkle'. He should have known it was nothing to worry about, but guilt insisted otherwise. Finally he went to Birley, who was 'astonishingly relaxed and worldly about the whole business. He sent me to the school doctor, an Old Carthusian rackets player, who thought it was a huge joke. "What, go in bare like a sailor, did you?" I said "No, she put a rubber on me." And he said, "Well, you're almost certainly alright, but what we'll do is take a Wasserman on you. You know what that is?" I said "Yes, I've read every single library book on the subject," which he thought was very funny. And he then said, "A Wasserman is no good until six weeks after the event, so you better go away for two weeks," which I did. And my blood was duly sent off and was of course negative.

'Then Birley called me in and said, "Look, I've just got one thing to say to you. The lesson you should learn from this, and the scare you've had, is to try and be a better person. This doesn't mean you've got to go round being kind to prostitutes and starting homes for dilapidated whores (ha! ha!), you've got to just try and be nicer." Very, very sensible, particularly when you consider how some headmasters would have reacted .... As for one's chums, I think they were rather surprised. One or two of them were a bit sceptical to begin with, but not after I'd spilled the beans to Birley. I don't know *why* they were quite so surprised. The West End was simply crawling with tarts. Finding one wasn't a difficult thing to do.'

But only Simon would have done it – or so Conrad Dehn insisted. Nobody else, he told me, would have *dreamt* of going to a prostitute; it was totally outside their imagination, let alone their experience. 'It wasn't that we approved, or that we envied him, but we were struck that here was this remarkable boy behaving in this way. "Do you know what Simon did?" Actually we said that a lot. And I suspect myself – though I never saw him glorying in it – that he rather enjoyed his notoriety. If he didn't, he's organised his life in an unfortunate way!'

By now Simon was the talk, not just of Saunderites, but of the whole school. Dick Taverne, then a junior boy in another house, said that masters he knew, as well as boys, 'were enthralled by Simon's reported misdeeds and spent a lot of time gossiping about him. He had an aura of disreputable glamour that was in stark contrast to the serious atmosphere of a public school in wartime.' Gerald Priestland concurred:

> Brilliant when he could be bothered, handsomely copper-headed but with a world-weary slouch and drawl, [he] moved through Charterhouse trailing an odour of brimstone. (*Something Understood*)

Conrad Dehn said 'brimstone' was an exaggeration (though naturally it delighted Simon), and he thought the slouch was not so much 'world-weary' as part of Simon's anti-militaristic pose. 'But Priestland's right about the hair. And what I also remember is that he had a sort of bronzed look – not bronzed in the sense of having been out in the sun but almost a sort of auburn sheen. It was really quite unusual and made him stand out. And he always reminded me a bit – this may be unfair – of a fox. I'm not sure whether it was his face or his demeanour – he was rather soft-spoken – but there was something slightly foxy about him. The fox hasn't got a very good human image and I don't mean untrustworthy. He just looked foxy.'

Look at a photo of the 1945 Cricket XI and you will see what Dehn means. So vulpine is Simon's appearance that he could almost be mounted on a huntsman's wall. His own view of how he looked then is rather more heroic. In *The Roses of Picardie* Jacquiz Helmut, a middle-aged don, wistfully admires a 'ginger-haired[2] youth with huge shoulders and calves' striding out to bat 'in dirty pads'. After hitting his first ball for a straight six he smiles 'awkwardly … out of a face that could have been Apollo's had it not been just too heavily jowled'.[3]

*

Even before Birley's 'sensible' advice Simon had resolved to pull his weight in the House and cease to mock the war effort. There were a number of reasons for this, beginning with the arrival at Saunderites of Myles, who had also won a scholarship. Always protective towards his younger brother – James Prior was struck by how 'very much closer' they were than other pairs of brothers at school – Simon realised he would be doing him no favours as a new boy if he soldiered on in the awkward squad. Luckily, he was now besotted with 'Alexis',[4] a contemporary who was 'keen' to the point of priggishness, so here was another reason for turning over a new leaf. Finally there was the prospect of 'Success my dears – Ah!', of becom-

[2] Simon's hair went from red to ginger to auburn.

[3] Margaret Viner (q.v.), then at Priorsfield, met Simon at a school dance and thought him 'incredibly beautiful. Like something on a coin. A god.' When she and her friends learnt of his sacking they assumed he'd seduced a housemaid – 'we were so naive in those days.'

[4] As with Colonel K I have retained Simon's pseudonym.

ing both a University scholar *and* a blood, after which you sauntered out of Chapel for the last time with a tear in your eye and a Leaving Exhibition, worth £80 a year, in your pocket.

To what extent Simon convinced those who knew him best that he was a reformed character I cannot say, but no one could gainsay the laurels that were showered on him as the academic year proceeded. In December he won the Thackeray, an important essay prize, and performed creditably in a trial run for an award at Corpus Christi, Oxford. In March Birley told him he was to be a House Monitor in the summer ('first step towards real power and place') and invited him to stay at his cottage in Somerset during the Easter holidays. He then went up to King's to take a scholarship, and on learning soon afterwards that he had succeeded, wrote this letter of thanks to the Provost:

c/o Birley,
Daisy Farm,
Coat,
2.4.45 Martock, Somerset.

Dear Mr Provost,

Owing to the efficiency of, I suppose, Mr Beves, my parents in Worral received a telegram[5] which apprised them of the fact that I had won a scholarship early enough to let me know here by Friday morning. My thanks are due for so quick a dispatch of good tidings.

I cannot say how much pleasure the prospect of coming to King's affords me. Although I told Mr Beves and Mr Lucas that I might try Oxford if I failed, I decided later that I would definitely come to King's again in December. Fortunately that won't be necessary now. Although I could almost wish I had failed simply because it would mean another opportunity of visiting a college I have already learnt to love before I actually became an undergraduate there – which, I am afraid, as things are going, will not be until after the war. I cannot express how much I wish I could come up this October and do a full three years' course, with the definite aim of a fellowship at the end of it. As it is, I should only have time for a year before being called up, and I don't think it would be advisable to split one's course in two. So I shall await better times with eagerness, and ambition will not provide me with any other object than eventually to become a Fellow of King's College, Cambridge.

Yours sincerely,
Simon Raven

[5] The Ravens were not on the phone at Worral.

Scrawled at the bottom of this letter, which is in the King's College archives, is an unsigned note:

> He won't be 18 till December. (?)[6] told him to think again about coming up in October – for 5 months of Classics *here* would surely be good for him.

Birley advised against this, ironically on the grounds that an extra year at school would 'stabilise' Simon's moral character. He had him pencilled in as a future Head of House, but was yet to be convinced that he was worthy of such an office. What was Simon's *code*?

> The Headmaster leaned forward in his chair and shook himself like a large, worried dog.
>
> 'You haven't been confirmed,' he said. 'Where do you stand – the question must be asked – in respect to Christianity?'
>
> 'Not an easy question, sir ... I find it hard to understand its prohibitions, its obsession with what is sinful or wrong. The Greeks put their emphasis on what is pleasant and seemly and therefore right.'
>
> 'Christ, as a Jew, had a more fastidious morality. And as the Son of God He had authority to reveal new truths and check old errors.'
>
> 'Did he?' I said.
>
> There was a long silence between us.
>
> 'The Greeks stood for reason and decency,' I said. 'Isn't that enough?'
>
> 'Reason and decency,' the Headmaster murmured, 'but without the sanctity of revealed religion ...? No, Fielding. It isn't enough. What you forgive or tolerate, I must know about and punish in order to *forgive*. Please bear the difference in mind .... Will you come,' he went on abruptly, 'and stay with us in Wiltshire?... there is more to be said on the subject we have just been discussing ...' (*Fielding Gray*)

But it would be wrong to infer from this that Birley invited boys to stay with him simply in order to vet them. Simon, who had been three or four times before, said he did his best to make life 'very, very civilised indeed. In the mornings one was encouraged to read because this was when Birley liked to work. In the afternoons – occasionally in the early mornings too – we'd cycle off to look at a local church. Birley knew a lot about churches. He implanted in me a taste for church-crawling which I've never lost. At dinner there would generally be something to drink, even if it was only beer. Birley's was the first table at which I drank a proper bottle of wine, ever. It was to celebrate my scholarship to King's.'[7]

On Sunday Birley and his family would attend matins. Simon usually

[6] Illegible.

[7] This was appropriate, given that it was Birley who suggested that Simon try for King's.

went too, 'not because it was expected of one – the choice was yours – but because it seemed to me he was being so civil. And I think the lesson Birley was trying to put across on these occasions, which I've since realised is a good lesson, is that on the whole Virtue is more *fun* than Vice. Because with Virtue there goes a quiet mind. It's more likely to bring worldly success. Virtue, unless as dictated by the most demanding people, is a pretty malleable concept. It needn't stop you eating and drinking and having a very agreeable time. And of course all the Arts are available to you. So one was made aware of how pleasant life could be within a civilised, virtuous, and still in his case, Christian context. But then he was old-fashioned C of E. No thumping and banging about it.... *And yet*, he had this tremendous conscience, which made him stand up in Chapel at the end of the war and say, "Look, nobody need think the Fair's about to begin. It's not party time, oh dear me No." Which wasn't exactly what people wanted to hear after six years of dreary war.'

> Wars were fought either to annex or to preserve [thought Fielding]. This one, as we had all been told to the point of vomiting, had been fought to preserve freedom, and freedom, to all present in the chapel, meant a return to life as it had been before the struggle started ... an end of rationing, of regulations, of being bossed about by common little men in offices, and of depressing notices about duty all over the place. We all wanted, we had all earned, some fun ....
>
> 'This,' said the Headmaster, 'is what the expected voices, the voices of common self-interest, are already saying. It is my duty to tell you ... that there can be no recompense and no return to the old life.' (*Fielding Gray*)

Birley did not of course put it nearly as bluntly as that. But he did advise the congregation that privilege now had its price:

> There is an immense duty before you, in the years after the Japanese war is also won, to make an England fit, not 'for heroes to live in' (the old phrase betrays itself in its exaggeration), but for ordinary men and women to live in with full and satisfying lives, as you yourselves are given so great a chance to live. The Nazis filled an empty house with the spirit of evil. There were days before this war when England was becoming spiritually empty. We can repay that debt that is ours, if we never allow this to happen again. (*Carthusian*, July 1945)

Birley's audience that day included James Prior and Dick Taverne, both of whom practised what Birley preached in their political lives.[8] Even

[8] '[Birley] is the only master at any school who had *any* influence on me at all,' said Lord Prior.

William Rees-Mogg, an 'Ultra' if ever there was one, had second thoughts about the merits of inequality. But Simon acknowledged no debt to Society. The only price he set on privilege was the skill and effort it took to earn it. If Providence had ordained that he should pass his time comfortably and agreeably as a Fellow of King's rather than toiling at a lathe, so be it. The last thing he would ever feel in the circumstances was guilt.

In Simon's defence I must point out that this was not entirely the result of selfishness and social conditioning. The Classics must share some of the blame too. As Peter Green pointed out in an essay on Classical influences in the modern world,

> snobbery, élitism and contempt not simply for trade but for all applied science, plus obsession with order and stability [are] all significant but often overlooked elements of the classical tradition.

One of the Uncle's predecessors, the seigneurial Frank Dames-Longworth, liked to embellish Horace: ' "*Odi profanum vulgus et arceo.*" And why did he hate them? Because they stank.' Simon's sentiments exactly. And yet he got on perfectly well with ordinary people individually, and in his books it is very often life's warrant officers who steady the line when the captains and kings have stolen away.

*

When in a sentimental mood Simon would say that nothing, not even his scholarship to King's or the publication of his first novel, could compare with the exultation of winning his First XI Cricket colours in a side that included a future captain of England and Chairman of selectors (Peter May), a future President of MCC (Oliver Popplewell) and a future Cabinet Minister (James Prior). The captain, Tony Rimell, was also a fine cricketer, playing for Cambridge in '49 and '50.

Although he had been awarded his XXII colours the previous year, Simon's selection was by no means a foregone conclusion. Rimell, May and Popplewell picked themselves, and at least two quick bowlers had to be chosen. Competition for the remaining six places was keen, with about ten players besides Simon who could justifiably feel they were in with a chance.

Simon's hopes rested on his abilities as an all-rounder. On the hard Charterhouse wickets he had developed into an aggressive lower-order batsman who preferred to come in 'when it was often one's duty to hit'. The lofted drive was his favourite shot and he also enjoyed the risky ploy of 'backing off a bit and cutting off-breaks and googlies against the spin'. But what Ivan Lynch remembered was 'how often he would succeed in turning a fast, straight ball off his stomach and down to fine leg'. This may be why, rather against his wishes, he was made to open after half-term. As a bowler of slow-to-medium off-breaks Simon operated in the shadow of Rimell, whose flighted deliveries bamboozled all but the best school batsmen. It was largely thanks to Rimell that Charterhouse's first two school opponents, Wellington and Tonbridge, were bowled out for 55 and 33 respectively. Simon broke a stubborn last wicket stand at Tonbridge but it was not until the third school match, against Bradfield, that he had a chance to shine. He took 3 for 19 in 12 overs, a tidy spell that guaranteed his place in the side against Eton three days later.

Simon was never a great fielder, so it is ironic that the chain of events which led to the award of his colours should have begun with a difficult catch he held at long leg to dismiss the Eton captain:

> I snatched at the ball with a panicky clap of the hands when it was a foot above the ground and about to strike the shinbone of my left and leading leg, a loathsome performance, as any half-educated cricketer will tell you. But the ball stuck and this, added to other fluky feats, procured me my colours, and I have remembered the split second of impact and the almost hysterical surge of joy ever since. (*Is there anybody there? said the traveller*)

So Simon became a major blood, one of the 'barons' whose swagger so annoyed Robert Graves when he had been at the school thirty years before.

> Oh, we are the bloods of the place,
> We shine with superior grace
> At the goal or the wicket, at footer or cricket,
> And nothing our pride can efface.
> The worms of the Sixth we despise ...
> We count them as dirt in our eyes.

In fact the division between brain and brawn was now much less marked. Most of the 1945 XI were in the Sixth, and four others besides Simon were Scholars. Nor, by the end of the war, was there much in the way of finery: First XI blazers and sweaters were not to be had for love or money, though if you were lucky you might get hold of a second-hand cap. Still, if the trappings were absent the privileges were unarguably in place. While lesser mortals were confined to the tarmac and gravel, a blood could walk on the sacred grass, arm-in-arm with his fellow bloods if he so chose, or with *both* hands in his trouser pockets. He could carry an unfurled umbrella and leave the buttons of his jacket or blazer undone. He was even spared any hassle at 'Crown', the school tuck shop, thanks to a cosy little annexe known as 'Blood's Window'.

Simon adored privilege and it was on the cards that his elevation to the peerage should go straight to his head and thence to his loins.

> By the midsummer of 1945 I was right out of control. Drunk with my own success in all fields, I had abandoned my reformed character, save only in the presence of Alexis himself, and with each day that passed I became more arrogant and more reckless. Here am I, I said to myself and often to the world, a scholar-elect of a famous college, a blood at a famous school, bursting with energy and curiosity at the beginning of a summer which has seen an end of war. There is only one watchword now – and that is pleasure. I will find it out and have it. Inflamed and justified by passages from my favourite poets, I roamed the fields at noon and haunted the evening copses. Nor did the great god Pan ignore his votary. I am grateful to Pan for that summer; as long as it lasted he really did me proud. (*The English Gentleman*)

Alexis was the priggish contemporary for whom Simon had fallen 'like a cannonball from the ramparts'. Almost 50 years later he described him to me like this: 'A Greek beauty with handsome, regular features, classic torso and legs and the most beautiful uncircumcised cock I have ever encountered. The prepuce went slowly back leaving a slightly damp and sweet-smelling surface. I was only allowed to feel it and never saw it come. Pity.'

Whatever he got up to with Alexis – there is a highly-charged seduction scene in *The English Gentleman* – their association was not one of the offences for which Simon was arraigned the following term. Nor indeed did hubris feature on the charge sheet, although in Simon's eyes this was the only crime he was guilty of. 'It is when a boy is most successful he should most beware ....'

Simon's apogee came at the end of June when he made 41 against MCC, earning himself this pat on the back from the *Cricketer*:

> S.A.N. Raven, a rapidly improving player, batted admirably on a bad wicket in the dark against a formidable MCC attack.

For a few days he kidded himself he might be chosen to play for the Southern Schools at Lord's. This delusion had no sooner passed than it was replaced by another, more serious one, about his performance in the Classical Sixth's annual examination. Despite a total lack of preparation ('What need had a scholar of King's to work?') he believed he had done quite well enough to earn high marks from the two external examiners, one of whom, [Sir] Maurice Bowra, was said to favour clever, amusing and handsome boys. But neither Bowra nor his equally distinguished colleague were impressed. Simon was placed near the bottom of the List, below boys who were a year behind him. This was the first sign that the Gods had turned against him. Not that he recognised it. Why should he have done? His failure in the exams was simply a gamble that hadn't paid off. There would be ample opportunities to recoup in the year ahead.

CHAPTER SIX

Farewell happy fields
Where joy for ever dwells.
Milton, *Paradise Lost*

An unexpected vacancy having occurred, H.E.D. Lloyd (D) was present as a member.
Minutes of the *Charterhouse Shakespeare Society*, 28 October 1945

Comforted by the knowledge that thanks to the Atom bomb he would not now be called up to fight in the Far East, Simon returned to Charterhouse for the Oration quarter in the best of spirits. Less than a month later – 'just as the leaves began to fall' – he was out on his ear. His nemesis was an unconventional master called Harry Iredale, a Christian Socialist who in Gerald Priestland's words 'was simultaneously attracted and repelled' by Simon and who 'wondered if he might not already have done his deal with Mephistopheles'.

Iredale had sniffed out scandal in the last weeks of the Cricket quarter. Unable to locate it precisely in July he had redoubled his efforts in September and soon found what he was looking for, a large dollop of incriminating evidence. According to Simon, Iredale deposited his 'repellent' trophy in James Prior's lap and demanded that he establish its provenance. Lord Prior told me he couldn't recall this, but acknowledged that as Head Monitor of Saunderites he must have been involved in the proceedings at some stage. One way or another Iredale's depositions found their way to Birley, who had no option but to investigate them.

There is an old saying, 'the more a turd is stirred the more it stinks'. So it proved now. Birley soon had proof of Simon's guilt, but the sheer scale of what was revealed to him about other boys, some quite unconnected with Simon, drove him in pursuit of every possible lead. (' "No Fielding ... What you forgive or tolerate, I must know about and punish in order to *forgive.*" ') This led to Simon's undoing.

'He went back on his word. To begin with he said, "Look, as things stand, I cannot have you as Head Monitor, which you would have been when James Prior left, but provided you tell me everything and promise to behave I've no objection to your staying here for the rest of this quarter. I shall also make every effort to see that this doesn't prejudice your scholarship to King's." He thought, you see, that I'd confined myself to boys my own age.

'And then, by sheer bad luck, he discovered that only a week previously I'd had a younger boy called Guy Halliwell. Not all that much younger: he was sixteen, I was almost eighteen, but it was clear from the way it happened that I'd been very deliberate. I'd put on my house cricket square – rather a pretty combination of black, blue and white – gone down to his house and had him in his study. Birley was very upset about this. He said, "If they'll have you at King's, well and good. You can go now. But I'm almost certain they won't." And indeed Patrick Wilkinson[1] rang up that evening to say they couldn't. So Birley then said, "I've got to renege on what I said. After what has become apparent about Halliwell, a younger boy whom you deliberately seduced, I can't have you here even for the rest of this quarter." Now it seemed to me then that he was taking an unnecessarily firm line over Halliwell, because I'd told him almost all I could remember and there were lots and lots of boys involved. I didn't think he'd want to hear one more dreary example. But he was adamant and so the next thing I knew was that I was packing my trunk and saying good-bye to my boyhood for ever.'[2]

Simon always suspected that William Rees-Mogg had urged Birley on at a crucial moment. 'I think Birley said to him, "What are we going to do about Raven?" And Mogg said, "He ought to go now, not at the end of the quarter." ' Lord Rees-Mogg denied this – 'I don't recall that Birley consulted me at all' – and insisted that he was as sorry as everyone else that Simon had to go. 'I think we all hoped that having sowed his wild oats Simon would settle down on a more conventional track. I don't think at that stage any of us realised that the wild oats would become disproportionately large in his life.'

Support for the belief that Birley alone decided to sack Simon comes from his son-in-law, Brian Rees.[3]

> Sir Robert's biographer was by no means the only person to assume, wrongly, that because he was very liberal in political and social matters, he must have been equally tolerant of homosexuality in schools. He may have been a little more understanding than other Headmasters of his generation, but by modern standards he was pretty strict. I remember him saying that the thing which shocked him most in post-war Berlin were the male prostitutes in the Kurfurstendamm. He was immensely happily married, you see, and it's inconceivable that he could have understood the wayward impulses

[1] Senior Tutor of the College. Old Carthusian.

[2] Simon did not set eyes on Halliwell again until 1971, when they met by chance at the Sydney Cricket Ground. 'Guy was in Sydney on business, doing very well by all accounts. Clearly one hadn't blighted his life!'

[3] Variously Headmaster of Merchant Taylors', Charterhouse and Rugby.

> of Simon's rather animal-crossed-with-Hellenic imagination. At the same time he was very fond indeed of Simon, who'd often stayed at Daisy Farm and was a great favourite with his daughters. To that extent the expulsion must have been more than usually painful for both parties.

Although they met at functions from time to time afterwards, the old intimacy between Simon and Birley was never re-established. In 1976, when *Alms for Oblivion* was completed, Simon sent Sir Robert a set of the sequence and was gratified to learn that he had put it in the guest-room, 'a great compliment'. But according to Brian Rees, Sir Robert was 'always rather dismissive when Simon's name came up in conversation and never showed any wish for a rapprochement'.[4] Rees added that the dialogue between Fielding Gray and the Headmaster 'rang very true. I can hear the style of my father-in-law in it very clearly.'

*

Traumatic as it undoubtedly was for Simon, his expulsion was not altogether unexpected. He had, after all, made no secret of his conquests and it was probably only a matter of time before rumours of these reached the wrong ears. But to the astonishment of people like James Prior and William Rees-Mogg, who likened the whole business to the Profumo affair, the net that snared Simon contained an even bigger fish, the previous Head of the School and Head Monitor of Saunderites, Hedley Le Bas.

Because he had already left, Le Bas escaped Simon's fate and was merely warned off the school premises for a year. But so good had been his 'cover' – he was very militaristic, a great one for 'showing up' – that his disgrace was all the more dramatic.

> When the scandal broke I was doing my basic military training at Brookfield Camp, Winchester [recalled Conrad Dehn]. And very shortly it became *the* topic of conversation among all the ex-public school, potential officer types who were there. And at that stage the involvement of Hedley Le Bas was very much more exciting. I mean we knew about Simon, but Hedley Le Bas was supposedly a pillar of rectitude, and I think people were amazed to discover that he was mixed up in something like this. Quite apart from anything else we'd always assumed that girls were very much his thing, not boys.

None of which was much consolation to Simon, who for two or three weeks felt 'like Adam and Eve did when they had to do a proper day's

[4] As Headmaster of Eton he vetoed a proposal by the Literary Society to invite Simon down to speak.

work'. Luckily, his parents behaved well, although as I have said, Simon mistrusted Arthur's motives. 'Expulsion equals failure. Failure equals disaster. He could afford to be nice about *that*. He stopped being nice when I duly went to Bangalore and got a commission. My mother was genuinely sorry for me, I think, and of course she liked having me at home. When I went off to India she changed her tune.'

Simon's immediate worry was the attitude of King's, where, like Fielding Gray, he very much hoped to become 'a wining and dining don. A witty, worldly, *comfortable* don.' Would they still have him? Birley had tried to reassure him on this point; indeed if Simon is to be believed he was rather put out when Patrick Wilkinson, on the telephone, had airily dismissed Simon's expulsion for homosexuality as of no consequence – 'of course we'll have him. Why ever not?' But there had been no room for him in College at such short notice and fearing that they might renege, as Birley had done, Simon went there in person soon afterwards and received confirmation of his admission from the horse's mouth.

Why then did Simon subsequently complain that he had been 'cheated' over his expulsion?

'I had been reared in the Arnoldian tradition which said that expulsion equals social death. No commission. No university. No clubs. The best one could hope for was total obscurity followed by an early grave. All bollocks, as it turned out. I got a commission, joined clubs and took up my place at King's as if nothing had happened. People just giggled when they learnt I'd been sacked "for the usual thing". At the time I was very relieved about this, because my expulsion had looked like being a terrible handicap. But later I did feel rather cheated. I had been a very bad boy. I ought to have been in permanent disgrace. But nobody took a blind bit of notice. It was so undramatic, in such bad aesthetic taste. One trembled in fear of the last trump and all that sounded was a wet fart.'

Pure sophistry, said Conrad Dehn, whose own view of what his expulsion did for Simon is given below.

> I've always maintained that if you followed Simon's example you'd pay your Headmaster a substantial sum to sack you because then you could earn pots of money writing about it for the rest of your life. That's what he's done: he has literally profited by his expulsion, uniquely in my experience. There must be hundreds of boys expelled from public schools every year, but he's the only one I know who's turned it into an investment.

On the other hand, Simon believed in retribution, the theme of so many of his novels. This was why he deplored Permissiveness: 'If everything's allowed, nothing is really exciting. You can't beat a little hell-fire to *flamber* any dish of pleasure.' Perhaps a part of him did regret that nobody noticed 'the hideous brand' on his forehead, just as years later he sometimes spoke wistfully of being 'drummed out of the regiment' – 'The humiliation is so intense, so *final*, that it breaks a man's heart for the rest of his life.'

Paradoxically Simon blamed Frank Richards for society's indifference to his disgrace. He thought the popularity of Billy Bunter and Co 'had made the whole punitive apparatus of the public schools, flogging and expulsion, the lot, a joke'. I think this demonstrates, yet again, how blinkered his education had made him, admirable though it may have been in other respects. The bloodiest war in history had only just finished and the full horror of Hitler's Final Solution, to say nothing of the Atom Bomb, was just beginning to sink in. Furthermore, it looked very much as if Britain was on the verge of a social revolution. Small wonder that nobody raised an eyebrow at the news of his sacking.

*

In retrospect Simon felt his expulsion had been beneficial – and not just because it proved such a fertile source of good copy. 'I am all in favour of premature dismissal,' he told the *Carthusian* in 1982.

> It shakes one up and concentrates one's mind. You get smug sitting in a place being Head Monitor till the end of the year .... If you are told to get out with your trunk it's a bit of a shock but does pull one together.

Naturally he did have regrets. It was a pity to forfeit the friendship of a '*good*' man like Robert Birley, and he was also sorry not to have collected a Leaving Exhibition – '*any* extra money would have been welcome at Cambridge'. He had mixed feelings about absenting himself from the 1946 Cricket XI, who were unbeaten. 'The question is, Would one have kept one's place? My form that summer in the Army was dismal.' Oddly enough, the night before we discussed this he had dreamt that he'd been dropped. 'Very shaming ... but I refused to stop wearing my colours and walking on the grass. Once a blood, always a blood!'

Exactly. He had already achieved, in four years, more than most boys aspired to in five, so that while it would have been very agreeable to sit in the Head Monitor's study 'bidding one go and he goeth and another come and he cometh', it could not compare with serving as an officer cadet in India, an experience he would have missed had he remained at school.

But Charterhouse had the last laugh, as he discovered when Myles returned home at the end of the quarter. 'What are they saying about me?' asked Simon, fully expecting a long, gossipy report.

'They're not saying anything at all.'

CHAPTER SEVEN

When the 'arf-made recruity goes out to the East
He acts like a babe an' 'e drinks like a beast ....
Kipling, *The Young British Soldier*

In January 1946, shortly after his eighteenth birthday, Simon reported for six weeks' Primary Training at Barnby Moor camp near Retford in Notts. In the normal way he would not have been called up for another few months, but by volunteering he acquired the right to nominate his regiment, a privilege coveted by aspirant officers. Simon chose the Parachute Regiment, partly so as to create 'a good, *keen* impression, because after all, one had a bit of ground to make up', but also because he rather fancied sporting the famous maroon beret.

Came the Spring and he found himself at the regiment's Infantry Training Centre on Salisbury Plain. Here recruits were knocked into shape[1] before proceeding to Jumping School, a prospect Simon did not particularly relish because parachutes then 'were by no means infallible'. But thanks to his cricket he was able, quite legitimately, to dodge the column.

'It was all pretty much as I described it in *Shadows*. The Colonel had played county cricket and the Training Centre's cricket officer was anxious to suck up to him by putting out a decent XI. This he managed until mid-June, at which time his three star recruits, myself included, were due to go to Jumping School. So he had us in and hinted that if we were to stay behind and play cricket, he would make it worth our while. The other two turned him down flat. I gave him to understand that eager as I was to get my "wings", I just might contain my enthusiasm if the price were right. My form had been patchy but he was desperate and we struck a bargain. I was given a stripe and installed as the Headquarter Company's mail clerk, a very pretty sinecure which meant that I did practically nothing before noon and absolutely nothing afterwards, except play cricket when required. Even better, I was moved out of barracks and given a berth in the company office, dossing down there with the company clerk, who was writing a book on the Blitz. In short I was practically a free agent, a very rare thing in the Army of those days.'

[1] Not literally. 'Milling' and other ferocious practices designed to test the mettle of recruits had yet to be introduced.

When he wasn't chronicling the Blitz, Danny, the company clerk, spent his off-duty hours servicing NAAFI girls, an office he was happy to share with Simon. There followed several 'heady and exhausting' weeks in the course of which Simon tried, unsuccessfully, to reconcile his carnal appetites with his cricketing duties. One flop followed another, culminating in a performance of such all round ineptitude that thanks largely to Lance-Corporal Raven, No. 1 Parachute Regiment ITC lost in the quarter-finals of the South West District Trophy. Meanwhile, one of the NAAFI girls had thrown up outside the Company office and the mess had been observed on the morning after by the legendary Regimental Sergeant Major Lord, on secondment from the Coldstream Guards. But just as it looked as if Simon would spend the rest of his military service scrubbing latrines, Fate, in the shape of the War Office, spirited him away.

'Before Mr Lord had a chance to interrogate me I learnt I'd passed my WOSB[2] and would be shipped out to Bangalore as an Officer Cadet. This meant that I had to leave the ITC and report *instanter* to the Transit Centre in London, one of the few occasions in the Army when I was only too happy to do exactly as I was told. Of course there was always the worry that if the truth did emerge then I would have to face the music. That hung over me for months to come. But in the end I got off scotters. If anyone took the rap it must have been poor Danny, whom I never saw again.'

(Old hands may wonder how Simon got round the problem of the certificate of 'moral character' which every candidate for a Commission had to get signed by a responsible body like a clergyman, JP or schoolmaster. In *Shadows* Simon said he simply forged the signature of 'Sniffy' Russell, a Charterhouse beak. In fact the certificate was signed by a Roman Catholic priest enlisted by Esther.)

Simon's luck continued to hold, for who should he find on the slow boat to India but James Prior, 'just the sort of chap to have with one in a tight spot, which it might very well have turned out to be if the Attlee government hadn't caved in so quickly. But nothing much rattled James. He was always very calm and very rational.' For his part Officer Cadet Prior was equally pleased to recognise at Liverpool docks Simon's 'smiling face and distinctive red hair'. It was now, on the 'unspeakable' voyage out, that their lasting friendship was forged.

Although they had been in the same house at school and played in the First XI together, Simon and James Prior had been in different forms and had different interests. Furthermore Prior was one term senior to Simon and immeasurably more responsible, particularly about the war effort;[3] consequently even before the events that led up to his expulsion Simon often said and did things which his fellow Saunderite could not condone.

[2] War Office Selection Board (for potential officers).

[3] For instance he persuaded Birley to allow him to keep pigs at school to supplement the rations.

'At the beginning of one Summer quarter I remember James saying, "We need plenty of rain between now and August. It'll help the farmers." And I said, "Fuck the farmers. What about our cricket?" All rather trivial, but indicative of the sort of things we disagreed on. James took the war very seriously. When it was over he became much less priggish.'

And a good thing too from Simon's point of view, because not only did he caricature James Prior in his memoirs, he also libelled him in *Alms for Oblivion*, where he is the model for Peter Morrison, an MP who becomes increasingly cynical and calculating as the sequence progresses. 'I've always thought it enormously to James Prior's credit that he has remained so fond of Simon,' submitted Conrad Dehn. 'After all, when you're as important as James became, being fond of Simon adds no cachet to you at all.'

*

In Britain the winter of 1946/7 was one of the coldest on record and also, because of severe shortages of food and fuel, one of the most miserable. I can still remember how my father, whose blood had been thinned by five years soldiering in the Far East, would put his feet in the gas oven to try to thaw them out. In Bangalore, by contrast, the climate was like a hot summer's day at home; there were ample supplies of food and drink, and, most satisfying of all for Simon, a hallowed system for turning aspirant officers into pukka sahibs.

> True, Urdu was abandoned after we reached conditional clauses [he recalled in the *Spectator*]; but in all else we were being prepared for a world that had every Kipling ingredient from chota pegs to punishment stations. On the military side, we received detailed instructions in Indian scales of rank and pay, Indian chains of command up to divisional level, mule transport, the dietary and religious vagaries of twenty different types of sepoy, and how to deal with homosexual jealousies among Pathans and Sikhs. Our social education comprehended the correct deportment when faced variously with a pundit, a baboo or a maharenee, conduct on the polo field (here and here only it was permissible to swear at a colonel or even a major-general), the excessive rates of interest charged by moneylenders in the bazaar, the impropriety of dancing with Eurasian girls in public, the degrees of deference due to the commanding officer's wife, which differed, apparently, according as to whether one was in a cantonment, on shikhar or at a hill-station ….
>
> Not the least ludicrous aspect of all this was the contrast presented between our own condition and that of cadets who had been left behind in the UK. For by now word had filtered through … that they were being treated as felons and paid as privates, required

> (without servants) to reach guardsmen's standards of turnout, lodged forty to a Nissen hut, tormented by exercises which demanded unbelievable efficiency and endurance, and were being failed ... at a rate of 30 per cent. We, on the other hand, were being paid as sergeants, waited on by bearers, and subjected only to the most gentle manoeuvres, which were usually interrupted for about three hours at midday while a squad of Indians erected a marquee and served us with a hot meal of four courses. (19.7.68)

How beguiling. But is it accurate? Up to a point, said Michael 'Barry' Walters, who was in Simon's company. 'I'm sure we were much better off than officer cadets at home. We had plenty of leave and there was a great deal to see and do at minimal cost. But they worked us hard. There was a two hour parade before breakfast and no siestas – much to Simon's annoyance, I seem to remember. I suppose some of what we learned was straight out of Kipling, but we also did a lot of jungle warfare training.'

Barry Walters had met Simon through James Prior on the voyage out. 'James and I were both in the Rifle Brigade draft. Simon was a Para but spent most of his time with us. He was very slim in those days and incredibly languid – what we should now call "laid-back". He made no secret of why he had been expelled from Charterhouse, but was not considered difficult in this respect. Neither then nor in Bangalore were there any scandals. It was only when I met him subsequently in Cambridge, and saw his friends there, that I realised he was genuinely ambidextrous. Again, he was selective about showing off his learning, probably because intellectuals were thin on the ground. But he was a great mocker. He mocked many of the things we had to do, and he mocked James Prior in an affectionate sort of way. James, even then, had a slightly pompous air about him. In general Simon did just enough to get by. He was good at the cerebral stuff like admin. and planning and he had enough natural athletic ability and timing to cope with the outdoor work. But he never wanted to be first in a race, which I still did. In that sense he was rather more grown-up than most of us.'

Simon always said that having shipped them out to Bangalore at great expense there was no way the Army was going to fail them. 'Even a cadet who had contracted gonorrhoea, not once but three times, received a commission with the rest of us – though he was warned, or so the rumour went, that a fourth bout would not be so easily overlooked.'

But James Prior, who was in Simon's platoon, thought he was 'really quite lucky to pass because he was very casual about the whole business. He had this romantic, Edwardian view of what being a subaltern entailed. It was vital to look the part – carry a swagger stick and wear kid gloves. I think he even tried to grow a moustache. You were there to lead your platoon over the top in the event of a fight. Otherwise, it was a case of, "Carry on, sergeant". I remember one famous occasion when it was his turn to lead the platoon on an exercise and we'd reached an impasse. What normally happened was that you'd consult your NCOs – the "O group" – and then give the orders. But Simon wouldn't budge until he'd picked the brains of another cadet called Bill Off, who was the platoon swot. "Send for the O group – and Bill Off" became a long-running joke between us.'

Fortunately for Simon the post-war Army wanted young officers with the gift of the gab. According to Barry Walters, 'They'd simply throw a subject at you – it could be anything from a cup of coffee to the Atom bomb – and expect you to stand up and give an impromptu five minute talk on it. A lot of people were absolutely tongue-tied, but Simon could think on his feet so it was no hardship to him. He could talk readily on any subject for five minutes, and very wittily too.'

And so, despite his limitations in the field, Simon was duly commissioned in May 1947. But instead of being posted to British units in India and the Far East (the official line), he and his fellow subalterns were simply shipped home again, as if their spell in Bangalore had been a bureaucratic oversight which had taken six months to redress. The absurdity of it all was underlined by the announcement, just before they left, that Independence would be brought forward a year, to August 1947 – 'so one got a crash course in the sudden fall of Imperial greatness. When we arrived the Raj was still in business. We knew the lease was running out fast, but nobody guessed we'd have put the shutters up within a year. At the time, I'm afraid, I was too busy preening myself as Raven sahib to shed more than a passing tear over its demise. Later, when it became apparent in India and elsewhere that we were better at running their countries than the natives, one did feel genuinely sorry for the administrators, particularly the old India hands who were the pick of the bunch. But one thing about a Classical education is that you learn about Necessity: what has to be, has to be. So although you may be sad and even resentful when something like this happens, you never get too bitter because you realise it is simply inevitable. *Ananké* as the Greeks said, or *Necessitas*, as the Romans said, is putting an end to this particular phase, so like it or lump it, on we go.'

But as Simon acknowledged in his Indian Army novel, *Sound the Retreat*, one man's Necessity is another's nightmare. Captain Gilzai Khan, an instructor at Bangalore OTS, reveres the Raj and anathematises Independence because it will set Hindu against Moslem. In a desperate attempt to make the British stay he resigns his commission and organises a pro-Raj campaign of civil disobedience among his fellow Moslems. This seals his fate because by now the British are determined to quit India at the double, and will trample on anyone who stands in their way. Second-Lieutenant Peter Morrison, the novel's hero, is ordered to put the boot in, a task he accomplishes so adroitly that the shine never leaves his toe-caps. This earns him a Viceroy's commendation and a backhanded compliment from the dying Gilzai Khan:

'Morrison huzoor,' he said, 'I wish you the long and successful career which your ingenuity deserves.'

That Peter Morrison *will* go far is predicted by Captain Detterling, a leading light of Simon's Old Gang and an assiduous follower of the world's game. '[Morrison's] got a lot of shit in his tanks,' he notes approvingly. And when a brother officer casts doubt on Morrison's probity, Detterling retorts that at least he 'knows what to wear and what noises to make.' Simon, for all his apparent sophistication, was still deficient in this respect. As he admitted to the *Carthusian* in 1982, 'There was a certain lack of strictly upper-class information [at Charterhouse] during the war.' It was not until he arrived at King's and began to cultivate its Etonian contingent that he became *sortable*.

*

After lording it in the 'military Cockayne' of Bangalore Simon came down to earth with a bump on Salisbury Plain. He had been commissioned into the Ox and Bucks Light Infantry, quite a smart Rifle Brigade regiment. But in the sweltering late summer of 1947 newly-commissioned infantry subalterns were as unrationed as the sunshine and about as welcome; the only way they could be accommodated was by secondment to one of the specialist arms like the Signals and the Artillery. To his dismay Simon was posted to the 77th Heavy Ack Ack Regiment at Rolleston Balloon Camp, very much an also-ran socially and professionally.

Away from Rolleston Simon tried to disguise his lowly station by styling himself a 'Gunner'. Gunner officers were deemed to be 'mounted' and Simon was mortified to find that he couldn't get into Fred Christmas's riding boots, which he would have been 'technically entitled' to wear with breeches and service dress.[4] Not that he could ever have appeared on parade like this. Lieutenant-Colonel Pugh, the Commanding Officer, had egalitarian ideas about turnout, insisting that his young officers wear battle dress and berets and carry, not riding whips, but 'mean little sticks of bamboo'. They were expected to muck in and get their hands dirty if necessary, which Simon considered frightfully infra dig. One day he was reprimanded by Pugh after an inspecting officer had found rust on one of his guns. When he ventured that it could only have been 'a very little rust', Pugh threatened to put him on a charge for insolence.

But as a general rule Simon was adept enough 'to glance the offending ball to leg in his inimitable style.' Conrad Dehn, who was also in 77th

[4] Simon had a minor fetish about such attire. What impressed him most about Granny Raven's chauffeur, 'Luffy', were his 'leggings'. Anthony Powell, no slouch on the subject of turnout, once consulted him about 'the duties, just before the war in 1914, when an infantry officer might be wearing breeches and top boots when in uniform'.

Heavy Ack Ack, recalled how he and Simon were sent on a motor maintenance course which consisted of 31 tasks, one for every day of the month. 'An instructor caught Simon slumped in the driver's seat. "What are you supposed to be doing?" he said. And Simon came up with what I thought was a brilliant answer: "Task 32. Testing the springs in the driver's seat." '

*

While Simon chafed in his 'prickly, plebeian' battle dress his father marched about in shorts and banged on about the need to economise. Hard-faced he may have been, but he had not done well out of the war and was down to his last hundred thousand. The shorts he wore were a legacy of several months in New Zealand, whither he had flown, at great expense, in a Sunderland flying boat. He had thought his money might go further there, only to discover that New Zealanders were just as hostile to unearned income as the Labour government. Next, he bought a house at Newton-le-Willows, near St Helens, because he liked the look of the local golf course. But this didn't work out either and by 1949 he and Esther were back at the Lodge Hotel, Hunstanton, where they had been staying when war was declared. The following year they bought a house in New Hunstanton but had scarcely moved in before they were looking round again. In October 1950 they took the lease on 'Brookfield', the house they were to remain in for the rest of their lives.

Brookfield was in Wodehouse Road, Old Hunstanton, exactly two doors away from Portland Lodge, which Arthur and his brothers had owned during the Twenties. The contrast between the two houses was stark, emphasising the extent to which Arthur's fortunes had declined since the days when he wooed Esther in his Bentley. Whereas Portland Lodge was a solid and substantial seaside villa which could be lived in comfortably all year round, Brookfield then[5] was a two-storey wooden box designed for summer use. In the winter, when the wind blew off the Wash, it could be bitterly cold, particularly upstairs in the bedrooms where there was no heating except electric fires. Esther was never happy there, but because it was only a short walk away from Arthur's second home, the golf club, her complaints were ignored.

To begin with Simon shared Esther's dislike of Brookfield, but later he decided that it was quite attractive 'in a knockabout sort of way'. Not that he ever took much notice of where he lived. 'I think Simon would be quite happy in a cell,' Anthony Blond told me, 'just so long as he was served three, or better still, four, meals a day.'

Pedantic note. Although Simon based the appearance of Fielding Gray's

[5] It has since been so substantially altered and enlarged as to become unrecognisable.

'common little house at Broughton Staithe' on Brookfield, he romanticised its location by removing it from prosaic Wodehouse Road and isolating it among sand dunes and crumbling gun emplacements at the end of the golf course.

CHAPTER EIGHT

Et in Arcadia ego.

Anonymous inscription on a tomb

'You must remember, what a thing a fellow of King's is.'

Thomas Gray, in a letter to a friend whose nephew had just been awarded a Fellowship

In May 1948, shortly before Simon entered King's, *Varsity*, the University newspaper, ran a series called 'Trends that made Cambridge men what they are today'. The part devoted to King's began by invoking Oscar Browning, the rich, eccentric, equivocal bachelor don par excellence, and then proposed that

> a Kingsman is the nearest thing in Cambridge to an Oxford man, and like him, has a queer accent, lolls about the place and doesn't believe in rowing.

Had Simon read this he would have been reassured, for it indicated that at a time of drab uniformity, King's was still a bit different.[1] Not that all cried '*Vive la différence*!' When Simon's contemporary, Martin Shuttleworth, told Max Rees, his History tutor at Wellington, that he had unexpectedly won a scholarship to King's, Rees was horrified. In his view, recalled Shuttleworth, 'they were all "Bloomsbuggers and atheistical Reds" at King's. He even wrote my father a "Don't put your daughter on the stage, Mrs Worthington" letter which my father, a retired Major-General, ignored. He was on his death-bed at the time and, besides, he was quite convinced my success was a fluke and I was going to the devil anyway.'

But the severest critics of King's were to be found in Cambridge itself, among the Roundheads who had congregated there, in one form or another, since the Civil War. What they objected to were precisely the customs and privileges that in Simon's eyes made King's an earthly

[1] When, in 1993, I sent him a cutting about the establishment of a creche in King's, he wrote back: 'Who is this horrendous Dr Hughes-Jones, with his pestilential baby and his gladness that the college is becoming "more like the outside world"? The whole point about King's – indeed any distinguished College – is that it is *not* like the outside world.'

paradise, beginning with its Royal Foundation. To the indignation of levellers, who were thick on the ground in 1948, this decreed that the Provost's writ ran within the College walls. [Sir] J.T. Sheppard, the Provost in Simon's day, liked to pretend that he was senile, but he could be spry enough when his sovereignty was challenged. On being informed by the University proctors that they knew of three ways back into King's after lock-up, he wrote back to say that there were in fact seven, four of them negotiable by bicycle.[2] And when Mark Boxer was rusticated for publishing a blasphemous poem in *Granta*, of which he was editor, Sheppard wrote to *The Times* to correct a statement suggesting that King's rather than the University was responsible for Boxer's rustication.

The levellers also resented the chains that bound King's to Eton, its sister college. Although these had been loosened in 1873, so that King's ceased to be an Etonian preserve, the links remained strong thanks to closed scholarships and long-standing family connexions. No doubt this led to injustices, as the levellers claimed; but Simon argued – and he was not alone – that the admission of a few upper-class nincompoops had to be set against all King's gained from the *Concordia Amicabilis* with Eton. He particularly relished the easy familiarity that existed between dons and undergraduates and which dated from the days when they shared the same alma mater.

But supposing they also shared the same beds?

This was the charge laid against King's by the puritans, and while it would have been difficult to prove, Counsel for the defence would have had to advise against taking the stand. Despite the conspiracy of silence about homosexuality in high places, people *knew* that from Oscar Browning onwards a succession of distinguished Kingsmen had been 'in the Club' (to borrow Simon's phrase). Consenting adults at King's could do pretty much as they pleased, the only proviso being that they must not offend either the porters or bedmakers. Before the war, it was said, glamorous dons like George 'Dadie' Rylands gave parties at which celebrities let more than their hair down once the ladies had retired and the servants been dismissed.[3] But even sedate affairs like sherry parties could be hazardous for the unwary.

> My father arrived from Bedales having been thoroughly briefed [said Christopher Moorsom]. At his first sherry party he thought he would be safe from prying hands seated beside a weedy-looking type with a beard. But to his embarrassment the beard led off by saying, 'Do you

[2] Climbing into College at night if you were late was not only condoned, said Simon, it was *encouraged*, since that way the porter need not be disturbed.

[3] 'I well remember the impatience of Robert Helpmann for the last woman to leave so that he could do his parody of the dance of the seven veils', recalled Patrick Wilkinson in his succinct retrospective, *A Century of King's*.

know I thought at first your eyes were blue, but now I see they're violet.' It was Lytton Strachey.

Strachey was typical of the Bloomsbuggers denounced by schoolmasters like Max Rees. Even before the appointment of Maynard Keynes as Bursar in 1924 King's had replaced Trinity, Strachey's old college, as Bloomsbury's Cambridge base. Not only did they share an ethos, based on tolerance, scepticism and intellectual integrity, but there were, besides Keynes, other dons with strong Bloomsbury connexions, notably Provost Sheppard, F.L. 'Peter' Lucas and Dadie Rylands, in whose rooms was held the luncheon described by Virginia Woolf in *A Room of My Own*.

Before the war King's could take pride in its association with Bloomsbury, which had yet to become a dirty word. As Patrick Wilkinson noted,

> As for the world of F.R. Leavis, it did not impinge much more on us than that of the athletic Hawks Club. (*A Century of King's*)

But by 1948 Leavis and his disciples, the exclusive brethren, were a power in the land, their sermonising strongly resented by those like Simon who identified with the cultivated élitism of the *ancien régime*. 'Leavis was the enemy, because Leavis was against enjoyment, against pleasure, was all for duty and so forth – very important too, as I've realised since. But in those days, in the piping days of '48 and '49, Leavis was the man we'd gladly have put in the stocks and chucked rotten eggs at.'

In fact it was not roundheads or even radicals who did for the old order but well-meaning liberals like Noel (Lord) Annan, elected Provost in 1956, at whose behest the College ceased to be 'a seminary for young gentlemen'. That is a different story. Meanwhile to Simon's great relief King's remained inviolate during his years up. Indeed it went a fair way towards recapturing its pre-war pre-eminence, when, in the words of T.E.B. Howarth,

> those who, like St Paul's Athenians, sought to hear some new thing, tended to gravitate there. (*Cambridge Between the Wars*)

This was the tradition with which Simon identified, and whose passing he always lamented. 'It was a very civilised place *in those days*,' he used to say. ' There was beauty, grandeur and serenity. There was learning, some of it on the margin of what one was reading, so that I for instance was encouraged to read English and European literature as well as Latin and Greek. There was very agreeable company. And above all there was gaiety in the old sense of the word. Now you may wonder what on earth there was to be gay about in 1948 when people were becoming heartily sick of sacrifices and austerity. But the *mood* in King's was inaustere, and this was due in large part to the efforts of dons like Dadie Rylands and Kenneth Harrison[4] to turn the clock back to 1938 and resurrect the old times, the good times. They were a wonderful lot, the dons there then …. They gave parties. They asked celebrities down. We met the celebrities. Got drunk with the celebrities. Went to bed with the celebrities, I regret to say! – No, of course I don't regret it. Nothing of the kind. And all this was exciting, it was fun, it was free. Austerity was on the way out and to hell with socialism, which wasn't really a very serious threat under Attlee, anyway.'

*

Although there were still several war veterans *in statu pupillari* in 1948, including a man on Simon's staircase who had commanded his own battalion, most undergraduates had only experienced national, rather than active, service between leaving school and coming up. Simon was no exception, but as Noel Annan noted, the officers' mess had left its mark on him, and he retained the air of 'an officer-in-mufti' or, more fancifully, 'a raffish Home Counties' condottiere amusing himself between wars'.

No doubt Simon made the most of his Indian adventures, to say nothing of his romps with NAAFI girls on Salisbury Plain; and with what Noel Annan called 'his magpie passion for collecting odd bits of learning and making good use of them', he still contrived, as he had done at school and in the Army, to seem older and more mature than his peers. 'He gave the impression of being aged about 40 and of having seen a great deal of life,' said the novelist, Peter Dickinson. 'He already had a slightly ruined look. There was a hint of danger about him.'

That he had considerable presence for a freshman is confirmed by another contemporary, Angus McKay:

> The first time I saw Simon he was playing billiards in the back room of the Copper Kettle or the KP – I forget which. Anyway, there he was, playing with such complete poise and sang-froid that I assumed he must be in his third year. It came as quite a shock to be told that he was a fresher like me.

Simon later wrote that at Cambridge he had modelled himself on Rhett Butler. Other exemplars were the film-star, George Saunders, famous for his suave cads, and 'smooth-talking cynics' from novels he had read like Mr Obispo and the young Rogue Herries. But the fictional character he would grow to resemble most closely in many people's eyes had yet to see the light of day: George MacDonald Fraser's Flashman. Fans of the

[4] Lay Dean, biochemist and authority on the windows of King's College Chapel; now revealed as the father of Penelope Mortimer's daughter, Julia. As Lay Dean Harrison was technically responsible for College discipline, regarding which he took a markedly more indulgent line than his successor, John Raven (q.v.).

'Flashman' stories will take my drift. All anyone else needs to know is, first, that Fraser's Flashman abhors cant; and secondly, that he's the sort of rotter who confounds authority by making his way in the world instead of coming to a bad end. Simon loathed cant, particularly fashionable progressive cant; and he was amused at the pain his literary success caused in certain quarters. 'According to the rules one ought to have found a pauper's grave at thirty. Instead, here one was in one's forties and fifties with cash in hand *and* cachet. Caused a lot of resentment, I can tell you.'

But during his first two years there was every reason to suppose that he would, in time, achieve his stated ambition of becoming a Fellow of King's. He took a First in Part 1 of the Classical Tripos and won two prestigious English Essay prizes, the James and the University Members'. He played cricket and squash for the College and royal tennis for the University (but not against Oxford). True, he was extravagant and dissolute, but after years of sobriety and austerity this was held by many at High Table to be no bad thing. 'Simon's a very naughty boy,' Dadie Rylands would say with a twinkle in his eye.

Although he was never taught by Rylands, who was an Eng. Lit. don, Simon became his protégé. No clever undergraduate could have wished for a more congenial mentor. 'Dadie was always a very strong general influence on everything from White Burgundy to what was, or was not, worth reading in a long book like *The Golden Bough*. He gave parties at which one met the *beau monde*. He lent one money, which was rarely, I fear, repaid. And he was also generous with his time. He was the only don to visit me in my dingy suburban digs after I'd been gated at the end of my third year, and what's more he brought along Arthur Marshall, whom I hadn't met before, to cheer me up.'

Now it has been urged against Simon by fellow Kingsmen that he is malicious at Rylands' expense in his books. I think Simon would dispute this and there was certainly no question of estrangement: Simon gave a 70th birthday dinner for Dadie and they were still corresponding 40 years after Simon had left King's for good. But as an act of reparation I propose to resurrect the second half of Simon's felicitous profile of his friend and mentor published by *Varsity* in 1952. Having given an account of Rylands' early career, he then proceeds to distinguish between the Man and the Legend:

> The Legend first. Its genesis is not difficult to trace. 'Dadie,' wrote Cyril Connolly in *Enemies of Promise*, 'was a charming, feline boy.' A fair start. Add to this the Cambridge and London of the Twenties; the dedications and the appearances in novels; the friendship of Sunday columnists, of Rosamond Lehmann, of Maugham, of the Oliviers; the gossip muttered in corners; the resounding triumphs and the seemingly interminable leisure; add, too, the gaiety, the charm, the wit – the *panache* – and then the trim, lithe little figure, tripping over the

lawn at dusk, leaving, one almost imagines, little rings of mushrooms in its wake becomes .... becomes a Faun. Pan's brother. Yes, one says, this is such a one as followed in the train of Bacchus; light of heart, light of limb; loved by the gods, disapproved of by the middle classes; brilliant, effortless, irresponsible; reared on nectar; a creature from another world, receiving (to the annoyance of the conscientious) all the prizes of this. That is what one says. It is almost totally untrue.

For Rylands has built his career on three virtues. They are just as much to be deduced from his history as the pagan attributes that legend would bestow, and are the triple foundations of this brilliance, whether as teacher, or producer; of his repute, whether as Fellow or Friend. They are these: the Lancashire virtue of sheer hard work; the Cambridge virtue of intense loyalty; and the Bloomsbury virtue of understanding. It was no supernatural dispensation that made Rylands one of the first Shakespearians in England, the producer of Gielgud, the originator of one of the finest *Twelfth Night*s ever seen: it was, in each case, unsparing effort, flawless loyalty whether to individual, author or institution, and deep and kindly understanding of everybody and everything concerned. Mere casual Bacchants are not made Bursars of King's, invited to lecture to the British Academy, charged with the production of Festivals, or permitted to adorn the Third Programme. Such functions require solid merit and sound learning; and many such functions has Rylands ably and gracefully fulfilled.

And yet ... and yet ... you see, what really makes Rylands the most entertaining personality in Cambridge today is that, for all his Northern conscience and outstandingly hard work, nevertheless, like Mrs Humphrey Ward's Uncle Matthew, he is never wholly serious; he has a forehead which betokens high intellectual distinction – and from which a Satyr's horns are perpetually on the verge of sprouting; he has a smile redolent of academic satisfaction – and asymptotic to the smile of Eros; he has eyes which gaze straightforward with what seems unwinking probity – and never is Rylands better favoured than when he winks. (11.10.52)

In addition to Dadie Rylands there were two undergraduates, now sadly dead, who by their idiosyncratic example helped shape Simon's lifestyle, then and later. Their names were Richard 'Dickie' Temple-Muir and Ian Murray.

Dickie Muir was a canny, cultivated Anglo-Scot for whom wealth was a means to a pleasurable end. Older, richer and considerably more *au courant* than most of his contemporaries at King's, where he arrived in 1947 after three years in the Rifle Brigade and short spells at Gottingen and the Sorbonne, Muir drank deep of the College ethos but never let it affect his head for figures. 'Dickie was always very sound about money,' said Christopher Moorsom. 'He used to keep a close watch on his gold shares, his "Freddies" he called them.'

Simon was never tempted to follow Dickie Muir's hard-headed approach to money-matters. Indeed he once confessed to Patrick Wilkinson's wife, Sydney, 'I always feel psychologically uneasy when my bank balance is not in the red.' But the good life and how to enjoy it was something on which they always saw eye to eye. As Simon wrote in his obituary of Dickie for the College *Annual Report*,

> I have never enjoyed the world so much as when I was with Muir. At Cambridge and for the next forty years, at cricket matches, race meetings, dog tracks, Casinos; cinemas, music halls, night clubs and even in front of television sets; motoring across Europe or (once) across Australia; arguing about where to have lunch in Macon ('We're not setting foot in that two-star job you're so slily looking up in Michelin, Raven, and that's flat'); sharing dubious hotel rooms ('There's a notice on the desk saying they don't take cheques, dear. We'll see about *that* in the morning') – all of it was so easy, so agreeable, so beguiling. Dickie was seldom epigrammatic; but his comments had a gentle sourness, not quite irony, not quite satire, a resigned pessimism, that turned the most dismal occasion into a kind of grey comedy and set up, on the most delicious of evenings, a salutory murmur of *memento mori*.

I myself met Dickie Muir in 1987, two years before his death and not long after he had sold *La Popote*, the popular South Kensington restaurant he founded in the Fifties. He was clearly not in the best of health, but the 'gentle sourness' was still in evidence: 'Finally had my fill of old poufs like Raven turning up at closing time expecting brandy on the house,' was his explanation for selling *La Popote*. And in response to my assertion that where copy was concerned, a writer like Simon would always put his own interests before those of his friends, he gave a wry cackle: 'Oh dear, oh dear. I think I've learnt that lesson very late in life!'

But it was clear that despite the occasional 'non-speaks' between them Dickie Muir regarded Simon as one of his oldest and dearest friends. 'I can't remember exactly how we met – it must have been at a party – but it soon became apparent that he was a very nice person to have around the place. He was physically rather beautiful – *then*. Highly intelligent. Knowledgeable about games like cricket and royal tennis, which he'd just taken up. Fond of gossip and determined to have a good time, which wasn't so easy in those days what with rationing and so on. I remember he got very excited when I told him that as Captain of the College squash team I got a special petrol allowance to take us to places like Eton in my car.' – What was so exciting about that? – 'I hope playing squash.'

'Dickie was Action, social and athletic,' said Simon. 'And, what you'd never have suspected from his British warm and Rifle Brigade tie, he was also gay in a very advanced way for those days. There's a famous story about the time he went to a tea dance at the Dorothy café in drag. "We old bags must stick together," he's supposed to have said to the mother of a friend who came too. Then his wig fell off on the dance floor. Exit Dickie, screaming. He screamed even louder when he met a crowd of drunken RAF men on the way back to King's. They tore all his clothes off, so Dickie had to sprint stark naked across the College court to reach his bed.'

If Dickie Muir had a fault in Simon's eyes it was his periodic bouts of stinginess. No such charge could be levelled against Ian Murray, who confirmed Simon in his belief that prodigality became a gentleman. A history scholar who had spent a year at King's during the war before joining the Rifle Brigade, Murray reappeared in 1947 and soon became famous for his good taste, generosity and extravagance. When Christopher Moorsom, who had just come up, crossed the corridor to borrow some milk, he was received by Murray in a silk dressing gown and offered champagne, cherries and Monteverdi (very much a 'Third Programme' composer then). One of Simon's earliest memories of King's was 'of seeing Ian heading for his rooms with a case of champagne like a box of Brock's fireworks'.

Murray's hospitality was legendary. At a time when claret too young to drink well was still being served at College feasts he made a point of offering his friends mature vintages. In later life his distaste for anything remotely second-rate proved a handicap, but at King's he flourished as *arbiter elegantiae*. 'Ian always had the first gull's eggs of the season at Tony's,'[5] said Christopher Moorsom, who also told me how Murray had once hired an aeroplane to go racing on the South Coast with a girlfriend.

Simon learnt much from Ian Murray about food and wine, and later regretted that he had not paid more attention to what his friend had to say about paintings and objets d'art – 'too busy scheming to get my end away I'm afraid'. But what impressed him most about Murray was the ease with which he obtained credit. 'Ian had *some* money, I think. But he could never have lived as he did without ample credit at local shops. This lesson was not lost on me and I made it my business to open as many accounts as possible.'

In the beginning Simon was quite well off. He had an allowance of two hundred pounds a year from Arthur and a further two hundred from either King's or the Army – 'can't remember which. By rights I should have received two hundred from both of them, making six hundred in all, which would have been princely. But the dismal egalitarian spirit of the times meant that if you had an Army grant and a scholarship you could not collect both of them. Is it any wonder that I was never tempted to become a socialist?'

This was where Simon and King's parted company. In politics the

[5] A popular restaurant in King's Parade.

conventional College position was pink liberal, putting it squarely behind the social reforms of the Attlee government. No doubt there was an element of hypocrisy here because 'in those days' the *cordon sanitaire* which protected King's from change was still intact, so socialism could be made to seem rather attractive, particularly if you had a glass of College port in your hand. But Simon's position was equally ambivalent, because he was indebted to the 'pinks' for their tolerance of sexual misdemeanour and blasphemy. 'Nobody minded what you did in bed or what you said about God, a very civilised attitude in 1948.'

What they could not abide, however, were 'flagrant assumptions of social superiority', the offence imputed to Simon by the College Tutor, Patrick Wilkinson. What did this mean? According to Simon in *Shadows on the Grass* it covered a whole range of items from hobnobbing with Old Etonians to guzzling champagne and smoked salmon while rationing was still in force. But when we discussed this he took a different tack, and attributed his Tutor's antipathy to left-wing, anti-militaristic prejudice.

'One was an ex-officer. One had served in India. *Ergo*, one was deeply suspect. Quite why he resented ex-officers so much I couldn't say. Perhaps it was because he never held a commission himself, though he passed the war very creditably doing decoding work at Bletchley.[6] At any rate he succeeded in alienating me thereafter and for ever when he read the riot act to me just prior to the Royal Visit at the end of my third year. He said, "This College is entertaining the King and Queen and Princess Margaret. If you or any of your friends disrupt their visit you will be sent down." And so I said – and he didn't forgive me for this, either – "It's not me or any of my friends who will make a row, it's all these damned lower-class boys who were corporals who will make the rows. We all held the King's commission and are not going to insult His Majesty." Very pompous of me, but Patrick should have known better.'

An alternative explanation was offered by Noel Annan, then Assistant Tutor. 'If Patrick did have a prejudice it was against the upper classes. He blamed them for the mess Britain was in before the war and would not have understood how an intelligent young man like Simon could identify with them. As Tutor, he was obliged to take Simon to task for not paying his College bills. But I think he was genuinely concerned for Simon's welfare. He taught him Classics. He knew how gifted he was and he knew of his ambition to become a don. So when he saw Simon dissipating his energies in a sort of grotesque parody of Evelyn Waugh it was not just his social conscience that was affronted.'

Lord Annan, born 1916, added that in his day undergraduates did not keep a well-stocked drinks cabinet. 'When you went to somebody's rooms after dinner for a gossip you had tea if you had anything, or just conceivably some beer. Certainly not whisky. Parties were different. You let go

[6] A very democratic place where uniforms were seldom worn and rank was unimportant.

then. But when Simon called in he expected wine or whisky and was very down on those who didn't have it.'

The gap between Simon's expectations and those of his elders is illustrated by this extract from *A Century of King's*, in which Patrick Wilkinson comments on the absence of refreshments at Provost Sheppard's Sunday evening 'at homes' before the war:

> This was good, in that it quietly propagated the idea that conversation, not food and drink, was the staple of human society.

Simon's reaction to this can be well imagined!

*

Dickie Muir went down at the end of Simon's first year and with him went any incentive on Simon's part to engage in College sport. He came to regret this. 'I'd have been much better off playing cricket or tennis than spending my afternoons at the flicks, though one did feel deliciously guilty coming out of the cinema when it was still light.'

Not that giving up games diminished his status, as would certainly have been the case at school. In the words of Julian Slade, who was reading Classics at Trinity, 'Simon occupied a very superior position in the arty-intellectual world of Cambridge. He had great charisma. People noticed him because he was tall, good-looking and had this striking golden-bronze hair that flopped over his forehead. He said and did outrageous things by the standards of the day and encouraged others to do likewise.'

This was what Noel Annan meant when he described Simon to me as 'a liberator', the same epithet he applied to Guy Burgess. 'Simon was one of those very assured undergraduates who by their example liberate their contemporaries from the shackles of family, school or class. He certainly had this effect on Francis Haskell. Not that Francis came from a narrow-minded family[7] – far from it – but even intellectual families have blinkers on and Simon saw to it that they were removed.'

Francis Haskell agreed with this. 'I once wrote a paper for one of the College literary societies, the gist of which was that for someone like myself from a conventional background, and rather timid with it, to meet a reckless fellow like Simon was very liberating.' – Reckless in what way? – 'In every way possible – emotional, financial, moral, in his attitude towards rules .... Not that this made him universally popular. Some people disliked him precisely because he behaved unconventionally. For instance he delighted in blasphemy and could be very cruel about people's beliefs. To say that now sounds as if you're going back to Victorian times, but in fact people were pretty reticent about their beliefs, or lack of them, 40

[7] His father was the balletomane, Arnold Haskell.

years ago. Simon wasn't. He was quite uninhibited and I'm very grateful to him. *Now*, I share very few of his views. And even then I didn't agree with everything he said, but I loved hearing him say it.'

Francis Haskell was reading History and it was through him that Simon became associated with a group of exceptionally gifted young historians who arrived at King's in 1949. They included Alan Caiger-Smith, founder of the Aldermaston Pottery, Jasper Rose, Martin Shuttleworth and Christopher Bennett, son of Stanley Bennett, the medievalist. This little band thought of themselves as being rather special. They read papers to each other, joined the Ten Club[8] and brought out what proved to be the last edition of *Basileon*, the occasional, esoteric College magazine which numbered E.M. Forster and Rupert Brooke among its earliest contributors.

Primus inter pares was Christopher Bennett, a rigorous and acerbic seeker after truth who unknown to the others became an Apostle. Determined that apostolic candour should prevail over cosiness and frivolity at their meetings, Bennett made them play the truth game, where his remorseless questioning reminded Alan Caiger-Smith of John Freeman on *Face to Face*: 'He wouldn't let people wriggle out of things or be inconsistent in their answers. He would reduce them to tears if necessary. It didn't matter that they were his friends.'

Simon gave an example of how brutal Bennett could be. 'He once asked Jasper Rose, "How could you have an affair with somebody as stupid as Jean? as plain as Jean? and as fat as Jean?" You were meant to take it on the chin, but Jasper didn't. That was the thing about the truth game. Everybody thought they were exempt from being asked the nastier questions, though they didn't mind asking them themselves .... I wasn't very taken with the truth game, but then I'm not really a fan of the Truth. It seems to me to be a dispensable commodity as often as not.'[9]

Verb sap. So it is hard to know how truthful Simon was being, 40 years later, when he insisted that it was only out of loyalty to Haskell, his bosom pal, that he took part. 'One was constantly being got at to answer questions of conscience which I found quite supererogatory. The great theoretical crux was, "Supposing someone is trapped in such a way that it is necessary to blow up King's to save his life? Do we save his life?" Everybody would say, "Yes, yes, yes, human life is sacred." And I would say, "No, there're too many people about anyway and there's only one King's College." Very, very tiresome.

'Haskell, I suspect, though he probably wouldn't admit this, shared my dislike of profound, soul-searching, undergraduates-going-on-till-the-

[8] A playreading club, open to dons and undergraduates alike, with a somewhat equivocal reputation.

[9] One very good reason, Lord Annan told me, why Simon was never seriously considered for the Apostles.

dawn conversations which we were all meant to know and love. He had a frivolous side to him, did Francis, which is why he was good to travel with. Christopher Bennett was not frivolous. He took himself so seriously that although he got a starred First in Part 2 of the Tripos he announced that he wouldn't put up for a Studentship because he wasn't a good enough scholar. Well ....!'

Bennett went into the Treasury and met a mysterious end. In September 1966 he disappeared while on a walking holiday in the Savoy Alps and was never seen again. Since he had just lost a bitter battle at the Treasury over diverting funds from defence to education, and since, moreover, he had given a series of intimate dinner parties before going on leave, Bennett was presumed by his friends to have committed suicide. That he did have a lighter side, even as an undergraduate, may be deduced from these verses, preserved in the commonplace book of another King's scholar, Norman Routledge.

'Coffee After Lunch'

O scholars of King's! You wonderful things
Whose emotions are wings, whose innocence brings
A rose to the cheek of a maiden that's meek
And a tear to the eye of a pansy too sly.

Your brilliance of mind illumines mankind;
Your intellects find no malice too blind;
But sparkle and gleam with analysis keen
And converse in a stream of gossip obscene.

Yet judgements too fierce are of all things accursed
Morality's pierce is considered the worst
Form of bad taste: facts must be faced. A
Grundy's displaced by scorn of the chaste.

Polite conversation is denigration;
The state of the nation's outside your patience;
But argument rolls round the state of your souls.
Pitiful things, dear scholars of King's!

May week 1950 C.S. Bennett

*

Simon's crush on the upper classes – in practice Old Etonians – had not gone unnoticed by his intellectual friends. As Martin Shuttleworth told me, 'We knew, for instance, that one of the reasons he played royal tennis was that you played royal tennis with people it was rather royal to play royal tennis with. He had a thing about rank. He was always going on about Fellow Commoners,[10] would give one lists of who was an Esquire and who wasn't, who needed to have a degree to become an Esquire and so on …. I don't think Simon ever belonged to the Pitt Club, but I'm sure he dined there. Whereas none of the rest of us would ever have been seen dead there because it was a High Tory haunt.'

Snobbery certainly accounted for some of Simon's interest in Old Etonians, but there was more to it than that. At the age of thirteen he had read H.A. Vachell's novel about Harrow, *The Hill*, and concluded from this that Harrow, set as it is on a hill, must be morally healthier than Eton, which lies in a river valley.

> From that day to this I have always imagined behaviour at Eton as corrupt and debauched, like Pompeii on its last day, and get a frisson of prurient pleasure whenever I go near the place. (*The Old School*)

Simon was impressed by the 'natural, easy manners' Etonians had, their savoir-faire and the fact that some of them wore Guards' blazers – 'though I could see that to wear a Guards' blazer was rather an absurd thing for an undergraduate to do, even then, so I was amused as well as impressed. But the point about these chaps was that they were amiable, funny, civilised and snooty – even at one's own expense, though this was usually expressed ironically: "You know your trouble, Raven, you don't quite hold your fork right." And one never held it wrong again, you see.'

If Simon was amused by Old Etonians, they in turn were entertained by him.

> I remember my first meeting with Simon [wrote Martin Shuttleworth]. It was near the bridge over the Cam, on a sunny morning during the Long Vacation term of 1949. Simon was with three or four others. He noticed me hovering nearby, asked if I'd just come up and invited me to join them. He did most of the talking and I remember the way the others, who'd all been to Eton, just listened and nodded their slow mugs and smiled occasionally at all the extraordinary stuff this fellow Raven was entertaining them with. They were not required to be amusing or interesting themselves. Just as Madame de Stael's lieutenant had his cock, so they had their broad acres or the promise of them. But I never saw Simon fawn on people like that. If there's the snob as fawner, there's also the snob as collector, and that was what Simon did. He collected these characters and put them on display, usually in somebody else's rooms, because although Simon

[10] An archaic class of undergraduate whose high birth or great wealth permitted them to dine at the Fellows' table.

was the greatest party-goer there ever was I cannot remember that he ever held a party of his own.[11]

Another friend, Alan Caiger-Smith, described how as time went by Simon's motives became increasingly mercenary. 'I think the word I associate most with him in the beginning is Amusement. He liked to entertain and worked very, very hard at it. If he wanted to make an impression on somebody he would do his homework and work up suitable gambits. He was very skilful. Then his money worries multiplied and he had to sing for his supper in earnest. You could sometimes see a glint in his eye and know that he was off on a hunting expedition to Trinity or somewhere. And indeed he'd say, "I'd love to talk to you about that, but I'm just off to see so-and-so. I think he's good for a couple of hundred and I must say that would come in handy just now." He looked rather like a "Questing Beast" when he was in search of money.'

[11] He held two in his first year, before Shuttleworth came up.

CHAPTER NINE

When days are long and sunny
The flower of youth is blown
We waste our parents' money
And time that is our own.
Cyril Connolly, after Housman

By the end of his second year Simon was heavily in debt. He could fob off friends and tradespeople but not the College: their bill for £75 had to be paid, on pain of banishment to lodgings in the town – 'a very dismal prospect, since some of the best things in King's happened after midnight, by which time one was supposed to be locked up in one's digs'.

By chance, Patrick Wilkinson had been asked to recommend an undergraduate for the job of bear-leader to the delinquent adopted son of a millionairess. If this was not exactly a sinecure it ought, he told Simon, to be well within the compass of an ex-officer. All he had to do was avoid any 'incidents' and not squander his fee, which would go a fair way towards settling his Buttery account. Simon was duly hired and midway through July sent this bulletin to Noel Annan on Savoy Hotel notepaper.

14.7.50

My dear Noel,

This is a line to say I hope you're having a lovely time, and to tell you something of my side of the looking-glass.

For Tuesday July 4 saw me deposited the other side of it in no uncertain fashion. Mrs P[leydell]-B[ouverie] (please call me Audrey) is a neurotic and dynamic woman who has been through three husbands and picked up a good deal of money on the way – quite apart from the very adequate settlement she started with. She has the rich woman's fancy for a variegated selection of expensive doctors and inbred dogs, and is now, by my calculation, undergoing her change of life. Her taste in flowers, pictures, wines, cars, and, for the matter of that, in adopted sons, is excellent. For the boy is extremely good-looking and very bright in the head; the trouble being that he is never, properly speaking, his own 16 years at all:– he is either a good 18 (existentialism, extra-sensory perception, Beardsley) or, more often, a bad 12 – toy soldiers, American comics, all the keys of an upbringing in a cosmopolitan Swiss 'school'. His sadistic and anti-social tendencies, so-called, I have managed to check by getting him to *say* or *draw* what he likes. The necessity for action is thus mercifully diminished. But I can understand that in most environments he is not allowed to subject people to a barrage of remarks like, 'I'm going to bite that puppy in half and smear its shit on its balls', and that he therefore gets rid of his devil otherwise than verbally – though perhaps not always quite so violently as the above quotation implies.

Situations follow each other fast and without warning. Thus a week ago I was suddenly left in charge of house, boy, dogs, servants, car(s), cash and well-stocked sideboard; nor shall I be relieved till about Wednesday. This week-end the house is to be filled with his younger brother (on long leave from Eton), Ian Hayward (who is to act as tutor to the younger brother during August and September), and finally Dr Csato, an Hungarian £30 per diem psychiatrist, who is coming to vet the boy. I am told the way to his heart is through his gullet and into his stomach, and propose following this route under careful cover, lest he should start vetting me.

Ian [Murray] and Margaret [Viner, née Heathcote][1] came for a drink yesterday (I have carte blanche to entertain), as did Malcolm[2] and George Dix last Sunday. Ian was very cheerful and is, I understand, contemplating taking rooms in St Edward's passage and writing a thesis. St Edward's passage will be very gay and fashionable next year it seems.

For the rest, I await Audrey's return, equipped with the two essentials for this job, driving-licence and passport, and shall then depart with boy whithersoever her surrealistic fancy may direct. It is thought that Biarritz is a likely target in early August. The one thing I do not have – despite a vast bedroom and private bathroom – is time to myself. Meanwhile, best love.

Yours ever,
Simon

Mrs Pleydell-Bouverie favoured Biarritz for snobbish reasons: it was here, at the Hotel du Palais, that the Windsors and their entourage spent August. When Simon and Angus arrived they were given a luxurious suite overlooking the front. A few days later Simon wrote a second letter to Noel Annan.

[1] The Zuleika Dobson of her day, she broke numerous hearts, including Ian Murray's. So besotted by her was Murray that after drinking heavily at her engagement party he knocked her fiancé, a Kingsman called the Honourable Hugo Phillips, down the stairs. She later married Henry Viner.

[2] Captain Sir Malcolm Bullock MP, a stalwart of 'the Club'.

CHAPTER NINE

11.8.50

My dear Noel,

The unofficial news sheet (on which one is forced to rely at this distance) has it that you are now back at Cambridge; so I'm sending you a line to let you know that my feet are still under me and there is a nice thick carpet under my feet. The boy and I are here till Mrs P-B arrives on Thursday, and for as long after that as the 'allowance' of francs holds out. While God, they say, disposes for man, Mrs P-B's proposals are made with such energy that God has so far showed insufficient strength of mind to refuse any one of them, and I await with interest the next movement. There is a lot to be said, I think, for the life of an animate backgammon counter who is always on the winning side: he feels, strangely if fallaciously, that he is entitled to some of the credit. In any case, tonight is Gala-night; and on such occasions a backgammon counter may well end up sharing a desirable square on the chess-board.

The antics of the P-B menage in recent weeks would provide a season for the Comédie Française. But it is so long since I wrote to you that a reconstruction would take me till long after the last rich Armenian had vanished from the Gala, so I must confine myself to outline.

Know then that the 30 guinea per day psychiatrist insisted so firmly on Angus (my boy) being kept apart from his brother that we immediately packed off to Aldeburgh – a good week before the brother was due, but under an arrangement for rooms that compelled us to return on the very day he appeared back from Eton. (God getting his own back.) The psychiatrist was then summoned to straighten out the confusion – all the way from London – on the very flimsy pretext that the boy had run a temperature of 101 (entirely due to overeating!)

On arrival, the psychiatrist set to on the gin with a will and a natty piece of self-analysis ('I'm drinking so much because I know there is so little left'); upon which I was sent to get 2 more bottles from the cellar, and returned with them to find Mrs P-B in a dead faint on the sofa, having heard that Angus' schizophrenia was now beyond any doubt and serious in degree. (Strictly confidential, this last, my dear.) The news went to her kidneys, with the result that a genuine illness of hers was substituted for the quasi-fictitious chill of the boy's, and the doctor's presence in the house became almost necessary. (God getting his own back again.) This was inconvenient because no one could play the gramophone; so we all settled grimly down to Canasta, and waited for instructions.

At length Ian Hayward and the younger boy set off for Scotland; while after a day or so there emerged, out of a confused mass of playing-cards, gin bottles, drugs, cheque-books and illegible telephone messages, a crumpled female secretary with 2 crumpled plane-tickets to Paris – regardless of the obvious fact that the younger boy was now safely at Drummond Castle and out of corruption's way. Still, I was never one to complain of inconsistency in others, and trips to France in one shape or another had been long on the books. So here we are; and in 3 days time Mrs P-B (who is now undergoing her change of life with more than the usual ferocity) will arrive to convalesce in the Casino. She is a woman whom I frankly adore: her driving gives one positive orgasms, and every time she smashes a car, she buys an even bigger one – thus speeding up the accident rate in geometrical progression.

Of home news I know little. Christopher [Layton][3] went to stay with Martin [Shuttleworth], invited a very dull girl to join them, and then denied all knowledge of her when she arrived. But his record isn't wholly vile, for he has completed a course on 'How to teach Economics to the Workers'. My suggestion that they should first be taught to work was not well received; and in any case, it seems, the course has baptized him in the idea of responsibility. If, with me, you read 'self-importance' for 'responsibility', you will doubtless join me in pronouncing this course otiose in theory, supererogatory in practice, and noxious in both. If not, the worst I can wish you is that you are shamed into doing one yourself – one with an equally improbable though perhaps different object, such as 'How to teach the Laytons that the Workers are unteachable'. Don't mind my fun. Music please Miss Dalrymple – or was that the Duke of Windsor arriving?

Yours ever,
Simon

When Mrs P-B arrived at the hotel she was not best pleased to find Simon and Angus occupying the Napoleonic suite at a cost of 'God knows how much' per night. From then on it was only a matter of time before Simon became surplus to requirements. When the axe fell it was not for 'the usual thing' – 'Never laid a finger on him, pretty as he was. I wasn't that daft!' – but for losing a pair of Angus's socks in the hotel laundry – 'Once she'd made her mind up, any excuse would do. An impossible woman.'

Not that Simon was complaining. He had tasted life in a grand hotel and found that it was very good. More important, he had found his vocation, albeit prematurely. For the gossipy letters to Noel Annan were the harbingers of an equally indiscreet novella which he began on his return to England and finished in three months flat. Provisionally entitled

[3] The Honourable Christopher Layton, a contemporary of Simon's at King's.

A Passage to Biarritz (a joke at E.M. Forster's expense), it describes how Esmé Sangrail Sa Foy, an indigent undergraduate, blackmails his way back to solvency while employed in identical circumstances to Simon. Although the plot creaks and we are told that Palm Beach is in California, the writing is polished and pithy, the characterisation deft and only a pharisee could fail to be entertained by Esmé's machinations.

Simon submitted his story to Putnam's where Roger Lubbock, an old Kingsman he had met a few times, was the fiction editor. Lubbock 'very properly' rejected it because it was libellous, but said that if Simon were to prepare a second draft, sans libels and preferably with a different title and setting, all might yet be well.

Once he had finished his Finals Simon did as he was bid and received an encouraging response from Lubbock. Alas, Lubbock's superior, 'a long, costive, creaking number called Huntington', got cold feet and insisted on further revisions. But by now Simon had other fish to fry and for 28 years no more was heard of *An Inch of Fortune* (its new title). Then the original manuscript resurfaced and since the libellees were now safely dead Simon's publisher, Anthony Blond, had no hesitation in issuing it. Reviewers, who included Peter Ackroyd,[4] were generally appreciative and it may well be that had the novel appeared in 1951, then as Tim Heald argued, 'it is odds on that it would have been seized on by Cyril Connolly and applauded as immensely promising.'

What would have happened next is anybody's guess, but Simon never really regretted his near miss. 'To publish a novel at 22, how satisfying … how envious one's friends would have been. They were envious enough anyway, some of them, when they heard it *might* be published. But didn't Connolly himself say that "early laurels weigh like lead"? The Army was a far better apprenticeship for writing than Grub Street, which is where I'd have found myself if Putnam's had published me.'

*

Roger Lubbock was not Simon's only contact in Grub Street. He was also on good terms with J.R. 'Joe' Ackerley, the eminent literary editor of the *Listener*, who in 1951 began to employ him as a reviewer. Of Simon's friendship with Ackerley I shall have more to say later, but at this juncture I should like to consider Simon and E.M. Forster, through whom he met Ackerley in the first place.

Forster had returned to King's, where he was formerly an undergraduate, in November 1946, following the death of his mother and the consequent loss of her house at West Hackhurst. In a typically humane

[4] 'He looks like a choir boy about to be goosed,' was Ackroyd's verdict on the passport photograph of Simon which adorned the dust-jacket. 'Wishful thinking,' riposted Simon, who said Ackroyd's moustache reminded him of Colonel K's.

gesture the College, having made him an honorary Fellow, then offered him a large room of his own as well.[5] To begin with Forster complained of feeling rather like the prize exhibit at a zoo, but by the time Simon arrived he was reconciled to his new circumstances and had begun to involve himself in College life. He joined the Ten Club, was re-admitted to the Apostles and held rather Edwardian tea-parties for undergraduates at which he would try to draw them out.

Simon got to know Forster in his second year, by the middle of which he had begun to call him 'Morgan' – 'though I always *thought* of him as E.M. Forster'. What Forster thought of Simon we shall never know for certain until his locked diary is opened,[6] but according to Bob Buckingham's widow, May,

> EMF was much amused most of the time, but shocked at some of [Simon's] escapades.

This is understandable. There was a Byronic quality to Simon that probably alarmed Forster, the quintessential 'muff', as often as it intrigued him. Nor can he have relished Simon's politics, or his cavalier way with personal relationships (though he evidently enjoyed the gossip they provoked). On the other hand Simon was good-looking, intelligent and witty, qualities Forster approved of in young men. And they shared an abiding distaste for religious faith in general and Christianity in particular, hence Simon's pert rebuke after Forster had broken his ankle climbing the belfry of Aldeburgh parish church:

> How unwise you were, dear Morgan, to go into Church where the Devil cannot look after his own.

Simon was flattered by Forster's interest in him. Of course he was. And while he may have had serious reservations about Forster's character even then, he carefully omitted them from the profile he wrote for *Varsity* in 1951. Under the heading 'Inveterate Iconoclast', it begins like this:

> As an old Tonbridgian of some distinction, Mr E.M. Forster was once invited to contribute to a series of articles on the history of Tonbridge Games. He replied that he would be delighted to write an essay on how he himself managed to shirk them. The editors did not accept his offer. Was there not something irresponsible, a trifle subversive even, about a grown man who could make jokes on such a subject? Mr Forster's tone was sadly at fault. A straight refusal could have been borne; but levity ....

[5] He used to sleep at Patrick Wilkinson's house in Trumpington Street.
[6] This will be at the discretion of the Fellows of King's.

> I am sorry for those editors. They are, in a minor way, among Mr Forster's butts. Together with Christianity, improvers, and possessive women, together with Mrs Grundy, officialdom and the public school tourist, they are among the number of inflated wine-skins that this shy old man has spent his life in lancing. Not, to be sure, in the manner of Don Quixote; but subtly and quietly, with a very occasional giggle, Mr Forster has inserted his pen-nib in the puffed out hides of the pretentious that lay about him, has stepped back (almost with a mince), and has slyly watched the dreary mucous of clergymen, rowing-blues and half-pay generals oozing across the floor and between the cracks in the boards, till it is dripping down, distractingly and infuriatingly, on to the Rugger Club Tea or the Prayer Meeting below ....

Forty years later Simon cringed. 'How could I have written such greasy rubbish?' But it is only greasy when compared to the astringency with which Simon would later write about Forster, notably in the *Spectator* and *Shadows in the Grass*. In a letter to me Forster's biographer, P.N. Furbank, allowed that there was 'a grain of truth' in Simon's description of EMF as 'bone idle' – though only a grain. As for Simon's charge that Forster was 'pathologically mean about money' – 'Nothing could be more *absurdly* untrue: he was, in a cautious, careful and well-thought-out way, quite astonishingly generous.'

Simon stuck to his guns. 'Morgan Forster was a mean old number who never bought anyone dinner in his life. Tea is about the only meal he's on record as having given anybody.' This said, Simon admitted that it was not entirely coincidental that his opinion of Forster began to drop following Forster's refusal to lend him £100 to settle some Army debts. By then, I suspect, Forster had concluded that Simon gave pleasure a bad name (as was also said of Cyril Connolly). In Bloomsbury circles, treats had to be earned.

'Everybody used to say, "Why can't you be more like Ant Blunt? He had a lot of fun like you, but he worked hard, he behaved nicely, he was a good socialist – you're not, you're just a beastly reactionary. *Be more like Blunt*," they said. So when Blunt was exposed I sent round postcards to all of these people who told me that and said, "Thank God I wasn't more like Blunt." Wasn't answered by many of them, I can tell you!'

Simon contrasted this with the same people's reaction to the defection of Guy Burgess in May 1951. 'They'd all known him and I think it did worry them, but they weren't going to show it. So what they did was make jokes: about how dirty Guy was, how homosexual he was and, in the end, how utterly unsatisfactory he was .... "But oh, my dear, *wasn't he charming*!" '[7]

[7] Whatever he thought of the Cambridge spies, Simon profited by them. He was paid a two-year retainer of £14,000 to dramatise Andrew Boyle's *The Climate of Treason*, but never had to write a word – 'The producers were worried that another scandal would break in the middle of the shooting, and eventually the project was aborted.'

*

At the beginning of Simon's third year, having failed to pay his Buttery bill, he was exiled to digs in Milton Road. Appropriately, it was now that he began to make a name for himself outside King's. His chance came through another Old Carthusian, Peter Green, who was editing the rather erudite dons' weekly, the *Cambridge Review*. Aware that there was intense debate at High Table over who should succeed Smuts as Chancellor of the University,[8] Green commissioned a piece about the election from Simon. What he got was pure 'Brideshead'.

'Time of Hope'

> It will not be long now before the bells of Great St Mary's ring to welcome a new Chancellor. But there is still a little time to pass, a time of deliberation and heart-searching for some, of intrigue and malice for others: a time of anticipation in many quarters, of indifference in few: to most people a time of interest, and to myself a time of hope. Hope, I regret to say, as frivolous as it is tasteless.
>
> For I am filled with a nostalgia for colour. I long for a return to the nice and decorative distinctions between nobleman and fellow-commoner, between pensioner, scholar and sizar. I long to see the golden tassel, the appropriate emblem of noble birth, proudly flaunted along the length of Trinity Street: nothing would please me more than to see the gilded arm of the fellow-commoner raised to beat the cringing but worthy sizar who had been so ill-advised as to burn his toast. I should like to see Porson drunk and obstreperous in Senate House Yard; I should like to hear the unyielding Bentley defying his College Council and announcing that his impoverished Fellows might receive no dividend for yet another year; and I should adore, above all, to attend a Midsummer Fair, where I could observe the orders of the Church, the statutes of the University, and the laws of His Majesty all alike being flouted in one joyous and scandalous kaleidoscope of bounteous misdemeanour.
>
> But I am told I am being at once sentimental and improper. My attitude betrays a lack of social conscience, a frivolous disregard for academic dignity, and a terrifying deficiency in Sense of Purpose. Now I am quite unregenerate in this matter; but I must still resign myself to accept the practical implications of the judgement made on me. Democracy, whether I like it or not (and I don't) is here to stay: Seriousness (drab, dingy monarch that he is) is set upon the throne: and *Il Penseroso* sheds universal gloom. There is, however, just one

[8] The Young Turks wanted Nehru, but Lord Tedder was appointed.

hope for me, and that hope is vested in the vacant office of Chancellor. For the function of the Chancellor remains, despite all that ill will combined with a sense of propriety can do, a delightful and decorative function. True, the medals of gold that once he gave are turned to dross; but he still has his robes and his processions, his feastings and his ceremonies: he still has speeches of good Latin in his honour, servitors clothed in good stuffs and ranged before him in menial attendance: he still has all the ornament that is the fit companion of pomp, circumstance and pride. So I am prepared to forgo the pleasure of seeing the servile sizar demurely seated on his bench, I am ready to deny myself the sight of the ruby-red decanter set gracefully before the arrogant elder son, if only the Chancellor's office is filled for me by a man whose qualities and tastes conform to the splendour and panoply of his office.

He must have a title. Not, for my preference, a Royal title, for these are somehow connected with the invidious notion of state subsidies; nor, on the other hand, must it be merely a paltry barony of sordid and industrial origin. It should be a title with the essence of poetry in it, a title with the romantic ring of ancient feuds and long-forgotten atrocities. It must be that of a duke or a marquis (with a string of misty earldoms that the glory of the family has outgrown): and its holder must be a nobleman of the old school, who has held his head high for all the malicious incursions of the proletariat, a man who drinks hock for breakfast, sets man-traps on his land, starves his tenants, beats his daughters, exercises the *ius primae noctis*, abuses his privileges with a laugh and ignores his responsibilities without a thought. He must have at least ten bastard children; and must have gambled away his wife's diamonds in a night.

But above all he must intrigue. He must blackmail Heads of Houses into giving fellowships to the most worthless of his nephews. He must have a posse of cringing followers, who canvass His Grace's pleasure from door to door, carrying in their breasts the gnawing hope of rich preferment. He must take his intrigues to courts and parliaments, making instruments of those even mightier than himself. His pleasure done, he must descend in rich apparel and feast gaudily for seven nights on end. His pleasure refused, he must appear silently, sullenly and suddenly, anger in his brow and potential disaster at his back for any man who has been so presumptuous as to arrogate to himself the right of conscience or free opinion. He must dominate and govern, he must threaten, rage and stamp his foot like Jove. He must drink deep, and call for another bottle when all the body of Doctors lie about him, prostrate and powerless in their scarlet.

He will be a subject for future Winstanleys to write about, my Chancellor. He will be a subject for poets and minstrels, the legend

> of Founders' Feasts in the dim centuries to come, when the University buildings will stretch as far as Bletchley and there won't be a drinkable drop of port in any of them. (4.11.50)

A few weeks after this appeared Simon went with another Kingsman, John Barton, to see a production of *The Cocktail Party* at the Arts Theatre Club. Barton was supposed to review this overnight for the *Cambridge Review*, a task he found was beyond him. 'So Simon said, "Tell me roughly what you think and I'll write the piece," which he did. This happened a few more times and then Simon took over as drama critic. He was very, very professional. No matter how chaotic his circumstances he always contrived to deliver his copy on time. He was never an idle person.'

Francis Haskell endorsed this. 'I've always thought that one of the bogus things about Simon was that he liked to pretend that he simply lived for pleasure. In fact he worked very hard as well. And even his pleasure was guilt-ridden: Simon has a terrific guilty conscience.'

Not that Simon had much time to feel guilty during his third year: he had too much on his plate, beginning with Part 2 of the Classical Tripos. Hitherto he had got by on the learning bequeathed him by Uncle Irvine and his colleagues, but this did not stretch to Ancient History and Philosophy, new disciplines for which he had the intellect but not necessarily the application. There were so many distractions, the most insistent of them a direct consequence of his chronic shortage of ready cash.

*

In his prosperous middle age, when he was given to laying down the law about manners and morals, Simon liked to quote the Duke of Omnium:

> Money is the reward of labour .... It is a commodity of which you are bound to see that the source is not only clean but noble.

How bourgeois he would have found this at King's! All that mattered there was *having* money: where it came from was immaterial. If, as an undergraduate, he resembled anyone in Trollope at all, it was Burgo Fitzgerald:

> Let Burgo's troubles be as heavy as they might be, there was something to him ecstatic in the touch of ready money which always cured them for the moment.

How did Simon raise ready money? Well, if all else failed he could apply to 'a gentleman in business near the Round Church', who would advance small sums against any item except bedclothes. But in general he relied on wit, ingenuity and sheer nerve. 'He was for ever devising shifts,' recalled Martin Shuttleworth. Noel Annan agreed. 'I always used to say that by the time he got to his third year Simon's life was as follows: that in the morning he went out and repaid some of his creditors, thus re-establishing his credit, and in the afternoon he went out and spent a great deal more which he had borrowed meanwhile.' – Robbing Peter to pay Paul? – 'Exactly. But it was so skilfully done that you had to admire the roguery with which he managed his life.'

Fenners was a happy hunting ground, particularly if it rained, because he might find himself sheltering with some easy marks. 'He had this list of prospects and it was the complete opposite of the sort of people you or I might suppose would be worth touching,' said John Barton. 'I remember Bishops came first because, he said, they were so surprised to be asked they paid up on the spot. This sort of worldliness was far beyond me at that point.'

On the other hand Barton did catch Simon out on one occasion by giving him, 'just for fun', a post-dated cheque. 'He didn't spot it and of course it screwed up all his transactions. He found me later on the same day and I altered the date, but I can still remember how agitated he was because he couldn't repay the people he was owing.'

Sometimes Simon's effrontery paid off in unexpected ways. Indignant that Barclays had bounced a cheque when he was still within his overdraft limit, he marched into the manager's office and accused him of ruining his credit. The manager was very apologetic, but Simon said, 'Apologies are not enough. I want something more tangible.' So the manager opened up his safe and handed over a pile of readies. How much? I asked Simon. 'Clean gone. But the legend has it that I received £200.'

Punctilious about repaying his friends, most of whom were no better off than he was, Simon could be unscrupulous with wealthy admirers like Philip Radcliffe, a music don whose ugliness, I was told, 'was so extreme as to be almost a form of beauty'. Radcliffe delighted in stroking young men's hair, a fetish Simon was quick to exploit – 'though I've no doubt Simon would have made a point of inviting Philip to any parties that Philip had underwritten,' said Francis Haskell.

Simon did not spend money on possessions, then or later: he was not bothered about objects at all, except possibly books. At Cambridge, every last penny went on having a good time, for which read wining and dining (sex came gratis and he was not yet a serious gambler). All are agreed that he was the most generous of hosts, his favourite thing being to entertain two or three friends to a lavish dinner at either the Arts Theatre Club restaurant or the Festival Grill, both a stone's throw from King's. College feasts excepted, he never ate dinner in hall if he could possibly help it ('the food was vile and one could eat perfectly well across the road for five bob'). Nor did he entertain in College after his second year, though before this there was a memorable twenty-first at which the champagne flowed so freely that several guests were legless long before the end (James Prior, said Simon, had to 'crawl home to Pembroke'), and a Pimms party at which Philip Radcliffe got so drunk that he couldn't take part in a recital that evening.

*

By the time he was thirty Simon preferred 'a good dinner to a good fuck'. But at Cambridge his appetite for sex was not only keen but indiscriminate: 'Simon would go to bed with anything on two legs,' said Peter Green ('Rich coming from Peter, who used to boast he'd had a one-legged tart in Westbourne Grove,' observed Martin Shuttleworth); and for once this quip was near the mark. Naturally he favoured partners who were young and personable, particularly if they were also strait-laced – 'Simon enjoyed a challenge,' said Alan Caiger-Smith. But if he thought it was in his interests to sleep with someone old enough to be his father, e.g. a celebrity like John Sparrow, he would generally do so. 'That's the way to get on, dear,' he told his friend Peter Dixon.'[9]

Simon used to say that where sexual conduct was concerned he tried to follow the precepts laid down in his notorious *Letter To My Son* (q.v.):

> Always be kind and considerate; but always make it plain, before you start, just what you are offering – which should not be a lifetime of devotion but merely a few hours' diversion.

But not everyone could cope with the latitude implicit in this matter-of-fact approach. 'I'm not going to bed with Simon ever again,' one disillusioned Newnham girl was heard to say. 'One day it's Boris,[10] then a choral scholar, then it's me, then it's back to Boris again. No!'

Simon's eclectic sex life excited considerable interest, not least because in 1950 bisexuality was still beyond most people's ken. True, there were plenty of homosexual dons who had married for the sake of convention, but they would not have described themselves as bisexual. To do so was unorthodox: you were assumed to be either queer or heter and that was that. In fact, as would become apparent from his novels, Simon reserved his deepest feelings for men; but his homosexual friends at King's were saddened to discover that he was not exclusively 'one of us'.

When people asked, as they sometimes did, how Simon could take on boys and girls concurrently, he would usually trot out his own translation of a Classical Greek epigram:

[9] Simon did, however, draw the line at Raymond Mortimer, who observed to Noel Annan how agreeable it would be 'to smooth the Raven down'. Simon thought him 'a creepy fellow with a clammy handshake' and kept well away.

[10] Boris Ord (1897-1961), celebrated organist and conductor.

Zeus, to catch boy Ganymede,
An eagle's form put on;
But when he wanted the lady Leda,
He turned into a swan.
Now some like boys and some like girls,
But as far as I can see,
If both are good enough for Zeus,
They're both good enough for me.

But for a more earthy rationale, nothing beats this exchange with Kingsley Amis' first wife, Hilly:

> Hilly: What puzzles me, Simon, is that you say it doesn't make much difference whether you go to bed with chaps or chapesses.
> Simon: It's quite simple, dear. It's all a matter of willies.
> Hilly: How do you mean?
> Simon: Well, dear, when I'm with a chap it's *his* willy, and when I'm with a lady, it's mine. D'you see?[11]

A corollary of this is that Simon 'never really cared for straight fucking because you can't see your willy'. The greatest sexual compliment he could pay a woman was that she was 'inventive', which attribute became mandatory in later life as the drink took its toll.

*

For most of his third year at Cambridge Simon was of no fixed abode. This came about through the negligence of his landlady in Milton Road, who allowed him to come and go pretty much as he pleased. Consequently whenever there was something to detain him in King's he dossed down there for the night, either with a friend or, if he were still sober enough to find one, in an unoccupied College guest-room. The strain of living like this took its toll. Simon was no longer raffish, but seedy, 'an unmade bed of a man'[12] who stuffed newspaper in his shoes and ransacked other people's wardrobes when his own clothes became too offensive for him. But however squalid his circumstances his Muse rose above them, notably at a meeting of the College Literary Society when Simon read a paper on *Pygmalion*. Alan Caiger-Smith was there.

At the Lit. Soc. you had to read papers on subjects that really

[11] 'I longed to show Hilly *my* willy,' admitted Simon. 'Too bad she never asked.'

[12] George Plimpton's description. Plimpton, shortly to found the *Paris Review*, had come to King's from Harvard. Simon said that he was 'always prepared to lend small sums of money without being unduly officious about their return.'

> mattered to you. It was not just an intellectual exercise. It had to come from the heart. Simon produced his Pygmalion talk at a time when he was behaving in a very rackety sort of way. It was one of his seediest periods. And out came this beautiful, radiant story which he'd worked on very hard, I know. Sheet after sheet of paper with only about six lines scrawled on it. And I think everybody was a bit stunned because it was so completely the polar opposite of everything he was doing and saying in everyday life. I suspect Simon was a bit shaken by it too: 'Where has this come from?' But he couldn't really explain it in words. It had just surfaced from some aspect of him which was always there and which was far more important than he liked to acknowledge. There was an Aegean quality about it. You could almost feel the quality of the light.
>
> Shortly afterwards I said to Simon, 'You obviously got a great deal of pleasure and satisfaction out of your Pygmalion story, yet as long as you pursue this seedy, hand-to-mouth, sexually-messy way of life you'll never have enough time for the things that really matter to you.' And he said, 'The trouble is I've got a daemon in me. I have to do these things.'

When Simon arrived at King's he had benefited from a concerted effort on the part of the older, fruitier dons to reimpose the status quo. But by 1950 the chill wind of social change could be felt in the Fellows' garden, one of its earliest manifestations being the appointment as Lay Dean of John Raven,[13] an austere figure from Trinity who taught Simon Ancient Philosophy. Immensely learned – as at home with Botany as with Aristotle and Plato – John Raven believed in high thinking and plain living.[14] Later, I was told, he mellowed. And Simon himself conceded that 'John seemed reluctantly to like me. He certainly argued my case for a First very strongly.' But given Simon's adherence to the pleasure principle it was inevitable that they should clash.

> I can still see Simon emerging from the Dean's quarters after a wigging [recalled Martin Shuttleworth], brazen of hair, face and manner as an animated second-hand lectern eagle, defiantly squawking that the vicar who'd just laid a heavy bible on his head was talking a load of balls.

[13] Son of Canon Raven, the sanctimonious Vice-Chancellor and Master of Christ's. Although they were not related, Simon found it convenient to hint at kinship with the Vice-Chancellor when opening accounts with tradesmen.

[14] There is a story, possibly apocryphal, that an amorous undergraduate in search of Simon was misdirected to John Raven's rooms. Finding no one at home he stripped off and arranged himself provocatively on the sofa. Enter John Raven, who simply said, 'Sorry. Wrong Raven.'

This must have been the occasion of Simon's three-week gating, imposed after he slept in a College guest-room once too often. John Raven agreed that this was harsh, but added that at least Simon would be able to devote his evenings to Aristotle, in whom he had shown scant interest up to now. Alas, it was too little too late. Simon could not conceal his disregard of *Metaphysics* from the examiners, who may also have been unamused by his jokes, e.g. his reference to The Good and The Beautiful as 'the fairy at the top of this particular Christmas Tree'. He was awarded a 2:1, a very good result for most people but less than was expected of a prospective Fellow.

But King's, as I have said, was a law unto itself, and Simon's stock was still high with the dons who elected Studentships – a sum of money that enabled you to exist as a graduate student. When it came to the vote, only Noel Annan argued against. 'In cases like this you have to put your feelings to one side and give an honest opinion of a candidate's capabilities. Everyone else said, "We must give Simon a Studentship because he's so obviously very bright." And he'd proposed a fascinating subject for his dissertation, the influence of Classics on Victorian public schools and their products. But I thought he wasn't cut out for research and I'm afraid I was right.'

Simon's joy at the award of his Studentship was short-lived. Barely a fortnight later he had some shattering news: Susan Kilner, with whom he had been having an intermittent affair for more than a year, was pregnant. The Furies had picked up his scent yet again.

CHAPTER TEN

> 'You know,' said Grimes, 'look at it how you will, marriage is rather a grim thought.'
>
> Evelyn Waugh, *Decline and Fall*

Susan 'Suki' Kilner, the daughter of a Yorkshire mill-owner, had gone down from Newnham the previous summer with a 2.2 in History and the ambition, which she soon realised, of a career in journalism. At Cambridge she had acted a good deal and also belonged to 'The Blue Nylons', described to me by her contemporary, Katharine Whitehorn, as 'a rather curious little club which was supposed to give us a forum for the intellectual stimulation we didn't seem to be getting at Cambridge as promised'.

Simon was vague about how he and Susan met. It could have been at a theatrical party, or in Noel Annan's rooms, where the Blue Nylons met, or, most probably, through a mutual friend like Margaret Heathcote. At any rate Kenneth Harrison, who took an avuncular interest in the couple, dated their affair from the Lent Term of 1950, Susan's penultimate term.

> Then, 'a look of understanding' – no mistake about it – appeared in Susan's eyes, and Simon began to talk of 'Tea at Newnham'.[1]

Simon, as we have heard, was promiscuous. 'Norman Douglas got it right,' he would say. ' "The only true aphrodisiac is variety." ' Furthermore, pursuit and conquest were as important to him as sex itself. So when he appeared to be 'going steady' his friends were intrigued. 'It wasn't at all what one expected of Simon,' said Alan Caiger-Smith. 'I think he was a bit disconcerted to find how eager Susan was. I remember him saying one afternoon, "Well, I must be off to Newnham. I'm having tea with Suki and you know what *that* means." '

But Simon continued to see Susan after she had gone down and there is no question that he was genuinely very fond of her. True, she was not a beauty, but she was 'wholesome', a quality Simon set great store by, 'particularly in those days, when even well-bred girls did not bathe as often as one would have wished. She was also kind (she lent me lots of

[1] Code for love in the afternoon.

money), intelligent, unprudish and great fun to be with. So it was very sad that it should all end as it did.'

Simon knew that if Susan meant to keep the baby he would have to marry her – or become a social outcast. The Permissive Society had yet to arrive and it was inconceivable that a male of Simon's background and aspirations should do other than 'give the child a name'. Since the prospect of marriage, even to someone as agreeable as Susan, appalled him, he immediately proposed an abortion. This was illegal in 1951, but if you had the right contacts it was possible to procure one safely and discreetly[2] – albeit at a price.

To begin with, said Simon, Susan favoured an abortion herself. But once it became apparent how 'ineffectual' he was at arranging matters, she rapidly went off the idea. Simon then raised the question of adoption, but Susan said she knew of too many mothers who had changed their minds about this after giving birth, 'and marched resolutely home with their babies under their arms'.

It was now, with Susan more than two months gone, that Simon came under pressure from her family – 'gentle at first, then not so gentle'. A rumour went round that Susan's brother, who was at Trinity, would appear any day with a horsewhip. Lord Annan was sure he arranged a meeting between Mr Kilner and Simon in the Fellows' garden, where Mr Kilner said that while he thought Simon ought to marry Susan, 'what happens after that must be a matter for both of you'. Simon denied that this meeting took place, but marry Susan he did, at Fakenham Registry Office on October 15th.

'I said, "Right ho, I'll marry you. That'll keep your family happy. But I won't live with you – ever." Very caddish of me, I agree. But I knew, you see, that if ever there were a born bachelor, it was me. And Susan accepted this. She was a brick. So once our union was legitimised I returned to Cambridge, she returned to London, and we resumed our separate lives.'

Compared with his expulsion from Charterhouse and the racing debts for which he was so nearly cashiered, Simon's shotgun marriage seems a minor blemish. Yet according to Francis Haskell, his closest friend at the time, 'It was very dramatic in a Trollopeian sort of way. Except on very rare occasions Simon is most reluctant to show that the wind has been taken out of his sails. This was one of those occasions.'

Alan Caiger-Smith agreed. 'He was genuinely horrified. No question about it. The thing Simon valued most in life was his independence. He saw life as a kind of game in which you had to be free to take risks, even if that meant coming a cropper. "We'll try it this way, and if it doesn't work out, well, let's face it, we can always pick ourselves up again, can't we? And if we can't, somebody else will come along and give us a helping hand – one

[2] As does Vanessa Salinger in *The Rich Pay Late*. But for an idea of how tricky this could be for less privileged persons, see *You Can't Have Both* by Kingsley Amis.

hopes." You couldn't do that with a wife and child. Of course he put a brave face on it. "Married I may be," he said to me. "But I shall be divorced *extremely soon* afterwards!" '

Susan gave birth to a son, called Adam, in March 1952. Simon visited them in hospital, but the sight of his offspring only served to reinforce his antipathy to small children – 'Until they reach thirteen or fourteen they are just a bloody nuisance.' Nevertheless he agreed to travel north for Adam's Christening a few weeks later. Alan Caiger-Smith takes up the story.

> Simon had asked Kenneth Harrison to be godfather but Kenneth couldn't come, so Simon asked if I would stand proxy for Kenneth. 'We'll hire a car and have a nice expedition,' he said. 'My mother and my little sister Robin will be coming too.'
>
> We'd hoped to hire something quite smart and drive up in style, but in the event all we could afford was a very ordinary old banger. Simon tried to look on the bright side. 'Off we go, my dears. It's all going to be great fun, isn't it?'
>
> Mrs Raven had a couple of bottles of gin with her. She was pretty tight before we set off and got progressively tighter as the journey went on. The plan was to stay the night at the Kilners', but something was wrong with the car's petrol feed and while it was being seen to we had to put up at a rather gaunt, 18th-century hostelry on the Great North Road. Mrs Raven soon went to bed because she was so tight and Robin followed her because she was still pretty young. Simon and I had quite a lot to drink and when we came down to breakfast the next morning our hangovers weren't improved by finding feathers in the scrambled eggs. 'Never mind,' said Simon. 'It wouldn't have been one's first choice, but at least the beds were aired.'
>
> Anyway we got to the Kilners' in the nick of time and were met by Mrs Kilner who said, 'None of us are going to enjoy this. None of us wanted it to happen. And I'm sure we would rather not be meeting. But since we are here together, and there are others present, I suggest we try and be as civil as possible in the circumstances.'
>
> And Simon said, 'I couldn't agree with you more. Here's my mother.' Whereupon Mrs Raven, who'd been at the gin again, went straight up to Mrs Kilner and tried to embrace her, which was not to Mrs Kilner's liking at all. 'Didn't you hear me?' she said. 'I'm not having any of that sort of thing.' And off she marched.
>
> Well after the Christening, which went off alright, there was a big reception with family and friends. And you got the feeling that although everyone knew it was just a charade, they were determined, for Susan's sake, to be polite to her rather difficult husband, his mother and sister, and his nice friend from King's. Now Mrs Raven

didn't just drink a lot, she chain-smoked as well. And with a fag in her hand she took up a position in the middle of the Kilners' drawing-room, on the floor of which was a beautiful pale grey Chinese carpet. She then got hold of Adam and announced, 'Isn't this the most gorgeous baby you've ever seen in all your life. I could lick him all over.' And proceeded to do just this. Whereupon Mrs Kilner rushed over and rescued Adam. 'For heaven's sake, not here.' – 'Oh, *do* give him back to me. I just love licking him. I'd love to lick him all over.'

Then Mrs Raven must have realised that she'd dropped her cigarette on this frightfully expensive carpet, so she plonked her foot down on the place where the cigarette had fallen and wouldn't budge an inch. And there were people coming up to her, 'Oh, Mrs Raven, wouldn't you like to sit down?' – 'No, thank you. But I would like some more champagne.' And after about an hour of this Mrs Kilner was heard to say, 'Somebody *please* take that woman out of the house.' But it wasn't until she'd drunk so much that she was in danger of falling over that she allowed herself to be moved, at which point the awful truth was discovered. So she was hustled away and Mrs Kilner exploded.

That was one side of things. The other side of things was that Susan's father, who was a charming man, had obviously thought long and hard about what he was going to do with this son-in-law of his. And he'd got hold of a Classical crossword puzzle, presumably in the hope that it would be of interest to Simon. And I thought to myself, 'My God, this is going to be a disaster. Classical crossword puzzle by the fireside after the Christening. Simon won't wear this.' And I was extremely apprehensive on Mr Kilner's behalf because he was so obviously a very nice man. But in fact Simon could not have been more cooperative. 'I think the answer might be Epaminondas ...', knowing perfectly well that it was. And, 'That's very good, Mr Kilner. Now, that should give us an "M" for here. How about Maecenas?'

This goes to show that although Simon liked nothing better than a good scene, particularly if it involved the sort of people whose values he detested, he could be kind and generous when the occasion demanded it, as was certainly the case here. Because if he'd been true to his principles, he'd have thought, 'Bloody Kilner family. Rich provincial bourgeoisie. Let's stir them up.' But like me he obviously felt that Mr Kilner was a delightful man who was making the best of a bad job, and so he played the game.

I enjoyed the expedition enormously. It made me very fond of his mother, even though she was a bit of a liability, because she was the only person there who wasn't playing a part. I think Simon would have preferred it if she had played a part! Still, at least he was word-perfect himself, which can't have been easy. He liked to improvise, to ad-lib, and always rather had his tail between his legs when this wasn't possible. It was the same when he had that tutoring job. He came back with a lot of very good stories about Biarritz, but it was clear that he'd had to toe the line. He'd gone 'King's Evidence', so to speak.

*

As soon as Simon knew that he would be spending a fourth year at Cambridge he determined to leave Milton Road and return to the centre of things. Luckily he was able to rent a room at the Central Hotel, 'a cheap, charming and disreputable *boîte* in Market Street, long since demolished to make way for some hideous modern development'. Even without the worry of Susan's pregnancy he had a lot on his plate, beginning with a long list of 19th-century tomes which would furnish the material for his thesis. Then there was the second draft of *A Passage to Biarritz* to be completed, plus 1,500 words a fortnight for the *Listener*, where Joe Ackerley had retained him as a quarterly novel-reviewer. Add to these commitments his drama criticism for the *Cambridge Review* and occasional pieces for periodicals like the *New Statesman* (where Susan worked briefly), and it is not surprising that something had to give.

'Scholarship was one thing, drudgery another. I very soon concluded that nothing would induce me to read, let alone make notes on, hundreds and hundreds of *very, very, very* boring books. So on the strength of Joe's seventeen guineas a fortnight, which went a long way then, I promoted myself "man of letters", when in fact I was just a tiresome and impecunious research student, neglecting his research.'

This was brought home to him the following Spring, by which time Putnam's had rejected the second draft of his novel and his reviewing had all but dried up. With not one word of his dissertation written his days at King's were clearly numbered. But what on earth was he to do next?

Commerce ('money-grubbing') was definitely out. So was schoolmastering, 'because I was on every blacklist in existence'. Grub Street would have been an answer because he could clearly write, but Simon still hungered for Experience, Adventure even. 'The thing about Raven and all the others who just missed the war,' said Dickie Muir, 'was that they felt they ought to have been shot at.' And there was another, more fundamental objection to Grub Street: it would bring him within range of Susan and Adam. This thought must have crossed Simon's mind when in May 1952 he reviewed a play called *The Trap* and complained of,

> interminable lectures from Miss [Mai] Zetterling on the rights of herself and her baby.

Of course there was always the Agony column of *The Times*, but Simon was no Peter Fleming.[3] Nevertheless, like the egregious Basil Seal he did wonder if he wasn't 'the kind of rascal' the cloak and dagger boys would welcome. Since Patrick Wilkinson was known to be a talent-spotter for British Intelligence, Simon applied to him. 'Patrick was friendly, but sceptical. "I don't think they'll really want you because you're too drunk and you're not reliable. But we can arrange an interview." So I was duly sent for, interviewed and politely notified that my services would not be required. The story I put about was that although quite queer, I was not queer enough to compete with Burgess and Maclean, nor was I socialist enough.'

But Patrick Wilkinson had an alternative suggestion, the Regular Army, who were, he said, so anxious to recruit graduates like Simon who had held temporary commissions that they were offering back-dated seniority. 'Yes, it was ironic that Patrick of all people should have put one on to this. I dare say he wanted to see the back of one. Probably there was a bit of pride involved too. Patrick was a great fixer. He would have regarded me as a challenge. But I'm grateful to him. Rejoining the Army was the best thing I ever did.'

*

Simon was sad to have forfeited the perks that came with being a don, 'comfortable rooms in beautiful buildings, free refreshments, possible attentions of good-looking students of either sex and so on. That would have been fun. But I am not sorry to have evaded educational responsibility because I wasn't cut out to be a teacher: I wouldn't have been good at it all. And I am more than happy not to have witnessed King's divesting itself of its privileges and embracing tertiary socialism. Noel Annan summed it up very well when he said to me, in the late 1960s, "You and I, Simon, are *liberals*. The place now is being run by *radicals*." '

Change was in the air even before Simon 'withdrew'.[4] Whereas he pursued knowledge for its own sake, the new men who began to arrive in about 1950 saw it as a means to an end. As Frederic Raphael[5] put it,

> They belonged to a generation that laid its ladders against the ramparts of the Establishment and swarmed up brandishing degree certificates ... (*My Generation*)

[3] Fleming's career as a bestselling travel writer began after he joined an expedition to the Matto Grosso advertised in the Agony column.

[4] The correct technical term for Simon's action.

[5] Raphael had entered Charterhouse the term Simon was expelled, 'a nine-day wonder'. During Raphael's first year at Cambridge Simon came to his rooms at St John's and tried to enrol him for the Cambridge University Old Carthusian Society. 'I declined, saying I hated the bloody place. He said I was probably right.'

It was the same with the Arts, where dedicated careerists like Peter Hall and Mark Boxer saw off the dilettantes and used Cambridge as a launching pad for Shaftesbury Avenue and Fleet Street. Simon was fond of Mark Boxer, who disguised his professionalism (and his liking for girls) beneath a flamboyantly camp manner. Perhaps Boxer did not care to be reminded of this. At any rate in a piece about King's written shortly before his untimely death he proposed that Simon's book about his Cambridge days[6] was 'largely invention'. But Boxer himself was wrong in saying that Simon provided Lord Rothschild 'with spermatozoa in a claret bottle for one of his experiments'. What in fact happened will serve to round off Simon's Cambridge career.

'Noel Annan said, "Victor Rothschild is doing research into breeding. He's exhausted the lesser animals and has now reached Man. He's not going to pay. But if you care to come down to his place he'll give you a decent bottle of wine, some books to look at – ha! ha! – and you can toss yourself off into a bottle." (It probably wouldn't have been quite like that because they'd have needed a sterile specimen, but anyway…) So I wrote a joke letter to Victor beginning, "My Lord," and saying how glad I'd be to be his Lordship's accomplice in his great programme of research. I gather it was well taken, but I was never called upon.'

*

Eleven months were to pass before Simon finally re-entered the Army. He spent most of them in London, living off his wits. 'I borrowed a lot of money. I gambled, sometimes successfully, on credit. And thanks to Joe Ackerley, I also had a basic income from reviews. It was exhilarating, instructive and amusing. I wouldn't have it again, not for anything. But looked back upon it was not without its delights.'

But before this 'wild, Catullan' period began he experienced a dismal couple of months at Hunstanton, where the air was thick with recrimination. 'My father, as usual, tried to have it both ways. He'd always disapproved of my reading Classics – "You'll never make any money at that" – so now I wasn't going to be a don, he could have a good crow. But at the same time he resented every penny that went towards my upkeep, and this made him very sour indeed. My mother was sympathetic but increasingly anxious. "There must be *something* you can do, dear." It wasn't certain, you see, that the Army would have me. I had to pass a Regular Commissions Board where they set one disagreeable practical tasks which I invariably buggered up. Luckily I did pass, but by then I'd left Hunstanton anyway.'

Simon left Hunstanton following the row that David Evers witnessed when Arthur accused him of watering the gin. He went to lodge in London

[6] Presumably Simon's memoir, *Shadows on the Grass*, some of which is about Cambridge.

with another old Kingsman called David Rowse, Dickie Muir's partner in a magazine publishing business. Rowse let him live rent-free, but London was just beginning to enjoy itself again after years of privation and it wasn't long before Simon turned up on Susan's doorstep with a begging bowl, 'which she very generously filled'. She also got him to review for *Time and Tide*, her current employers, but they paid so little – 'two quid a go' – that broke as he was, Simon soon gave this up. He had a pretty fair idea of his worth, even then.

The *Listener*, Simon's most regular employer, was not particularly generous either, but Joe Ackerley regarded Simon as a 'real find' and pushed all manner of books his way. Their relationship, said Simon, was 'extremely moral' – this despite his claim that Ackerley had signed him up in the college urinal at King's. 'We had the same sense of humour (which encompassed jokes at Morgan Forster's expense), and we'd exchange notes about possessive women, because Joe had this neurotic sister in the background who made his life a misery. But I never went to bed with Joe. We were chums, that's all.'

Ackerley, said his friend and literary executor, Francis King, was genuinely fond of Simon, but thought he went a bit too far. 'What a cad,' he would sigh, when the subject of Simon's treatment of Susan came up. Since Ackerley was a notorious misogynist, then as King points out, 'Simon's behaviour must have been very bad indeed to cause this shock.'

Did Simon remind Ackerley and his colleagues of that other unrepentant libertine, Guy Burgess? If so, it would help to explain why, despite his looks, his charm and his undoubted ability, he made such a small splash in the literary pool at this time. Nor was his reputation improved by an incident involving Graham Greene, whom he and Martin Shuttleworth went to interview for the *Paris Review*. When Greene answered the door to his flat in St James's he was greeted by the spectacle of Simon being noisily sick into his hat. In vain did Simon blame 'last night's oysters'; his character had acquired another stain.

But if Simon was not welcome in the genteel world of belles-lettres, he had a free pass to Fitzrovia, recalled here in his review of Julian MacLaren-Ross's *Memoirs of the Forties*:

> A world of vapour and vomit, of sickly and surrogate Lotus, of afternoon lust in borrowed beds, a world of Billy Bunter's postal order; a world which smelled of feet.
>
> And yet … What fun it was, particularly on those days when, against all expectation, Bunter's postal order had for once arrived. What fun they were, those randy middle-aged women with their ingenious perversions, those long draughts of rancid wine which did such wonders for the bowels, those truly Roman nights in the old Gargoyle – the militant Sapphists fighting it out with teeth and nail-files, a minor poet or two being sick into each other's beer, the

hilarious rush down the fire exit to escape the bill. What fun ... (*London Magazine*, November 1965)

Randy middle-aged women were all very well, but what Simon preferred were the 'hard-up striplings' he found in the West End pubs and dives that catered for homosexuals. You knew where you stood with boys: all they ever asked for was money. It was now that he began to accumulate the material for 'The Male Prostitute in London', which essay became a collector's item when *Encounter* published it in 1960.

In December Simon had his begging bowl out again, this time thrusting it under Philip Radcliffe's nose. He needed money to join Dickie Muir in 'The Great Lyndall Hunt', which Muir got up after his fiancée, Lyndall Hopkinson,[7] decamped to Rome with William Mostyn Owen. Although Muir was still quite keen on boys he had recently concluded that a wife would be a social and professional asset. And besides, as he told Peter Dixon, 'I'm far too unattractive to live my life alone as a homosexual.' Now, just as he was on the verge of marrying, his fiancée had sacked him. He took it very hard.

'Dickie was rather spoilt. He'd come into money young and was used to getting his own way. I think he thought he could *buy* Lyndall back – wrongly, as it turned out. But I was more than happy to accompany him there, particularly since he was picking up some of the tab. I'd been to Rome for the first time that Spring (also on borrowed money) and was eager to return, not least because the Roman attitude to sex did not seem to have changed at all in 2,000 years. Nor did the Romans make much of Christmas, I'm glad to say. So it was a very agreeable interlude, the only snag being that we had to keep changing hotels, each cheaper than the last, as our currency allowance dwindled.'

*

Simon ought, by rights, to have been back in the Army by now. But owing to a mistake by the venerable Colonel of his old regiment, the Ox and Bucks, he was to remain in limbo for a further five months. In October the Colonel had assured Simon that there was a vacancy he could fill on the regimental roll. But there wasn't, which meant that he had to reapply elsewhere, meanwhile losing his place on the Junior Officers' course he would otherwise have attended at the School of Infantry, Warminster. In the long run this hiccup worked to his advantage because it enabled him to join the King's Own Shropshire Light Infantry (KSLI), a regiment that was tailor-made to his requirements. The price was five more months of cadging, scrounging and sponging, by the end of which he had acquired another expensive habit, the Turf.

[7] Younger daughter of Antonia White, now Lyndall Paserini.

Simon's gambling merits several pages, but for the moment all that needs to be told is how he became a regular punter. Funds were low on his return from Rome and since David Rowse had had enough of him he moved in with Ian Murray at 71 Cromwell Road. 'Then I thought it was about time I made more of my club, The East India and Sports. The food was uninspiring, but it was cheap, as was the drink. More to my purpose, they had a "racing room" with a ticker tape where you could bet on credit. I never paid much attention to form, so I lost more often than I won. But when I did win it was usually at long odds, which allowed me to keep the bookies at bay and still have a bit left over for treats.' (Another advantage of belonging to this club was that you could cash cheques for up to £50 using the club's blank cheques. The Easter before he rejoined the Army Simon managed to cash six cheques for the maximum, beginning on Maundy Thursday.)

Despite his conviction that 'everybody should experience a thoroughly dissolute interlude like this', Simon was more than ready when in May 1953 he was ordered to proceed to the KSLI Depot at Shrewsbury. The futility of badly organised pleasure and raffishness had begun to oppress him. It smacked of the 'personal incompetence' he had seen so much of in Fitzrovia, and which he was determined to avoid from now on himself. 'Let's face it, one's record was not very good. All it needed was another unwanted pregnancy or some other catastrophe along those lines and one might as well have slit one's wrists in the bath.'

And so, to adapt Housman, Simon 'went where he was wanted/For a soldier of the Queen'. But unlike Housman's hero he was not a Shropshire lad, so what led him to 'the Fifty-Third'? Quite simply, because he'd hit it off with the officers of their Territorial unit, the Herefordshire Light Infantry, when on reservists' camp[8] the previous summer. 'We had a very drunken two weeks and I concluded that if the Herefords' Mess was anything to go by, the KSLI would be right up my street. Naturally I had a different tale to tell the Colonel, Jack Grover,[9] when he looked me over at the In and Out. But he evidently approved, because a month later I was told to report for duty at Copthorne Barracks.'

[8] Simon was a 'Z' reservist, in effect an able-bodied ex-national serviceman. As such he was liable to attend occasional camps.

[9] Major-General J.M.L. Grover, CB, MC.

CHAPTER ELEVEN

I will go back this morning
From Imbros over the sea;
Stand in the trench, Achilles,
Flame-capped, and fight for me.
Patrick Shaw-Stewart, Untitled poem

> Soldiering – that pleasant, clubbable occupation compounded equally of regimental duties, minor imperial skirmishes and field sports.
>
> Michael Howard, *Three People*

When Simon received his marching orders his first act was to buy a sword at Messrs Wilkinson of Pall Mall. As he had just had a heavy lunch the one he chose 'was subsequently about as much use as Excalibur for taking on parades'. But that was not the point. The sword was the symbol of the paladin. By acquiring one of his own (an expensive luxury for an impecunious subaltern) he was establishing a link, however tenuous, between himself and a tradition of aristocratic heroism that stretched back via Avalon and Roncesvalles to the Trojan War. For Simon had been weaned on the *Iliad*, 'the oldest and the best story of them all', and although there was more in him of Alcibiades than Achilles, he retained a sentimental attachment to the Homeric ideal.

'One had these fantasies. Riding in with the Forlorn Hope – that sort of thing. In fact the discomforts, to say nothing of the physical fitness required for riding in with the Forlorn Hope, were always rather beyond me. But not all my fantasies had to do with heroism. I fantasised about high rank as well. Clearly one would never be a Field Marshal. But how about "Major-General Sir Simon Raven"? That sounded good, and for a short while I thought it might even be possible. Generals then were not all as lean and mean as they are today, despite Lord Montgomery's best efforts. So although my motives for rejoining the Army were mixed, I was serious about it to begin with.'

We have only Simon's word for this because the evidence suggests that his ambitions were always far cosier than his fantasies. For instance he once wrote,

> I loved the Army as an institution and loathed every single thing it required me to do.

Shurely shome mishtake? 'No. Though a better word than "institution" would have been "club". Just as some MPs who never make a single speech in their entire careers regard the House of Commons as an admirable club, so I regarded the Army as an admirable club. But when it came to spending the night in a slit trench or going to the lavatory in a ditch, this had less appeal. And therein lies the dichotomy.'

Simon's distaste for roughing it may have been unusual, but 40 years ago there were still plenty of other officers about who regarded the Army as a comfortable refuge from industrial society. Luckily for Simon, the KSLI had its fair share of them. Not that this was immediately apparent, for no sooner had Simon reported to Copthorne Barracks than he was sent on the exacting two months' Platoon Commanders' course he had missed before.

Given the way he had spent the past five years it was right and proper, said Simon, that he should be 'smartened up' in this way. The trouble was that the School of Infantry did not confine itself to practical instruction; it also went in for the sort of 'quasi-moral indoctrination' that he found repugnant. Too much was at stake for Simon to complain about this at the time; but as we shall see he cut loose five years later in *Perish by the Sword*, a polemic that could still call forth an indignant seven-page rebuttal from the Commandant of Sandhurst 30 years after it first appeared.[1]

After so much 'military hysteria' (one of several 'Simonish' expressions relished by his peers in the KSLI Mess), Simon was delighted to return to Shrewsbury in time for the regimental cricket week, in practice a two-day affair since most of the unit was in Germany. Inspired by the occasion and the copious refreshments he celebrated with some spirited hitting: 22, including a straight six, against the Herefordshire Gentlemen, and 64 – 'Raven hit the ball hard and was out to a good catch' – against the Shropshire Gentlemen. Already he was beginning to feel at home, so that when, shortly afterwards, he set out for the pretty university town of Gottingen, it was with the same heightened anticipation as had marked his progress to Cordwalles, Charterhouse and King's.

*

Simon had been admitted to the KSLI as a replacement for one of two subalterns killed in Korea, where the regiment had acquitted itself with distinction. The news of his recruitment disquieted those Regulars, a majority, for whom brains came a poor third behind breeding and charac-

[1] See *Friends in High Places* by Jeremy Paxman (Penguin 1991), pp. 226-7.

ter in respect of officers. As the then Adjutant, J.D. 'Oscar' Whitamore, explained, 'The KSLI was an old-fashioned county regiment, very keen on sport and with strong landowning connexions. I remember thinking when I heard there was a University entrant coming to join the Mess, "Oh God, I hope he's not one of those wet, intellectual types." '

So Whitamore was pleasantly surprised when he met Simon at the door to the Mess and found himself shaking hands with 'a tall, well-built fellow who was good-looking in a caddish sort of way and presumably used to taking regular physical exercise'. Whitamore was soon disabused of this last notion, but by then he had discovered 'what excellent company Simon could be. He was very amusing, often at the expense of people and things I'd been brought up *not* to laugh at. He was full of original ideas, so that things one had taken for granted suddenly appeared in a new light. In short, he was a revelation. I can't overemphasise what an influence he turned out to be on me.'

Simon, for his part, was delighted to find that with the exception of 'one or two hard-faced ex-rankers left over from the war, who didn't care for me', the KSLI Mess was every bit as congenial as he had hoped. Although a fairly ordinary upper-middle-class regiment – 'not a bit smart by Brigade or cavalry standards' – it just happened to have, both among its national service officers and its regulars, 'a lot of rather eccentric, intelligent, sceptical, drunken, "gambly" sort of people. It was one of the last regiments to remain pretty firmly bachelor, too, which was a great relief, because there's no fun to be had in the Army if everybody's married and the Mess is deserted after four o'clock.'

Simon's impact on the Mess was recalled by John Ogden, another subaltern. 'Simon pounced on and developed our taste for good food, drink, gambling and sex. You may wonder how we found time for such amusements. The answer is that within the garrison we left as much of the routine stuff as possible to the NCOs, who were very competent. It was different on manoeuvres, but they didn't happen that often.'

The KSLI, said Ogden, was first and foremost a front line unit. Provided you had the makings of a fighting soldier your private life was your own affair. 'Most of us lived well beyond our means. I once lost half a year's pay at chemmy and another officer borrowed literally thousands of pounds on the strength of a Trust fund which he didn't in fact have. There was also a homosexual undercurrent, particularly among the younger officers, though this didn't preclude some brothel-creeping in towns like Brunswick. So all in all Simon was in his element.'

For Ogden and the other subalterns Simon's appeal lay in his 'intriguing combination of gravitas and levity. He was obviously much better read than we were, yet he never condescended. He was amusing, amenable and generous. He didn't set out consciously to entertain, but he was a fascinating conversationalist who never rationed his time or his wit. I shall always treasure our Rabelaisian evenings at the "*Alte Krone*", Gottingen's best restaurant. Somebody might be throwing up under the table but that wouldn't prevent Simon from explaining, in great detail, what one could learn about the sex life of the Ancient Greeks from their vase paintings.'

On at least one occasion Simon put his learning at the disposal of a brother officer who was faced by a task for which he did not carry enough guns. Lieutenant Rodney Haszard, in later life an Estate Manager, was obliged by virtue of his age and rank to compete in a Divisional Essay competition. Simon wrote the essay for him and Haszard was declared the winner, receiving £25, which he passed on to Simon, and invitations to lecture, which he politely declined.

*

One of the lessons Simon had learnt as a National Service officer was that in the Army, 'it was more important that nothing should go wrong than that anything should go very right'. As a platoon commander he took just enough trouble to ensure that this was the case, but otherwise employed a very loose rein. 'He was good at cutting corners,' said Oscar Whitamore, 'and in general they worked. I can't remember anything going seriously wrong.'

Himself something of a martinet, Whitamore acknowledged that Simon's men '*adored* him. He was so funny with them, outrageous even. When everybody else was being frightfully serious, he'd be light and amusing. And yet they had confidence in him, particularly the NCOs. Whenever a problem presented itself he had a knack of hitting on the very answer that would put everyone to the least trouble.'

Occasionally he miscalculated. Whitamore told me how, during an exercise, Simon was entertaining his men in a *gasthaus* when he was warned that 'Big Sunray' himself would inspect their position in the morning, and that he would expect to find them properly dug in. Unfortunately the ground was very rocky, and the best they could manage by morning was a line of shallow scrapes which Simon ordered them to squat in – 'perhaps he'll think we are dug in'. But the General wasn't fooled. 'These defences are lamentable,' he complained. 'They offer no protection whatsoever. They're not even bullet-proof.'

'I grant you that, sir,' conceded Simon. 'But at least they're blank-proof.'

The General's reaction to this witticism is not recorded, but Whitamore added that by and large Simon got on well with Generals because he was much better company than most junior officers. 'No question of "Yes Sir, No Sir, Three Bags Full, Sir," with Simon. He was prepared to have a proper conversation with them and even be mildly ironical about the Army, which they didn't seem to mind. I couldn't have got away with that, but Simon had the poise to carry it off.'

How did Simon see himself as a subaltern? I think we need look no further than this passage from *The Feathers of Death*, in which the narrator sets forth the military credentials of the hero, Alastair Lynch.

> Two of his qualities became immediately apparent. Firstly, he was excellent company for days at a time; never intrusive, always ready for a little conversation, quick to pick up and share private jokes about the situation or activities in which we were involved. The only thing which made him disagreeable was the occasional necessity for making a bad or hurried meal, when he would point out that one's meals were as surely limited in number as one's days upon earth and that it was a positive duty to enjoy them. The second thing I noticed about him at once was his interest in, and very quick understanding of, the theoretical side of mortaring, as opposed to a total disinclination to investigate such minor and practical details as the way in which the weapon worked or ought to be cleaned. He was, in short, given to generalisation – like most intelligent yet lazy people. Indeed, intelligence and laziness were the two qualities for which he became famous throughout the Battalion .... Successive company commanders recognized his undoubted competence and deplored or condoned, as their natures might dictate, his infinite capacity for doing nothing and his complete refusal to move a foot in any direction unless he was firmly and personally convinced of the necessity. In fact, however, he was never guilty of a major *bêtise* and his attitude was on the whole approved and appreciated in our Regiment. As [Colonel] Sanvoisin used to remark, Alastair's idleness might equally justly be described as economy of action – a pleasing thing in an army where so many officers rushed around and shouted their heads off merely in order to deceive or impress their seniors. In the end it was arguable that Alastair commanded and administered his troop in an efficient and unobtrusive manner, giving the minimum of trouble or work either to his men or himself. This the men were quick to recognise, as they were to appreciate his undeniable friendliness and fairness .... Thus one could say that Alastair's two years with our Regiment had made him a popular and respected figure both with the men and with his superiors .... True, two or three of the more severe officers ... looked upon Alastair as 'dubious' or 'equivocal'. But they were a definite minority. His contemporaries ... were at once proud and fond of him.

Simon's first commanding officer, Lieutenant-Colonel Percy Jones, was a Classical scholar who read Horace and Virgil in his spare time and enjoyed a joke at the Army's expense, foibles that were right up Simon's street. The two men collaborated on a history of the regimental silver, and it was Simon whom Colonel Jones chose to accompany him as an umpire on 'Operation Battle Royal', a big atomic warfare exercise similar to 'Apocalypse' in *The Sabre Squadron*. An unrepentant divorcee, Colonel

Jones agreed with Bardolph (and Simon) that 'a soldier is better accommodated than with a wife', so it was ironic that the one serious rebuke he gave Simon arose out of a complaint by Susan.

As a married officer with a child Simon received an allowance which he was supposed to hand over to his spouse. This he had not so far done, his negligence resulting in a legendary exchange of telegrams. In response to Susan's WIFE AND BABY STARVING SEND MONEY SOONEST, Simon wired back SORRY NO MONEY SUGGEST EAT BABY. Susan was evidently not amused because she took her complaint to the War Office, who passed it on officially to Colonel Jones. Oscar Whitamore takes up the story.

'As Adjutant I used to deal with most of the Colonel's mail. One day this letter arrived from the War Office saying that Mrs Raven hadn't been receiving her allowance. Not what you'd expect to hear from an officer's wife, and a bit of a slur on the regiment. I told Simon so at lunch. "Don't worry, Oscar," he said. "It won't happen again." So I agreed to put the letter into Simon's personal file and lock it away in the safe without mentioning it to the CO. Two months later another letter came and this time the CO himself opened it. I said to Simon, "Now you've dropped *me* in the shit as well, you bloody swine." '

Luckily for Oscar Colonel Jones accepted his explanation. 'But he was very cross with Simon because the last thing any decent CO wanted was people from Whitehall poking their noses into regimental affairs. Simon was told to go home, "And for God's sake get your wife to withdraw her complaint." '

Indignant that things had come to this pass, Simon at first tried to bully Susan, who stood her ground. Then, ashamed at his boorishness, he appealed to her good nature. 'I said, "Look, I haven't any money besides my pay. I simply cannot afford to give you this allowance, which you don't really need anyway." And Susan, as usual, was a brick. She officially withdrew her complaint.' There were unforeseen repercussions, but they belong to a later chapter.

*

Simon's disorderly private life was a reminder that he had yet to resolve the inherent contradiction noted by Alan Caiger-Smith and articulated even earlier by the actor, John Carson, who served with Simon in 77th Ack Ack: how could someone be so shambolic and yet such a dandy? For despite looking like a tramp during his last two years at Cambridge, Simon *was* a dandy – not in the foppish sense (though Oscar Whitamore said he had 'a good leg for a boot'), but in his attitude to life and art. 'I can't write clumsy English,' he told Maureen Cleave, adding that he preferred 'a good phrase to an absolute truth'. And if, as someone said, the dandy is the epitome of social irresponsibility, then Simon surely qualifies on that score too.

Frivolity is another mark of the dandy and it was this, said Whitamore, that caused Simon to fail his promotion exam from Lieutenant to Captain, the only exam he ever failed in his life. 'He would give facetious answers to questions like, "In a malarial area, what anti-malarial precautions would you take?" Instead of saying, "Roll your sleeves down and take some Paludrine," Simon wrote, "Roll your sleeves down and take whatever pill of the moment the Army favours." ' (Simon's explanation, no less frivolous, was that he couldn't be bothered to learn 'footling details like the number of tanks in a battalion [*sic*]'.)

A potentially more serious threat to Simon's progress occurred after he had been in Gottingen about a year. He had arranged to spend some leave with Francis Haskell in Florence, but could not resist stopping off en route at San Remo to sample the tables. As usual he was drinking 'prodigious quantities of whatever was going', for which the penalties were at worst mild indigestion or diarrhoea. But all of a sudden his bowels erupted 'like Vesuvius', something that hadn't happened since Bangalore, and he suffered acute dyspepsia. So instead of proceeding to Florence he limped home to Hunstanton to recover.

Brookfield was not the ideal destination for someone in need of a teetotal rest-cure and although Simon was still feeling unwell, he made full use of the drinks cabinet, with predictable consequences. 'If it wasn't one end, it was the other, sometimes both at once! Eventually I passed out on the bathroom floor and was discovered lying in a pool of blood and vomit by my mother.'

When he came to in King's Lynn hospital Simon learnt that he had had a peptic ulcer which had burst, resulting in a severe loss of blood. He convalesced in a private bed, at a cost of fifteen guineas a week to the Army, read copiously and angered the Matron by sending out bets every morning via the hospital switchboard.

The Army took the news of Simon's ulcer very calmly, their only stipulation being that before rejoining his unit he should have a medical. This he passed with flying colours, but the 'splendid' MO insisted on giving him a parting word of advice. 'He said "Look, you will be told that you must live on bread and butter pudding and never again drink or gamble or do anything that will cause you a moment's anxiety. Absolute bollocks. But one rule which may or may not see you through is, 'Do not drink strong drink on an empty stomach.' " Very sound advice which I've followed ever since and on the whole it's worked. I get bad diarrhoea from time to time, but that's about all.'

So from being an indiscriminate tosspot Simon became a heavy, but disciplined, drinker who never had more than one aperitif if he could possibly help it. His ulcer gave him a perfect excuse for ducking out of 'unspeakable' gatherings like cocktail parties ('Civilised men entertain their friends to dinner in small parties and to wine after dinner in large'). But as the years went by he became increasingly inflexible about his timetable. 'Dinner at eight *meant* dinner at eight,' a friend told me. 'If you weren't there on the dot he'd start without you.'

*

As he prepared to clock up two years as a Regular Simon could afford to feel rather smug. His wants were few, his duties light and his entitlements substantial, including as they did generous leave, first-class travel on the cheap, an artificially high exchange rate and (unofficially) the deference accorded by Germans to a representative of the occupying power. 'They weren't supposed to kowtow any more, but they did. German policemen still clicked their heels together when they addressed you and café owners had to listen if you queried the bill. Made quite a change from England, where deference was already on the way out.'

But the regiment's days in Germany were numbered. They returned home in March 1955, just in time to celebrate their bicentenary with a big parade at the Depot. Soon afterwards they sailed from Liverpool for Mombasa, with orders to assist the Kenyan Security Forces in mopping up the Mau Mau, whose rebellion was almost at an end.

Sorry as he was to be exiled from salubrious spots like Baden Baden ('my very favourite place for a few days' leave'), Simon was not unduly put out at the prospect of active service in the bush because it was clear that the Mau Mau were on their last legs. 'They were riddled with clap, most of them, and surrendering in droves. So to think, as some chaps did, that we were in for a real scrap, was nonsense.' And what of Kenya? Simon rather hoped it would be like Bangalore, with an agreeable climate, plenty of servants, racing, cricket and so on. True, 'Bwana Raven' lacked the resonance of 'Raven Sahib', 'but at least one would not be served curry three times a day'.

No sooner had the KSLI been assigned quarters near Nairobi than they were pitched into 'Operation Dante', whose objective was the elimination of two large gangs of Mau Mau lurking in a region of the Aberdares known as the Kikuga Escarpment Forest. If all went well the Mau Mau would be flushed from their lairs by intensive bombing and shelling, and then ambushed by a cordon of security forces, including the KSLI, as they tried to make good their escape. Alas, the plan had two major flaws. First, there were no less than 90 square miles of dense bamboo forest within the cordon and only a limited amount of firepower, so the chances of panicking the two gangs were extremely slim. Secondly, syphilitic or not, the gangs' mastery of forest craft was infinitely superior to that of their pursuers.

The folly of sending untrained troops into the forest was immediately underlined in the most tragic manner when Colonel Jones' successor as CO, Colonel Brooke-Smith, was accidentally shot by one of his own men who mistook his CO's native trackers for Mau Mau and let fly with his Bren. Before he died Colonel Brooke-Smith is said to have congratulated the man on his marksmanship and told him not to worry. By chance, one of the other participants in Dante was (General) Frank Kitson, then learning the counter-insurgency trade as a young Captain. Noting that a mere 30 terrorists were killed in three weeks he pronounced the operation 'a colossal and expensive failure', adding, with unconscious irony,

> In all fairness it is necessary to add that many more terrorists would have been killed had the soldiers shot straighter. (*Bunch of Five*)

Simon did not take an active part in Dante and was far away when his CO died. But the Aristotelian implications of Colonel Brooke-Smith's death – 'he was warned against disturbing the ambushes but he would go' – were not lost on him and they furnish a cautionary climax to the last chapter of his memoir, *Bird of Ill Omen*.

Dante was the only operation of its kind that the KSLI took part in while Simon was in Kenya. Henceforth constant patrolling was the order of the day, with each company maintaining a Headquarters outside the forest and a number of smaller camps within it. As second-in-command of 'D' Company Simon's place was at Headquarters; his rare visits to the forest were made with the ration wagon. It was while returning from one such visit that he had his sole brush with death. As his jeep emerged from the forest, a thunderbolt 'like a red football' bounced across the road ahead – 'Great sucks to Zeus!'

When he came to write *The Feathers of Death* Simon created a colony called Pepromene which owes almost as much to Evelyn Waugh's Azania as it does to Kenya during the Emergency. And the influence of Waugh can also be detected in this Company report which appeared in the Regimental Journal.

> 'D' COMPANY
>
> We have now moved from the Rift Valley (dust and settlers) to the Fort Hall District of the Kikuyu Reserves (dust and officials). Therein we are settled on a series of hill-terraces by the village-cum-fort-cum-prison camp of Kigumo. Everyone there has been extremely kind; the surroundings are pretty and sometimes impressive, and you know very well what we haven't got.
>
> Company H.Q., at Kigumo, where there is generally one resident platoon, is a ritzy affair of marquees and perilous mud-and-wattle buildings. The NAAFI and the stores (sure signs of sound and established soldiering) will soon be in permanent buildings. The Officers' and Sergeants' Messes are already built, and are probably the two most inflammable erections in Africa. We have showers, some dogs, a tent full of Dhobis; charming neighbours, who have

'The Sunday lunch-time of the soul' – Simon in his fat middle years.

Arthur and Esther Raven in the 1930s.

Myles padded up to face Simon in August 1938.

Lismore, the house at Virginia Water where the Ravens lived from 1933 to 1938.

Esther in her running kit, Simon in regulation grey.

Picnic at Holkham on the North Norfolk coast.

Charterhouse First Eleven 1945. Simon seated far right, Oliver Popplewell far left, Peter May second from left. James Prior standing third from right.

Simon, Myles, Robin, Honey and Esther at the bird sanctuary near Brancaster, 1945.

Gottingen 1954. Lieutenant Raven fraternising with a German employee of BAOR.

Rome 1959. Ian Murray and Simon.

Simon, aged about 21, looking 'like a choir-boy about to be goosed', according to Peter Ackroyd.

The Trogs, *c.* 1973. Simon standing at left in cap, Myles seated in the middle with Peter Budden behind him and Michael Webb second left in umpire's coat.

Cyprus 1994. Simon, Oscar Whitamore and Andrew Whitamore.

Dickie Muir, aged about 65.

Andrew McCall as shown on the dust cover of his novel, *The Au-Pair Boy*. Photo: Hans Feurer.

Santa Monica 1979. Simon sketched by Don Bachardy (detail).

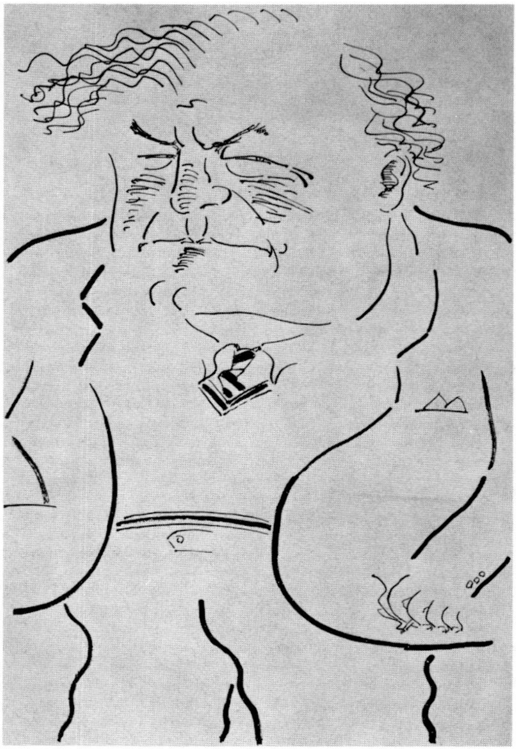

Mark Boxer's caricature of Simon for Alan Watkins' *Brief Lives*.

provided us with endless material and no bills; terrible roads; and, as a shopping centre, the several streets of identical Indian shops popularly known as Fort Hall.

'*Dulce est desipere*' in Kigumo, but the two 'forest' platoons live on a more hazardous basis. They have various rather uneasy resorts – Fort Lancaster, with a superb view of the famous Elephant Ridge and apparently unending rain; Fort Mitchell, where the native population do nothing but steal donkeys; Fort Thompson, which is (nearly) slap on an elephant trail; and the celebrated Forest House, as leaky a locale as anyone ever played pontoon in. From their hide-outs our patrols go forth in steady succession, and have achieved finds as various and substantial as a V.H.F. set (lost by the Police), three donkey carcases (eaten by the Mau Mau), several captures and one or two incidents of a sufficiently bloodthirsty nature to annoy Dr Edith Summerskill[2]...

... We had a most successful celebration of our arrival in the form of a Retreat Parade, followed by parties in the Officers' and Sergeants' Messes. Apart from Administrative big-wigs who graced the occasion, a number of local chiefs and, paramount among them, Senior Chief Njiri, were present. Senior Chief Njiri expressed his appreciation, on departing, by some well chosen signs; while some of the more obscure local functionaries seemed to forget that there was any necessity to depart at all.

In general, however, life – rough but not unpleasant – is rather humdrum. We look forward to our promised holiday in Nairobi this February with gratitude and appreciation, '*memores alios fecere merendo*'. Meanwhile, our fishermen prosper, a little game is gathered, the whole thing is no doubt very healthy, and no one would mind if he never saw a tent again. (January 1956)

Kigumo was an important village, the seat both of the local District Commissioner and of the local Chief Inspector of Police. Simon got on famously with Arnold Hoff, the District Commissioner, a colourful survivor of pre-war Fitzrovia and the Spanish Civil War who is the model for Matthew Sachs in *Feathers*. His relations with the Chief Inspector were cordial enough, but he had no time at all for the 'short-contract' men under him. 'They were reminiscent of the Black and Tans, brutal and insensitive, but with even fewer pretensions to commissioned rank, though this didn't stop them trying to infiltrate our Officers' Mess. My Company Commander would have let them in, but I was adamant. I said, "We can't have these oiks in here. They're no better than corporals." He said, "We mustn't slight them. They're very sensitive." – "So am I," I said.'

In Gottingen Simon had not wanted for food, drink, sex and gambling.

[2] Labour MP noted for her vigorous opposition to Prizefighting.

Naturally he could not hope for the same amplitude in Kigumo, but he managed pretty well all the same. Visitors like Oscar Whitamore would invariably be urged to 'come and have a drink of something nice' (instead of bothering about some tedious duty). And it was only with great reluctance that Simon would eventually acknowledge that it was 'time to get back to that *nagging* set'. If, said Oscar, you were lucky enough to be staying for dinner, then thanks to 'Grandad', 'D' Company's resourceful African cook, you could expect a delicious alternative to the usual bush fare of corn-beef hash or tinned stew. Arnold Hoff was a regular dinner guest, so when one of the 'oiks' arrested Grandad on a trumped-up charge of rape, in revenge, it was said, for being excluded from the Officers' Mess, Hoff soon had the truth from the girl concerned and the cook resumed his duties.

At Warminster Simon had been publicly rebuked for advocating a system of regimental brothels in an essay on Administration in the Field. But Warminster's writ did not run at Kigumo, where as Temporary Company Commander Simon connived at the establishment of a 'rough and ready knocking shop' in a store-room behind the NAAFI. 'I did so on three conditions: that the girls, who were local, were inspected three times a week by our medical orderly; that they were paid in advance; and that there must be no violence.'

There was, admitted Simon, an element of self-interest in this, for he had begun sleeping with a private in 'D' Company – 'a bit of a misfit, but attractive in a butch sort of way' – and there would be less likelihood of resentful muttering – ' "Why should officers have all the fun?" ' – if his boyfriend's mates had a cheap and cheerful alternative to Mrs Palm.

That left gambling, or gaming as Simon liked to call it. Among themselves the officers played backgammon, piquet, pontoon and bridge. Then it occurred to Simon that since there were no casinos in Kenya, some of the local settlers and their wives might leap at the chance to play roulette, so he passed the word around and there was a favourable response. To accommodate his guests, who would want to be home by nightfall, Simon arranged for play to commence after lunch. On one occasion they were ready for the 'off' when a Land Rover weighed down with Mau Mau deserters crawled into camp. The driver, an NCO in another regiment, insisted that the rest of the gang were there for the taking. He begged Simon to act on this 'A1 info' and 'jack up' a patrol forthwith. But Simon was unimpressed. 'How very tedious,' he said. 'Here's a hundred shillings to take your "A1 info" elsewhere.'

This is worthy of Fingel, the regimental reprobate whose machinations Simon celebrated in a series of witty and subversive yarns.[3] Fingel's code is at odds with Queen's Regulations and he would certainly not be welcome

[3] *The Fortunes of Fingel*, Blond & Briggs 1975.

in the Army of today. But regiments were more tolerant then. When Simon submitted the following article to the *KSLI Journal*, it was printed in full:

'The Pleasures of Life in Kenya'

As I hate wide-open spaces and wild animals and, indeed, any manifestation of The Great Out of Doors, I am not a suitable person to appreciate or write about any Colony. However, a guide to the urban delights of Kenya, such as they are, might be of use to some of you destined for this country, and in any case the subject has not really received proper attention yet in this Journal. Everyone seems so determined to produce evidence of healthy, John Buchan enthusiasm. Being unashamedly a lover of cities, and believing as I do that civilization hardly exists outside them, I shall do my best to describe the Restaurants, Theatres and places of Assignation – in short, the decent, urban pleasures – as they are to be found in this country.

Kenya starts with the terrible disadvantage of being inhabited by Puritans. The people who made this colony, courageous and generous as many of them were, came here, in general, either out of desire for the money to be made or else with some very forbidding ideal of duty or endeavour in mind. The money-grabbers come and go, but the idealists stay. So do their children and grand-children. Like their forebears, they are generous, friendly, industrious and brave; but they do not really approve of pleasure. They come of hard stock and they still live hard lives. That which in London, Paris or Rome would constitute a very modest degree of refinement, therefore becomes, in Kenya, the height of degenerate effeminacy. To be sure, like the Africans they so frequently resemble, Kenyans are prone to long and disastrous cocktail parties.

However, Nairobi is just recognisably a capital city, and it is my business here to say what is worth doing rather than to bemoan obvious shortcomings. Food and drink first. The best cuisines in Nairobi – leaving aside private clubs – are to be found in the Swiss Grill, The Lobster Pot and the Grill at the New Stanley Hotel. The Swiss Grill has rather tiresomely decided to encourage music and dancing, as opposed to its proper business of caring for the stomach. This means prices will rise and quality and service will fall. But they can still produce fair dishes:– notably their *Rognons Flambés* and the *Suprême de Poulet*. The latter has some subtle Eastern additions to distinguish it from the products of Provence and the boulevards. Then they have a drinkable Vin Rosé, and a notable Chambertin at a reasonable price. The Lobster Pot is uninspired but comfortable and pleasant. The New Stanley Grill, finally, will provide very good *Escargots Bourguignons* (enough garlic for a whole battalion of

> Frenchmen), the panache of a very French headwaiter, and several passable white Burgundies ...
>
> ... The Nairobi Club has the rather heavy air of many London Clubs, but has the great good sense to confine the ladies to a certain very limited number of rooms. (As for the Muthaiga Club, ladies swarm all over it like the more inquisitive type of warrior ant.) But both keep good kitchens, fair cellars, well-stocked libraries and comfortable bedrooms. Both have a decent, easy air – the very antithesis of the usual atrocious, open-necked-shirt bustle-about-nothing sort of atmosphere which is the Black Death of the Colonies. In the Muthaiga Club there is leisure and, praise heaven, artificiality. There is time for good manners and even, though it is rare, elegance. One is back in the world one understands. One is away from the abominable wide-open-spaces, from the appalling wild life[4] which is so importunate everywhere. One has escaped from Kenya.

By the time this piece appeared Simon had escaped from Kenya for good. After several months in Kigumo he had concluded that he was not cut out for command in the field, and that unless he wanted to wind up as a 'pear-shaped Major doing the PRI accounts' he must find a new role in the Army. The one that appealed to him most was military attaché, for which he would need to gain proficiency in a language that was neither over-subscribed, like French, German, Spanish or Italian, nor deservedly unpopular, like Serbo-Croat or Czech. Seduced by the prospect of being en poste at 'Constantinople' (Ankara would have been more realistic), he applied to go on a Turkish course. But the new CO, Lt. Col. Dawnay Bancroft, vetoed this.

'He said, "I know you've been pretty slack about rounding up the Mau Mau, but you're too good to lose. So I'm sending you home to command the Training Battalion at the Depot. It's not a very demanding job so you'll have plenty of time to read for Staff College, which is where you ought to go next." '

And so, as the 'D' Company scribe noted,

> Captain Raven, to our regret but not his, packed his playing cards and form books and departed on leave and ultimately to the Depot. The sound of a voice saying, 'Now if we put 5/– from the catering fund into messing, buy eggs to feed the pigs, we can sell them and provide money for the catering fund', will be sadly missed.

[4] Simon's ignorance of wildlife was profound. A visiting officer, admiring some tiger skins in the Officers' Mess at the Depot, asked where they were shot. 'Africa, I suppose,' said Simon.

CHAPTER TWELVE

> This is the third time, thought Jacinth, that I've left somewhere important in a hurry .... That business at school, that business at Cambridge, and now this. Always in October .... But I'm really getting very tired of it, thought Jacinth: if only, just for once in my life, I could contrive to leave, as it were like all the other boys, at the appointed end of the term.
>
> Simon Raven, *Brother Cain*

Once it was put to him that he ought to be reading for Staff College Simon abandoned all hope of military advancement and settled down to enjoy himself until such time as the Army decided to dispense with his services. In this he was considerably assisted by 'the old-fashioned notions and sheer good nature' of Major Bob Garnett MBE, the Commandant of the Depot. A veteran of Arnhem, Major Garnett believed that the 'social obligations of regular officers in their own county' took precedence over mundane military chores like recruit training, which could safely be undertaken by NCOs and National Service officers. Since these social obligations included cricket and racing, Simon, for the first and only time in his Army career, was able to demonstrate some genuine enthusiasm.

'In summer one was expected to turn out for the Depot or the Shropshire Gents two or three times a week. That was no hardship. In winter those who were able, hunted, while the rest of us did our share of rough shooting – not very expertly in my case, though I believe I did once bag a partridge – but being there was what counted. As a reward for my cricket and shooting I was given plenty of leave to go National Hunt racing, which flourished round about, and in due course this led to my downfall. But I had my moments on the way.'

Of course Simon could not evade all military responsibility. He willingly undertook the onerous task of improving the food in the Officers' Mess, and it was thanks to his efforts with the ground staff that some sort of consistency of bounce was achieved on the cricket square and tennis courts. But he knew his limitations, as a brother officer noted in the *Journal*:

> Captain Raven settled down to organise his life, believing that ability to delegate authority was the true mark of a leader of men. He speedily delegated 100% of his. Routine played a large part in his life.

> Every day at 14.00 hrs he would retire 'to study for Staff College' with a pile of books. Sad to say *Officers and Gentlemen* was the most military of them that I ever saw. (January 1958)

This was the work of Captain Jack Hands, the Depot Dentist, 'a very droll fellow' according to Simon, with whom Hands had quickly established a strong rapport. 'From the moment we were introduced I became intrigued,' Hands told me. 'I'm rather aggressive with people when first I meet them – it's defensive. Now Simon and I were the same rank and about the same age, but he was a soldier whereas I was a dentist. *And* he'd clearly been to a posh public school, whereas I was a grammar school boy, so I felt the need to assert myself. But he totally disarmed me. He didn't even have to say anything: his eyes spoke eloquently enough. "I know you. I know what you're about." But said with amusement, not as a challenge. And we instantly became good friends. He knew he could tell me anything, however outrageous, and I would simply find it interesting.'

Hands was already in place when Simon arrived. He had been posted to the Depot after a very dispiriting time at the Dental Corps HQ in Aldershot, where they were so formal that 'even if a Major entered the Mess you were supposed to stand up'. The KSLI, by contrast, 'were so relaxed it didn't seem like the Army at all'. The other thing that struck Hands was 'how feudal the set-up was. At Corps level this would have spelt trouble, but in a field regiment like the KSLI it was permissible. The squaddies were country lads for the most part, and very docile. Once one of the officers received a complaint from the Other Ranks' dining hall that the rice pudding wasn't sweet enough. He told them to put more sugar in and they said there wasn't any, so he said, "Put a tin of condensed milk in," and that's exactly what they did.'

Mind you, added Hands, some of the officers weren't too bright either, 'though that didn't stop them taking themselves pretty seriously. I used to take the piss out of them sometimes. So did Simon, come to that. He had these nicknames for his subalterns. Julian Johnson was "Madam" and Rodney Haszard was "Aunt".[1] "Poor old Aunt", he'd say, "looking down her long nose. She won't like having to go on this night exercise. Still, it's either her or me ...." '

But in general, said Hands, Simon preferred not to inconvenience people if he could possibly avoid it. 'It was all a question of good manners. He set enormous store by these and they certainly paid off. For instance I never heard him call anyone "Sir", not even a General, yet nobody seemed to resent this and I can only assume it was because he was so facile. The people he took the most trouble with were the men who'd risen through

[1] In fact Colonel Jones bestowed this soubriquet after seeing Haszard skiing. He said that with his spindly legs and voluminous plus-fours, which from a distance looked like a tweed skirt, Haszard was like a maiden aunt from the waist down. It is only fair to add that in the opinion of Jack Hands, the men would have followed Haszard 'to hell and back'.

"the back door", like commissioned Quartermasters. "They can do you a lot of favours," he'd say, "or totally fuck you up. So it makes sense to have them on your side." '

In theory all the recruits under Simon's command would join the regiment in Kenya once they had done their basic training. But, said Hands, Simon 'protected' key personnel like the chefs and the Mess waiters (chosen for their good looks) and the most promising cricketers and footballers (to the delight of the RSM, a keen footballer). 'He thought most of them would rather stay at home near their Mums anyway, and as far as I know there were never any complaints.'

A problem Simon faced during the cricket season was that although Major Garnett loved the game and wanted as many matches arranged as possible, he was a pretty indifferent player. So in collaboration with Hands, who was the cricket officer, Simon devised a scheme to keep 'old Bob' happy. 'He said, "If we're playing a weak side we'll put him in first, give him a chance to make a few before the bowlers find a length. Otherwise we'll shove him down the order and cross our fingers. And we'll always let him bowl against the tail-enders, so he might pick up a wicket or two." Good manners again, you see, because although it was clearly in Simon's interest to accommodate his CO, not everyone would have gone to that sort of trouble.'

Hands described Simon as an aggressive batsman who liked to go for his shots. 'It was no use expecting him to batten down the hatches and play for a draw. Most of his runs came from boundaries because he was very short of puff.' As a bowler he could manage short spells of slow off-breaks, but he was a dead loss in the field – 'he used to position himself at first-slip and make lewd asides about the batsmen'.

Unlike Hands, who always played to win, Simon enjoyed cricket for its own sake, regardless of the result. The one time he threw a wobbly was when a ploy of his backfired. 'We had a needle match against a Gunner regiment at Oswestry and Simon thought it would help our cause if we could get them pissed at lunch time. "They're a stingy bunch," he said, "so if we offer them plenty of our booze they're sure to gulp it down." But the chap who drank most was our star bowler, who'd taken six wickets before lunch. In his first over after lunch he just keeled over. And Simon couldn't see the funny side of this. "Would be a fucking education officer who'd do that to me. Typical bloody grammar school boy. Can't hold his liquor." '

This was a rare set-back. Simon, said Hands, had a genius for arranging matters to his advantage, a classic example being the '18th-century fiddle' he engineered with Hodge, the Mess Sergeant (who was no stranger to such enterprises).

> Simon decided he must improve the Officers' Mess cuisine. We didn't eat badly, by the way, in fact by most people's standards we ate bloody well. There was certainly no shortage of anything. But Simon

was a bon viveur. 'We've got a good cellar,' he said. 'We must have food to match.'

The problem was that all this lovely grub would have to be paid for out of the existing catering fund, because those of us who ate our evening meal at home, the majority, were not going to pay extra so that Simon and his chums, the bachelors, could sit down to a five-course dinner with wine each night in the Mess. So Simon had to make a profit out of what we paid every day for our lunches, and he did this by producing curries and casseroles in addition to the soup and cheese that we usually had. Nobody complained. It was bloody good food and well worth the extra few bob. But what I only found out later was that we were eating meat that had been commandeered from the men's rations. Meanwhile Simon had this pool of surplus cash, which went towards oysters and lobsters and the best cuts of meat and game. Now I've always regarded that as a very 18th-century fiddle, and had Simon lived then I think he might well have become a General. He certainly hadn't the makings of a modern Major-General.

*

Simon believed that you would always pay for your pleasures somehow, and the price he paid for his gluttony was all too apparent to a fastidious old friend like Joe Ackerley, meeting him for the first time in three years.

> A disaster has happened to him, I fear [Ackerley informed E.M. Forster]; he has got plump. His one-time crowning glory, that abundant Titian hair, crinkles thinly and gingerly now above a fat pink face, with creases of fat about the eyes .... Suede boots, and a loose, short, shapeless, not very clean camel-hair coat – or wd it be called duffle? He looked like the kind of person who asks for a light in the Long Bar of the Trocadero and to whom one replies with only a regretful mutter as one edges away. A sudden ulcer, not long ago, which, as he put it, 'gushed blood at both ends', has imposed a rigour of diet, no spirits before meals. (But brandy is allowed after, and the bill at the Escargot came to £3-10-6). On the other hand he has won at baccarat from a fellow officer who had staked and lost all the cash he possessed, a splendid Bentley[2].... He has his intelligence still, and indeed his charm and warmth of manner, but I did not accompany him to his homosexual club (the Rockingham, a dull expensive place, I have been taken there before) after dinner, nor did I allow him to put himself to the trouble of lifting me home in the Bentley. Most of the officers – subalterns – in his depot are queer, he says, and where

[2] A fib. See below for how he really came by the Bentley.

the guardsmen now hang about is Grosvenor Square. They still cost a pound. (Forster papers, King's College archives)

Whatever Simon did with guardsmen in London while on leave, he forbore to try with recruits at the Depot. On active service overseas, as in Kenya, the Army tolerated 'deprivation homosexuality' provided it was not detrimental to discipline. At home, Queen's Regulations were rigorously enforced. Not long before Simon was posted to the Depot a senior officer there who rejoiced in the name of Julius Caesar made the mistake of writing some indiscreet letters to a Mess waiter, whose mother discovered them and went to the police. Caesar was hounded out of the regiment and into prison, a lesson that was not lost on Simon.

But in the Mess Simon made no secret of his bisexuality. Jack Hands remembered him saying, ' "I like all four types." – What do you mean by that? – "Amateur and professional men and amateur and professional women. Nothing would suit me better than if I could have them on alternate nights going along."[3] That took me back a bit. And then he went on to explain who you could pick up where.'

Hands was more charitable about Simon's appearance than Ackerley. 'He was good looking but a bit effeminate, like a rather large, cuddly teddy bear. He had very wavy hair which he used to plaster with pomade,[4] but so did the other bachelors. They all used cologne and bath oil too. Their lotions looked exotic because they weren't emulsified, but separated out in a whirl of greens and yellows. There was a lot of equivocal chatter. "I'm very cross with Madam [Julian]," Simon might announce. "She's made a silly mistake over the Mess account and had to go and confess." But if they did get up to anything among themselves it didn't show. Simon never touched anyone that I saw.'

In his two Army novels, *The Feathers of Death* and *The Sabre Squadron*, Simon gets carried away with his descriptions of regimental finery. Thus Martock's Foot wear 'scarlet full dress … and a busby worn with a plume of feathers of royal purple', while Earl Hamilton's Light Dragoons sport 'decorative trousers of deep pink … [and in winter] cloaks lined with silk of the same colour and trimmed with collars of white fur, to buy one of which absorbs the whole of an officer's dress allowance for about ten years'.

This taste for extravagant display was not reflected in Simon's turnout at the Depot. Comfort was his priority there, hence his preference for service dress over battledress ('made one *itch* so!'), for a fore and aft cap

[3] Compare with Gore Vidal's belief, '[that] it is possible to have a mature sexual relationship with a woman on Monday … with a man on Tuesday, and perhaps on Wednesday have both together'.

[4] Shortly after Simon arrived in Gottingen Colonel Jones called for his company commander. 'This man Raven reeks of unguents,' said the Colonel. 'Is he *suspect*?' – 'Well, sir,' said the company commander, 'I have never felt it necessary to press my backside against the wall when he came into the office.'

(known, by virtue of its design, as a 'cunt' cap) over an officer's peaked cap, and for ginger chukka boots over walking shoes or, heaven forfend, 'ammunition boots'. Mess kit, a casualty of the war years, had yet to be re-introduced; on formal occasions in the Mess Simon wore either a dinner jacket or Number One Dress, consisting of a dark green tunic and navy blue trousers ('but not alas boots and spurs: only officers who were deemed "mounted" were entitled to strut around in them!')

In any case it was not Simon's turnout but his manner that put him in a class of his own. One afternoon he invited Tim Lewis, a national service subaltern, to come with him to the cinema. 'So we drove down in Simon's newly-acquired Bentley, parked outside the cinema, and were just about to go in when we met Major-General "Woolly" Cox, who had succeeded General Grover as Colonel of the Regiment. He took one look at Simon, who'd left his Sam Browne belt off and was wearing chukka boots and bright yellow socks, and ordered him back to barracks. "You're improperly dressed," he said. And Simon said, "Oh Woolly, don't be so tiresome," and walked on into the cinema.' (Simon said Lewis had imagined this. 'One *always* wore plain clothes outside the Depot.' But Lewis, who subsequently became Managing Director of Blackwells, the Oxford booksellers, was adamant. 'It's not the sort of incident you forget.')

*

Simon's Bentley, a green drop-head coupé model, cost about £950, roughly a fifth of what he won in October 1956 with a complicated four horse accumulator known as a 'Yankee'. John Ogden, who had recently rejoined the regiment after an unhappy two years in the City, was in the Mess when Simon got the news. 'It was tea-time. Simon came downstairs after his bath and asked for the evening paper, took one look and said, "My God, they've come up!" I said, "You'd better phone just to check." No reply. They'd all gone home. So a rather nervy evening ensued with Simon obviously hoping for the best but fearing the worst. Next morning he was on the blower first thing and it was bubbly ad lib.'

No wonder. For this mighty win redeemed Simon at a time when his credit was all but exhausted. From being £3,000 in the red, he found himself £2,000 in the black. Being the sort of person he was he immediately bought the Bentley – 'impressed the locals no end' – and set about living up to it. But why spin Joe Ackerley that yarn about baccarat?

'Because I knew he'd tell Morgan Forster, who in turn would tell Patrick Wilkinson, and both Morgan and Patrick would absolutely shit themselves with self-righteous socialist indignation. Just imagine! A young officer staking his all on the turn of a card. Why, it was positively Tsarist! ... Of course I soon had my comeuppance. God saw to that.'

Simon expected to be punished for his follies, indeed there were times when he could not wait to bend over and receive six of the best. Hence, in large part, his addiction to gambling, as he admitted to readers of the *Listener*.

> People with superficial minds condemn gambling as an essentially arid pursuit; even if you win, they say, you merely get something for nothing, which is bad for your character, while if you lose it is pure waste. But this is to ignore a whole psychological treasury of terror, guilt and perversity. Unwholesome gambling may be, but it is not arid. Take only one motive, and that the most commonplace, for gambling: desire to be punished. There is nothing arid in the deep, the almost sexual satisfaction,[5] which comes from an evening of steady and disastrous losses, and from the knowledge that the Roulette Wheel, that Mummy-Nanny figure, is dishing out the chastisement one so richly deserves. (11.1.62)

Betting on the horses, particularly when done at a meeting, was less reprehensible in Simon's eyes. Not only was it healthier – 'fresh air rather than fug' – it was also a good deal chancier, particularly if you tended to eschew form in favour of intuition, association or fancy. 'At roulette you can fall back on arithmetic. But horse-racing is full of imponderables. You don't know how the horse is feeling, or the jockey. And the market depends on how many people back the horse, not how good it is. I did once keep a ledger but it got so depressing I gave up. If I were the kind of person who could go days without making a bet and then put down £200 to win £300 I suppose I might have done better. But I wouldn't have had nearly as much fun. I'd rather put down 50p to win £500 any day.'

One afternoon Simon ran through that day's bets for me. ' "Bertie Wooster". I like the name, and he does occasionally win races. "Penny Forum", because I once had a girlfriend called Penelope with whom I nearly went to a May Ball. "Welsh Pageantry", because I saw it run quite well at a meeting two years ago. "Green Seago". He's a good painter, Seago, and I used to know his son. "Montpelier Lad", because I like Montpelier. "Mr Chris Gateau" because Chris is the name of the Headwaiter of the Stafford Hotel, where I've eaten some wonderful meals. That's my kind of gambling.'

With Major Garnett's blessing Simon 'represented the regiment' at Cheltenham and Chepstow, Hereford and Ludlow, Haydock, Uttoxeter, Worcester and Leicester, to all of which he would go by taxi – 'so in the long run the Bentley might have saved me some money'. Unfortunately fate decreed that he should take delivery less than a month before the Suez crisis, in the wake of which there was such stringent petrol rationing that the car was only serviceable for trips to Ludlow and back. Its subsequent

[5] 'Simon used to *come* when he had a big loss,' said Anthony Blond.

history was monitored by the *Journal*, which in April 1957 reported this 'heartening stop press news':

> The Gold Cup at Cheltenham has, in all likelihood, prolonged the life of the resident Bentley, even if there is a local bookmaker pacing his floor with a pistol at his head.

The bookie survived, the Bentley did not. Its obituary appeared in the next issue.

> Another departure, after a very much shorter and more hazardous career, has been the famous Bentley. Amid much grieving that child of chance has returned whence it came.

Simon's Gold Cup win was exceptional. Almost every other horse he had backed since the previous autumn had lost, wiping out his winnings and plunging him even deeper into the red than before. The bookies were becoming importunate but not, as yet, threatening. It was left to a tradesman to cast the first stone. Jack Hands was a witness.

> It was a gorgeous Spring morning and Simon and the others were having coffee served to them on the lawn outside the Mess. Then through the barracks gate chugs this baby Austin, which finally pulls up near where Simon and Co were sitting. Out gets a little man in a mackintosh and a bowler hat who makes his way towards them with something in his hand. 'Any of you gentlemen Captain Raven?' – 'Yes,' says Simon. 'What can I do for you?' – 'I'm sorry, sir. Got to give you this.' And slaps a writ on him. It was for about £250 worth of men's toiletries, owed by all of them but bought in Simon's name from Floris or somewhere like that.

Simon's reaction to this was to have a good laugh. But there were other debts, much closer to home, which could not be dismissed so nonchalantly, beginning with his laundry bill and his garage bill. If he didn't pay these the regiment's name would suffer and Major Garnett for one would not be amused. Then there were various cheques drawn on the Mess funds which had yet to reach the bank months after they were written.

'A bit like having an interest free credit card, I agree. Luckily we had a very understanding auditor who'd say, "Hullo, this cheque seems to have been here for a couple of months. Well never mind, cheques don't go out of date for six, ha! ha! ha!" And when they did go out of date one simply tore them up and wrote another one. Creeping embezzlement really, not straight-out theft. But contemptible all the same.'

Contemptible or not Simon made no effort to economise, although one or two of his friends like John Ogden sensed 'an undercurrent of unease'.

His situation was not improved by Susan's unexpected request for a divorce. 'I said, "Why don't we go on as before?" because one was getting this marriage allowance. But she would have it. So we got one of those bogus divorces where you write a letter saying you're leaving for good, and back-date it two or three years.

'The trouble was that the Army got wind of this and reminded me, in the most unsporting fashion, that the whole time I'd been in Kenya I'd been drawing a special allowance for married officers abroad without their spouses. And I said, "Yes, I was still married then." Whereupon they came back and said "Yes, but you'd already sent the letter saying you were leaving for good." So I had to repay a lot of that allowance, which didn't help.'

In fact it was Arthur Raven who kept Simon's non-bookmaking creditors at bay during the summer, but this was a stay of execution rather than a reprieve. ('A thousand quid would have put me in the clear but my father, in his usual stingy way, said six hundred was all he could manage.') Matters came to a head in October when an exacting new auditor arrived. Unlike his genial predecessor the new man required all outstanding cheques to be honoured in full and without delay. Since his credit was now exhausted and writs would soon be as plentiful as the autumn leaves, Simon had no option but to tell Major Garnett.

Once he had recovered from his initial surprise – 'either he didn't think I was a plunger, or that Yankee had convinced him I was lucky' – Major Garnett, to Simon's great relief, did not turn 'spiteful or tiresome. Instead, he simply gave me a rather Edwardian look and said he would sleep on the matter.'

Next day, said Simon, the Commandant remained uncensorious, 'but he reminded me that by incurring debts which I couldn't pay I was guilty of conduct unbecoming an officer and a gentleman. Once an official complaint was made I'd be court-martialled and in all probability cashiered, which would be very disagreeable for the regiment, for him and for me – in that order. He then remarked that in his youth they'd had an adage, "If you can't pay the bill, look for the fire escape."

' "This is your fire escape," he said. "You will send in your papers today and I will undertake to get your resignation through within six to eight weeks." (It normally took six months, but he had a chum at the War Office who could speed things up.) "You'll still owe the bookies, but it'll be no concern of ours. Meanwhile leave here and *lose* yourself until such time as your resignation is gazetted. If you can't be found, you can't be court-martialled." '

So that was that? – 'Well no,' admitted Simon in the tone of voice he used when someone found him out. 'Although I was told to push off on leave pending my resignation it was made very plain to me that somehow or other those Mess cheques must be honoured before I left. Luckily my father came across with just enough to calm things down, though I've since heard that there were quite a lot of people who said, "Let's get that bugger Raven." But others said, "No, he's been here for five years, given us all a lot of fun. So let him go." Whether they were new-fangled or old-fashioned, the vengeful voices, I don't know. I suspect new-fangled. You know: "It's got to be the same for everybody. If he's done wrong, he must face the music." The old way was: "Get him out. Then we won't have the embarrassment of a court-martial and cashiering." Not that I'd have been stripped on the square. That was no longer in order. You could be cashiered but they wouldn't bother with the ceremony.'

*

'All creative artists,' Simon once wrote, 'are natural anarchists.' With his Butterflies tie, his chukka boots and his grog blossom Simon did not in the least resemble the conventional idea of an anarchist; but then neither did his exemplar, Evelyn Waugh. Both, however, were temperamentally unsuited to a profession like soldiering, where a measure of abnegation was required. Simon had better manners than Waugh, so his subversive tendencies were not so apparent. But at times his impudent insouciance recalls Basil Seal during his interview with the Lieutenant-Colonel of the Bombardier Guards:

> '… Can you imagine yourself leading a platoon in action?' [asked the Lieutenant-Colonel].
>
> 'Well, as a matter of fact I can, but that's the last thing I want. In fact that's why I want to keep away from the line regiments. After all there is always a number of interesting jobs going for people in the Guards, isn't there? What I thought of doing was to sign up with you and then look round for something more interesting. I should be frightfully bored with regimental life, you know, but everyone tells me it's a great help to start in a decent regiment.' (*Put Out More Flags*)

Waugh lamented that it took him so long to learn that he was not cut out for Action. Simon was much more sanguine. With the exception of his two months at Warminster he did not regret one moment of his Army career, but he was glad to have escaped when he did. 'I now had a world I could write about and a style I could write in, this last derived from the Army's admirable rule of composition: "Be Brief, Neat and Plain." But I got out just in time. Any longer and I'd have lacked the energy to put myself about a bit, so those slow horses were luckier for me than any quick ones ever were.'

Simon had been advised to leave the Depot as inconspicuously as possible. 'No tender farewells, I was told. Just shove off as if you were going on leave in the normal way. "We'll send your kit on afterwards – or flog it if you prefer. But for God's sake, no fuss." '

As Simon was preparing to slink off he ran into Jack Hands, who'd been on leave. 'We had a brief chat and then Simon put out his hand and said, "Well good-bye, Jack, I'm going." – *Why*? – "Little bit of money comes into it here, old bean." And then he explained about the debts and so on. "I shall get a taxi," he said. And I said, "Don't be so bloody stupid. Why waste money on a taxi? I'll take you to the station." So I fetched the car, and out he came to meet me, walking in a rather funny sort of way with his hands behind his back. And then he walked round the back of the car, got in and sat beside me. "Now I shall add the final touch," he said. And like a conjuror he produced a bowler hat and put it on his lap.'

CHAPTER THIRTEEN

I'd had a good run for my money, but now the bill was due. So it was a case of, 'Either you work, or you die'.

Simon Raven, in conversation with his biographer

Although experience is the best of all teachers, her fees come exceedingly high.

Dean Inge

Just before the balloon went up at the Depot Simon had attended a Reunion Dinner at King's where Noel Annan, now Provost, had offered to recommend him as a reviewer to his friend Robert Kee, the new literary editor of the *Spectator*. 'I didn't advertise my predicament because long faces are unseemly at revels, but perhaps Noel sensed that all was not well. At any rate his offer was timely in more ways than one. It meant regular work and regular money, because Kee soon put me on to fortnightly novel-reviewing. And it also meant cachet, because if you were an aspirant man of letters, as I was, the *Spectator* was one of the best places to display your wares.'[1]

Simon also renewed his connexion with Joe Ackerley at the *Listener*, but Ackerley, aged 61, was not a good long-term bet. He and his peers – Cyril Connolly, Raymond Mortimer, Alan Pryce-Jones, John Lehmann et al. – were in the process of being elbowed aside by a younger generation who had different priorities. 'I think the old literary intelligentsia knew they'd been living on borrowed time for years. What surprised them was how long it took for the new men – the barbarians, as they feared – to emerge. It must have been rather nerve-racking, this limbo. And everyone said, as they do in that poem of Cavafy's, "Why *aren't* they here? At least these people would have been some sort of an answer." '

Not that Simon saw further than his next review to begin with. 'One of the dangers of looking back is that everything seems neater, tidier and more logical than in fact it was. I lived from day to day, anxious for work from any source and grateful when a chum suddenly popped up in a position where he could be useful.'

Karl Miller was a case in point. He had known Simon at Cambridge and

[1] Other regular contributors included Bernard Levin (Taper), Alan Brien, John Braine, Frank Kermode, Robert Conquest, Isabel Quigly and Leslie Adrian.

was now helping to produce *Monitor*, BBC television's new flagship Arts programme. This would be launched with a film about Kingsley Amis, the subject of one of Simon's longest reviews to date. On the strength of this review Miller recruited Simon to interview Amis in Swansea. Although they hit it off together and remained friends for many years, the interview was not a great success (all Amis could recall were the 'endless' reaction shots needed of Simon nodding his head). But Simon could console himself with the knowledge that he had been paid to appear on television – 'an infinitely more significant achievement then than now'.

In his piece about Amis Simon contrasted the lower-middle-class Amis hero – 'four-square, robust and beery ... [but] in matters of politics or social welfare, the most ineffable prig' – with his upper-middle-class predecessor and rival, the Huxley-Hartley-Powell hero – 'amusing, facile, sexually flexible, willowy, non-moral or Roman Catholic, dirty-minded, pretty and corrupt'. Simon favoured the latter but he now realised, rather belatedly, that Lucky Jim and his mates were in the ascendant.

'I left Cambridge before people like that had begun to make themselves felt. And in the Army, particularly when one was serving abroad, it was still possible to believe that nothing much had changed since the Generals got rid of Hore-Belisha. We'd lost India, of course, but there were still plenty of interesting places left. Then came Suez. I think that was when the penny dropped for me. Quite a few Regulars were dubious about it, and although I think we might have pulled it off if that brute Dulles hadn't blackmailed us, once we had to back down it was clear to me that the Durbar, so to speak, was done. This was what I was trying to say, politely but firmly, in *Perish by the Sword*: "Sorry, chums, the Raj is over. I really *am* sorry, but it really *is* over." '

Perish by the Sword, a Memoir of the Military Establishment, launched Simon's literary career. It was written at the behest of Hugh (Lord) Thomas, who had resigned from the Foreign Office over Suez and was now juggling journalism with research for his projected history of the Spanish Civil War. Thomas had overlapped with Simon at Cambridge but did not really get to know him until they had both gone down. 'We used to run across each other at the old Cavendish Hotel where I lived for a time, and would dine together regularly in Soho – slightly too well, I fancy. Simon was primarily interested in literary affairs, whereas I was keen on politics – I was Labour candidate for Ruislip in 1957 – but this did not in any way upset things. I remember explaining to him that the charm of Ruislip as a constituency lay in its proximity to The Bell at Aston Clinton, a famous restaurant frequented by such as Dickie Muir.'

Anthony Blond, a new and enterprising young publisher, had commissioned Thomas to edit a series of essays on 'The Establishment', which epithet had recently come into vogue. In his preface Thomas described the Establishment as 'the present-day institutional museum of Britain's past greatness', and accused its members of being 'in thrall to what is, or is not, "done" – which derives from notions one hundred years old'. Thomas must have known that Simon subscribed to many of these notions.[2] But he had no hesitation in persuading Blond that there ought to be an essay on the Army, and that Simon was the man for the job.

I have already invoked Alastair Lynch, the hero of Simon's first novel, *The Feathers of Death*. I shall now do so again, since in Alastair's objections to Sandhurst, quoted below, you have the gist of Simon's case against the post-war infantry officer in *Perish by the Sword*.

> The trouble with Sandhurst lies in the moral and disciplinary side of the institution. Military subjects are taught capably and broadly, academic subjects with sympathy and even liberality; but there is with all this a nagging insistence on the Arnoldian virtues and a distinct tendency to employ Arnoldian methods .... Alastair had been prepared for this, and he had also been prepared, up to a point, for a return to the conditions of existence in a public school; but he had hardly been prepared for the positive barrage of moral influence with which authority bombards its pupils at the R.M.A. To indulge in irony at the expense of the establishment's values was a dangerous and unpopular pastime; to accept them whole- or even half-heartedly was quite out of the question. Alastair was thus in the uneasy position of having to simulate enthusiasm and responsibility and similar virtues for days on end, with almost no one to whom he could turn for the release of a compensating bout of cynicism or satire. For most young men at Sandhurst are only too ready to accept the military-cum-moral values upheld there, since in the centre of these is the assumption that only very superior people are capable of absorbing them and that, by extension, each cadet belongs to a morally superior caste. This neo-feudal conception has a strong appeal for young men of uncertain intelligence and uncertain social backgrounds, and so there were few cadets willing to listen to Alastair while he analysed the Sandhurst *credo* into its absurd components and mocked it for the nasty, incongruous and ugly edifice of the spirit it was. Still, uneasy as he might have been, he remained unconverted, though hardly unaffected, by the intensity of the moral atmosphere he had to live in. It might even have been a valuable educational experience for him, had it not turned a light-hearted eighteenth century scepticism into an almost paranoiac distrust of any kind of moral excellence.

Simon insisted that *Perish* had been 'largely *contrived* to fit Thomas's

[2] Simon's attitude to the Establishment was like Lady Edward Tantamount's in *Point Counter Point*: 'For her the traditional hierarchies were a joke – but a picturesque joke and one worth living for.'

bill', but he was sincere in his condemnation of an officer-caste, as opposed to -class, whose claim to authority was based upon its supposed moral superiority. Quite how much of a stir this would have created had it been confined to *The Establishment* is open to question: with national service on the way out fewer and fewer people cared two hoots about what was, in effect, a closed shop. But publication of the book was delayed until mid-1959, by which time Simon had made a name for himself with his Army novel, *The Feathers of Death*. On the strength of this *Encounter* agreed to run *Perish* in its May issue, prompting encouraging letters from among others Major-General J.F.C. Fuller, Sir Basil Liddell Hart and (Professor Sir) Michael Howard. But the gauge was picked up by B.A. Young,[3] who was clearly at a loss to know what someone with Simon's 'particular cast of mind' had been doing in the Army in the first place.

> The fact is that the type of man who so offends Captain Raven, and the 'feudal' attitude to life which he adopts, happen to be rather effective in the business of soldiering.

Simon was given the chance to reply to Young in the next issue. By this time he had just finished his second novel, *Brother Cain*, about a sinister right-wing organisation dedicated to cleansing away 'the dirt and corruption which breed communism'. Perhaps this is why he went so far as to suggest that the puritanical young officers of today might, just possibly, be the junta of tomorrow,

> for such men are apt to dislike very strongly the vague mixture of sloth, liberalism, petty corruption, cultural freedom and political time-serving which informs (beneficially, on the whole) the affairs of this country.

But as Noel Annan pointed out years before, 'the officers' mess leaves its mark on you'. Simon concluded with this 'purely personal reflection':

> that during one's time in the Army some of the iron has probably entered one's own soul. Even now, having had no official connection with the Regular Army for some considerable time, I find myself glaring with anger at private soldiers who are walking in the street with their hands in their pockets. Why can't I mind my own business? Why indeed?

Like his arteries, Simon's attitudes had begun to harden. Hitherto his conservatism had been balanced by the lively curiosity which King's, in

[3] Assistant Editor of *Punch*; subsequently dramatic critic of the *Financial Times*, 1964-91. Army officer 1939-48.

particular, had encouraged. The Sixties – 'Did any era have more to answer for?' – cured him of that. All his energy went into clearing a patch of jungle and erecting barriers against the barbarians without. When he did raise his head above the parapet the view was so appalling that he registered only its barest outlines before turning away in disgust. This is why, in his novels, Simon is happiest when dealing with post-war society before 1963. When focused on events since then his mirror tends to blur or distort.

*

Since leaving the Army Simon had been lodging in Chester Street with his friend and fellow Kingsman, Peter Dixon, who after spells in Italy with the *Daily Mail* and MI6 was now working at Lloyds. Like others before him Dixon was struck by the contrast between Simon at work and at play.

> He had a strict timetable. Mornings were for writing, which he did in a squiggly longhand. Then about one-thirty he'd pop out to a pub for a beer and a sandwich, come back for a snooze, and then revise and type up the morning's work and perhaps do some reading until it was time for a bath and a drink. 'Right,' he'd say, rising from his desk, 'that's done.' And he'd switch off completely. We'd usually eat out, either locally, or, if Simon fancied a boy for the night, in Soho. There was a dive in Dean Street where you could usually pick up someone without any fuss. Simon was kind but firm with these boys, a bit like a good prep-schoolmaster. At my insistence they were always out of the house by breakfast.

To his great relief Simon's resignation was duly gazetted before any duns found their way to the Depot. And since gambling debts were unactionable in civil law, he could pay them in his own time and thus avoid bankruptcy. But following a complaint by one of his creditors he was warned off the Turf as a defaulter, and did not attend a major race meeting for several years. He also had to resign from his club.

> 'You must understand, my dear Jacinth' [said Colonel Hamilton], 'that though we're making all this as respectable in the short run, as possible, you can't go on being respectable for very much longer. Very soon now you're going to find yourself *outside Society*. You are the man who resigned because he couldn't pay his debts and didn't want to be court-martialled. In my club, for example, the rule says: "If a member of the club be sentenced by Court Martial to be cashiered or dismissed the service; or if he be known to have resigned his commission to avoid Court Martial, he shall thereupon cease to be a member

of the club." You see what I mean. You may have "resigned" but you're still not welcome in the pavilion at Lord's.' (*Brother Cain*)

Or, as we shall see, at smart golf clubs like Royal St George's and the Royal Cinque Ports. But by then Simon had begun to trade on his notoriety, so he did not repine. Meanwhile in April 1958, when he completed *Perish*, he was still 'an obscure hack'. It was to better himself, professionally as well as financially, that together with the finished copy of *Perish* he submitted to Anthony Blond the synopsis of what was to become *The Feathers of Death*.

'Luckily Blond liked it. In fact he liked it so much he not only gave me an advance, he also contracted to pay me £10 a week while I was writing it, a sum of £50 on completion, and a further £50 on publication. Anthony and I have since had our differences, but I shall always be *immensely grateful* to him for his support at the beginning. He positively put me on the map.'

Blond did, however, set a tough condition: the novel must be finished by the end of June, in ten weeks' time. So Simon would have to write 10,000 grade A words a week *and* keep up his reviewing – 'a vital stand-by for years to come'. There was no way he could follow such a punishing schedule in London, besides which he was flat broke. And so, 'with every kind of misgiving', he arranged to go and stay with his parents in Hunstanton.

If there was one commodity Simon valued above all others it was independence – 'the denial of, or freedom from, the power of others'. Judge of his melancholy then at finding himself, once again, beholden to Arthur and Esther, the two people on earth he had striven hardest to cut loose from. What succoured him was his contract with Blond, which he could wave in their faces should they doubt the worth of his labour. And labour he did: twelve hours a day, seven days a week, until at last, on June 27th, the task was finished. Another six months would elapse before reviewers gave their verdict, but Blond was certain he had a winner: 'As the MS flowed in week by week I experienced that sense felt by Isaiah Berlin when he was listening to Namier talk, "of sailing in first-class waters".'

With nothing to occupy him but reviewing and no money for treats Simon took refuge in brandy, which he obtained locally on his parents' account. In October, as so often before, there was a row, following which Simon hastily sent off the synopsis of *Brother Cain* to Anthony Blond together with a request for an advance of £50. This duly arrived, the brandy bill was paid and Simon pulled himself together and began work on his second novel; it is time we had a closer look at his first.

Simon once described *Feathers* as 'a story of homosexual romance in the Army'. This is a good departure point. The narrator, Andrew Lamont, is the Intelligence Officer of Martock's Foot, a very laid-back regiment of 'mounted infantry' which owes something to the KSLI and also, it seems to me, to the sort of pre-war Yeomanry regiment immortalised by Keith Douglas in *Alamein to Zem-Zem* (although Simon claimed never to have heard of Douglas when I put this to him).

Martock's Foot have been posted to Pepromene, a colony east of Suez whose fierce mountain tribes are on the brink of insurrection. The regiment's job, which it doesn't particularly relish, is to establish a cordon of fortified camps round the perimeter of the mountains and wait for the tribesmen to attack. Lamont accompanies 'D' company to Gikumo, which is identical in most respects to Simon's Kenyan command, Kigumo. He is thus able to observe the growing intimacy between his friend, Lieutenant Alastair Lynch, and blond, blue-eyed Drummer Malcolm Harley, a soldier in Alastair's troop.

It soon transpires that Lynch and Harley are lovers and that Lynch is not prepared to give him up – 'You keep out of this, Andrew …. It's the most exciting thing I've ever had. I will have it, do you hear?' Then Lynch and his troop are ordered into the foothills, where a little later they are attacked. When reinforcements arrive they discover that among the casualties is Harley, shot dead by Lynch. A Court Martial is convened to decide whether, as he maintains, Lynch had to shoot Harley because he had disobeyed orders under fire and was endangering the troop; or whether, as Harley's mucker Simes alleges, Lynch murdered Harley because Harley had publicly rejected him – 'they all think I'm just a little nancy boy and it's all *your* fault'.

Lynch is acquitted, but not before he has admitted to Lamont that he and Harley had a vicious quarrel the night before the attack – '[but] I don't think I killed him because of that'. Retribution follows swiftly, for as Lynch is borne away in triumph on the shoulders of his troop, Simes darts out of the ruck and stabs him in the back with a bayonet. It only remains for Lord Nicholas Sanvoisin, the Commanding Officer, to deliver a measured funeral oration in which his late comrade's many qualities are set beside the one flaw that sealed his fate.

And what was this flaw? Not, I think, 'the abuse of trust' Lord Nicholas refers to at the graveside, but another defect he identifies earlier:

> 'Anyone … who, like Alastair, dares to be an open pederast must combine a number of very dangerous qualities … [he] is openly arrogant, openly rich, openly sceptical. And hence the offence openly given to Mrs Smith of Birmingham, to our "young and lovely Queen" in Buckingham Palace, to trades' union leaders, to good-form conservative politicians – to everything and everybody in the Mediocrity State. The open homosexual, however likeable to you or me personally, is just a pure bloody nuisance in the sort of world in which you and I are forced to live and run an army.'

Simon detested this 'manky' world and its 'middle-class values', and there is obviously a good deal of him in Alastair Lynch. But they differ, crucially, in their attitude to love and sex. Simon would never have lost his head over a private soldier. Sleep with him, yes. Fall in love with him, no. Later he became more vulnerable, but for many years yet he would maintain that love was a disease against which he had been immunised by Classical literature and personal experience. 'By the time I left Cambridge I was aware that if ever one got keen on someone, sex tended to introduce an additional, and in the end, *intolerable*, complication. What did work, for a time at any rate, was friendship plus sex, but one could really only be friends with one's peers.'

*

The first intimation Anthony Blond had that others shared his high opinion of *Feathers* was this puff from 'Whitefriar', the doyen of book trade columnists:

> I'd like to be the first to say it. In *The Feathers of Death*, Simon Raven has written one of the year's most striking, most controversial novels. It is a *bombshell* of a book.

Publication day was January 28th. That evening Blond threw a launch party at the Reform Club to which he invited, I was told, every homosexual bookseller in the country. Whitefriar was there too and in his next column he reported Blond as saying that the book was already into its second printing, propelled towards the bestseller lists by appreciative reviews in the *Observer* (Anthony Quinton) and the *Sunday Times* (J.D. Scott). The latter found it extraordinary that such an 'absurdly romantic, preposterously *reactionary*' novel should be so praiseworthy. His amazement was shared by Walter Allen in the *Evening Standard*, who pronounced Simon's point of view 'so outrageously snobbish as to be at once comic and faintly touching. His favourite word of contempt is "middle-class".'

Scott and Allen could be forgiven for thinking that Simon was writing against the wind. They had been the first critics to establish a link, however fragile it subsequently proved, between emerging writers like Kingsley Amis, John Wain and Philip Larkin and the social revolution that was supposed to have taken place since 1945. In fact Simon had rather more in common with Amis, at any rate, than was immediately apparent. Meanwhile it was not until some weeks later, when an unsigned review appeared in *The Times*, that *Feathers* received its most perceptive tribute:

> The main pleasure to be got from it is due to an exceptional gift for story-telling. The story [Mr Raven] tells is not an agreeable one, but it is set in a masculine prose so good, and told with a narrative verve

> so rare, that his future will be watched with eager interest by those who mourn the decline of the classical novel.

By chance Simon had just urged the merits of the classical novel in *Smith's Trade News*. Wearing his reviewer's hat he complained that too much of what he had to read was 'sterile' and 'incestuous':

> The job of novelists is to write about MAN .... And now that both Epic and Tragedy seem dead as art forms, it is the job of novelists to write about Man in an Epic or Tragic fashion (polished little tales about art critics squabbling in front of gas fires are merely irrelevant).

'A man must have fire in his belly for such a task,' Simon concluded. Was he referring to brandy, the drink Dr Johnson prescribed for aspirant heroes? If so, he should certainly have drunk more rather than less when writing *Brother Cain*, because it is a tepid effort whose hero simply doesn't measure up. Simon admitted this. 'He was just somebody for it all to happen to. I had a certain set of events I wanted to narrate, certain ideas I wanted to parade, and I'm afraid I took rather a nonentity to lead through them.'

One of the points Simon was trying to make was that Western Governments could be just as ruthless, just as capable of 'dirty tricks', as their Communist adversaries. He concluded this from his observations as an umpire on Exercise Battle Royal, when extreme measures to neutralise 'resentful peasants' in the aftermath of a nuclear explosion were rehearsed. In 1959 reviewers thought such 'silly' notions should be left to Ian Fleming, particularly when they came gift-wrapped with sex, snobbery and expensive meals; only the *New Statesman's* Paul West credited Simon with having started some 'disquieting trains of thought'.

Although Simon's stock dipped slightly following the muted reception of *Brother Cain*, he could console himself with the knowledge that thanks to the sale of paperback, film and American rights to *Feathers*, his independence was restored. After a month's holiday in Italy with Dickie Muir, Ian Murray and their respective wives, he quit Hunstanton for good and rented 'bachelor chambers' in London (actually a very basic bedsitter off Gloucester Road). He also became friendly with Burgo Partridge, whose *History of Orgies*, published by Blond, had enjoyed a *succès de scandale*.

Burgo, born 1935, was suckled in the bosom of Bloomsbury, being the son of the diarist, Frances Partridge, and her beefy husband Ralph, who was lusted after in vain by Lytton Strachey, himself the unrequited love of Ralph's first wife, Dora Carrington. As is apparent from his mother's diaries Burgo had been a source of anxiety to his parents ever since running away from Millfield at the age of fifteen. He was neurotic, prone to fits of depression and had few friends his own age. Nor did he have an occupation, being in possession of an ample allowance and sharing his father's distaste for hard work. His book, it was said, was a flash in the pan, and at the time he met Simon he had no plans for another.

In one of Simon's later novels an undergraduate whom Fielding Gray has befriended compares Fielding to 'indulgent Mr Worldly Wiseman, who dispenses shrewd advice and pleasurable suggestions'. This, broadly speaking, was the role Simon filled for Burgo Partridge, to the relief of his parents, both of whom had long since vowed never to 'interfere'.

> Simon was a good influence on Burgo in all sorts of ways [said Frances Partridge]. He stimulated him, shook him out of his moodiness, and encouraged him to work hard – something that didn't always come easily to Burgo, any more than it did to his father. At the same time Simon, for all his apparent manliness and worldliness, would get in a 'feminine fluster' about tickets and things, and this brought out the practical side in Burgo, who was quite good at arranging things without too much fuss.

Frances Partridge's first glimpse of Simon was 'pink and naked' in their swimming pool at Ham Spray. This was misleading: Simon hated swimming and exposed as little of his sensitive skin to the sun as possible.[4] He had only gone in to cool off on what was a very hot summer's day. On subsequent visits his preference for indoors was marked. 'He never took any exercise, not even a walk, which at his age was rather odd. There was rather a feeling of fug about.'

But, conceded Mrs Partridge, there was nothing stuffy about Simon's sense of humour or his conversation. 'The more one got to know Simon, the more one appreciated his geniality. But at the same time it was clear that we had a lot of values that weren't his. He had no time for love, as opposed to sex. Friendship he would allow. We had ethical values. I don't think he did then. Sin had a great attraction for him. He used to describe, over and over again, how it was that he'd had to leave the Army because of debts. He seemed proud of this. And he could be rather brutal, albeit with the best intentions. After Ralph died Burgo tried to discuss his childhood feelings for him with Simon. "You never liked him, did you?" was all Simon said, which was very obtuse of him. I think this lack of delicacy comes over in his writing.'

But there is no question that like many before him, and many to come, Burgo fell under Simon's spell. Following one of his subsequent visits Frances Partridge recorded in her diary the essence, as she understood it, of Simon's 'Regency, cynical, materialistic outlook':

> Simon said at lunch today that he was horrified by the younger

[4] Ian Murray's wife, Joanna, remembered Simon sitting on the beach at Positano in a grey flannel suit.

generation's seeming to believe in fidelity. He thought marriage should begin for a man not before 30 or 35, and then leave room for escapades on both sides. No romance. The nearest to love he will admit is sex plus getting on quite well together. Jealousy hardly accepted. I don't know whether he would admit any pleasure in mental intimacy. Doubt it. Conviviality, good living, comfort and luxury are all rated high. It's too highly seasoned and unsubtle a diet for Ralph and me and we escaped yesterday afternoon and walked down the valley feeling – anyway I did – the sort of refreshment natural beauty, wind and sun give after a night spent in a stuffy room, full of smoke, drinking too much and a hangover. It's not our view of life at all. But we both agree that Simon has done a lot for Burgo; he has a good head and good nature and a very likeable style about him. (1.8.60 – unedited entry)

Simon described Burgo as 'a good companion, though he could be terribly morose. Rather like Oscar [Whitamore], Burgo would have a kind of male period about once a month when he would alternate between being very quiet and very quarrelsome. He wouldn't say anything for hours and then he'd suddenly burst out with "Fuck you. Fuck you. Fuck you. What am I doing here with you? I don't want to go out to dinner to that wretched restaurant. It's much too expensive and I shall have to pay." Then another six hours of silence. But apart from these monthly traumas he was a good companion: funny, observant, perceptive, malicious – not least about his mother, whom he was nevertheless very fond of.'

Because of Simon's reputation and Burgo's youth people thought there must be something on between 'Partridge and Raven, the two game birds'. This was not the case. Burgo preferred women and was 'too dark' for Simon's taste. 'The trouble with Burgo, Blond used to say, is that if you're in Israel they all think he's an Arab, in Egypt they all think he's a Jew, and wherever you are they all think he's a terrorist. When we were in Cyprus together RAF policemen were always darting out and wanting to question us. He was all things to all men, but all things bad. This made him a bit paranoiac from time to time. He had two horrors. One was that people at Poste Restantes were not letting him have his mail because they weren't checking properly. The other was that restaurateurs were discriminating against him. He'd spy someone tucking into something that he thought he hadn't been offered. And I'd say, "Look Burgo, it's more than probable that these people ordered the dish in advance. It's the sort of thing they only do on order." But he wouldn't be convinced. He'd sit there glowering with paranoia. Every now and then he got rather too drunk for anybody's good. But it's a measure of him as a companion that we spent three nights together cooped up in a wagon-lit compartment between Ostend and Athens without falling out.'

*

Simon now had the bit between his teeth, which was just as well because he needed every single penny he could earn, and more besides, to make ends meet in London. Mindful of the fact that before the war the kind of writers he admired were always on the move, setting their novels wherever they pitched their tents, he sold the idea of a novel with a Greek background to Anthony Blond and invited Burgo to come along for the ride.

Blond had no qualms about underwriting Simon's part in this enterprise, but he 'very prudently' refused to hand over a lump sum. Instead he promised to pay monthly instalments via American Express. Burgo, meanwhile, took an 'enormous' amount of money with him, to the consternation of his father who thought Simon had infected him with his love of gambling. In fact, said Simon, Burgo didn't feel secure unless he had 'wads of lolly on him – luckily, in this instance, because Blond forgot to send the first of my instalments and Burgo had to keep us afloat until the money arrived'.

In the course of their four months' odyssey Simon and Burgo went from Athens to Crete to Athens again, thence to Hydra, back to Athens, onwards to Cyprus and back to Athens for the last time, via Alexandria, Beirut and Baalbek. Despite these changes of scene, and accommodation that was far from princely, Simon was still able to complete a novel and write several essays. The latter included his study of London's male prostitutes, referred to above, 'which for some reason was very well received on the Stock Exchange'.

In the age of AIDS 'Boys Will Be Boys'[5] seems rather tame, but in 1960, seven years before the Sexual Offences Act, it was, well, seminal. Here, announced Simon, is a branch of human activity which I, as a novelist, am curious about. Who is involved? What do they do? And where do they do it? In pursuit of some answers he considers five representative 'boys', from the Guardsman who only does it when he's short of cash, to the 'full-blown courtesan', as at home in the salon as the sack. He observes them in the pubs, clubs and coffee-bars where they meet their clients ('some of whom have an unmistakably officer-like manner'), notes how much they charge, and for what, and follows them home as far as the bedroom door.

Had Simon published this in a risqué magazine like *Lilliput* he might well have received a call from the Vice squad, for it was clearly the work of a client. But because he wrote it for *Encounter*, at that time a forum for the great and the good, he was in the clear. Not that he ever saw himself as a campaigner, except against the cant which was common to both sides in the debate about homosexuality. He loathed cant whatever its provenance. 'I cannot write out of political, social or economic expediency,' he

[5] The title by which it came to be known.

once told me, adding that 'in the modern world, people are far too afraid of giving offence'.

Simon was soon giving offence again himself, this time to Zionists, who objected to some mild criticisms of Israel he made in the *Spectator* following a visit there with Anthony Blond. 'Blond contacted me in Athens and said he wanted me to come with him to Israel. "I'll pay," he said, "and in return you can write an essay about the place for a book I'm planning on modern Jewry."

'So we went to Israel with Ant's knowledgeable cousin, David Sussman, as our guide. I had a very enjoyable time, which since this was the land of Jehovah was a pleasant surprise. But it was clear to me that Jehovah's followers, the orthodox Jews, had a baleful influence on the government out of all proportion to their numbers. And Israelis themselves, although in many ways very admirable, were in danger of forfeiting one's sympathy through their pride, their self-righteousness and their intransigence …. And have duly done so. But you weren't supposed to say this then.'

Nettled by the hostility of Zionists to his *Spectator* piece Simon gave them both barrels in the essay he was writing for Blond. Alas, Blond's book never materialised, but Simon was able to include his contribution in *Boys Will Be Boys*,[6] and I can only say that as a guide to the Israeli mentality it still takes some beating.

This would seem the moment to say a word or two about Simon's robust attitude to Jews, among whom were numbered his publisher and some of his oldest friends. Why, I asked him, did he risk offending them by using expressions like 'jewy'? – 'It is just because I have known and liked a lot of Jews,' said Simon, 'that I've always thought that one should talk to them like other people and make no concessions to their Jewishness. And they mostly take it in good part – as indeed the Blacks I knew at Cambridge did when you used the word "nigger". Provided they knew you were being friendly they didn't mind. But I suppose one does have to be more careful these days. Everyone's so sensitive, so *compassionate*.'

I thought it worth canvassing Frederic Raphael about this, first, because he still bears the scars of bigotry at Charterhouse; and secondly, because he once wrote of Simon, 'No one has succeeded in making bad taste more palatable.' Here is his reply:

> Simon on Jews is not a matter which gives me nightmares or much pause. Those who trade in shock-horror are obliged to outrage as fancy cooks are to raspberry vinegar. What is obvious is that he is nostalgic for a time when making naughty remarks about Yids and Jewboys was a sign of casual superiority not of moral delinquency; he seeks at every stage to pastoralise his prejudices (not at all the

[6] A miscellany which includes Simon's essay on male prostitutes, from which it takes its title.

same thing as pasteurising) .... Take it seriously? Should we take sorbets, custard tarts or mutual masturbation seriously? Really, I cannot contrive a balanced response to yah-boo-sucks uttered by a fat, empurpled old pouffe whom I really like to see when I see him and rarely think about otherwise.

This, I guess, is the sort of passage Frederic Raphael has in mind when he refers to Simon 'pastoralising his prejudices'. It is supposed to describe the beginning of term at a prep school in the 1980s, but the language is cod-Edwardian:

'This is Marius Stern,' Canteloupe would say, 'my old friend Gregory's boy.' And to Marius, 'This is "Gin-Sling" Carhart-Harris, who downed ten Tom Collins in five minutes and then hit the ball clean over the Pavilion at Bangalore – and won a bet for a monkey.'

'How do you do, sir,' Marius would say, giving a smile at once manly and flirtatious. 'Where did you keep the monkey afterwards?'

'Haw, haw, young'un. A monkey means five hundred quid.'

And Marius, who knew this perfectly well as his mother used this kind of slang, would be led on to 'Whiffy' Cave-Browne, while 'Gin-Sling' Carhart-Harris said to his daughter, his son-in-law and his three grandsons, 'By Jove, what a fine little chap'; and the son-in-law said, 'But isn't his father a Jew?'; and 'Gin-Sling' riposted, 'Eton and the Brigade. Poor chap can't help the other thing. Anyway, if Canteloupe likes the boy, the boy's all right. I remember when Canteloupe – "Detterling" we called him then – used to cut the ball later than any man in England.' (*The Face of the Waters*)

To conclude this topic, here is Conrad Dehn's theory as to why, despite his saloon-bar anti-semitism, Simon relished the company of Jews. 'Maybe his liking for them is because it is among Jews that he has had the most uncritical friendships. They've liked him for what he was and were not concerned to try and reform him. He might not have come across such tolerance in the more conventional Christian community.'

*

In *Kingsmen of a Century*, Patrick Wilkinson writes of Simon's novels, 'They are widely read, not least (with mixed feelings) in King's, which features in some of them as "Lancaster College".' Dr Wilkinson's unease is understandable. He was recognised to be the model for Dr Walter Goodrich, the worldly, manipulative don whose machinations come horribly unstuck in *Doctors Wear Scarlet*, the novel Simon completed in Greece.

Dr Goodrich thinks he has a winner in Dickie Fountain, one of those personable paragons who combine academic and athletic success with a pleasing manner. Goodrich's plans for Dickie include marriage to his loyal, frumpish daughter Penelope. But Dickie is not the responsive thoroughbred he appears: for one thing he has a vicious, sado-masochistic streak, for another he is impotent – flaws which are exploited by a blood-sucking siren whom he meets in Greece. He is rescued from her by some Cambridge chums and reinstalled at Lancaster. But once a vampire, always a vampire, as poor Penelope discovers to her cost.

In later years the novelist Angela Carter used to put it about that Simon had tasted human flesh. I dare say *Doctors* contributed to this canard,[7] but in point of fact Simon did not set out to write a vampire story. It was only when he was faced with the problem of settling Dickie Fountain's hash that he realised, following some research on Hydra, that vampirism was the answer.

> '[T]he vampire is in fact a living human being with a peculiar type of sado-sexual perversion [said Dr Holmstrom]. The sexual element is quite obvious; you might consider, in this context, such relatively normal practices as *fellatio* or *cunnilinctus* [*sic*].[8] Nor is it difficult to see that vampiric intercourse, in a quiet way, has a deeply sadistic tinge to it. It follows, of course, that the victims of vampires tend to be of a masochistic type – and like most masochists, capable of assuming a sadistic role in their turn. You should also be aware that sadistic practices – and among them this one – are liable to have a strong appeal for impotent males or frigid females.'

Simon's solution did not impress reviewers like Maurice Richardson, who complained that 'vampirism simply will not do in 1960 .... Mr Raven must give up this habit of suddenly turning in front of our eyes into a kind of intellectual's Dennis Wheatley.' Although Simon approved of Richardson, who later wrote a most perceptive introduction to *Royal Foundation*,[9] he cited this as an example of criticism that missed the point.

'I write in order to entertain, which means I must first entertain myself. At that date vampires were considered off-limits to proper novelists (though I notice they're quite acceptable now); *ergo*, one was breaking ranks by writing about them. But they had then, and still do have, a fascination for me that I tried to convey in my novel. If I failed to do this, then by all means say so. But don't tell me I ought to be writing a different novel.'

*

[7] 'I'm not aware of having done so – except, of course, in bed. But I wouldn't be averse to trying it ... although I do draw the line at necrophilia.'

[8] One of the more entertaining howlers inflicted on Simon by Blond's typesetters.

[9] Simon's first television play and also the title of a collected edition of his radio and television plays, published in 1966.

After Israel Simon returned to his Gloucester Road bed-sitter and a summer of what Dylan Thomas called 'the capital punishment'. However hard he worked – and he had begun to write radio and television plays in addition to reviews, essays and a new book, *The English Gentleman* – he could not seem to earn the '£10 a day' that life in London apparently cost.

> Simon was very easily influenced by his peers [said Anthony Blond]. Because they liked to go to expensive restaurants, because they drank only the best vintages, because they always ended up with brandy and cigars, he felt he must follow suit. The trouble was that people like Dickie Muir could afford to live like this and Simon couldn't. So every morning he would be on my doorstep asking for more.

Eventually Blond put his foot down, but not before an incident which measured the huge gulf, not simply in resources, but also in attitudes, between rich people like Dickie Muir and impoverished writers like Simon.

'I persuaded Dickie to take me as his guest to one of John Aspinall's private chemmy parties. I'd sat in on these twice before, in '53, I think, and '56, and come away £900 to the good, which went a very long way then. But Dickie warned me that banks now started at £300, not the £20 or £30 I remembered, so I arranged to take ten per cent of his gains or losses, hoping that this would not commit me too deeply.'

But it did. Dickie lost £20,000, ten per cent of which was about as much as Simon could hope to make from his writing in a year.

> I remember wandering round Berkeley Square in the very early morning [said Dickie Muir], and Simon was saying how awful the whole thing was and of course he'd repay me. So the matter was left at that and we all shed tears and had a good breakfast somewhere. Well much to my annoyance Simon then wrote a piece about all this for the *Spectator* in which he described Lord Derby, who'd also been playing, as looking like 'a failing salesman in a hired dinner jacket'. He didn't actually say it was Lord Derby, but anyone in that milieu would have seen through the disguise.[10] I thought then, and I think now, that this was disloyal of Simon, particularly since he never did repay me. We were on non-speaks for quite a while.

But, as I pointed out to Dickie Muir, a writer in Simon's position could not always afford to be loyal: everything and everybody was grist to his mill ('Oh dear, oh dear. I think I've learnt that lesson very late in life!').

[10] Simon called him 'Eddie Lancaster'.

Simon admitted as much in an autobiographical passage from *Boys Will Be Boys*.

> [But] in the end, my code is just a worldly, weary de-Christianised version of the public school code – *or would be if I had the strength of character to live up to it* [my italics]. I believe in fair play, keeping one's spoken word, not telling tales, not kicking a man when he's down, paying one's debts (in fact I bilk mine whenever possible), and in backing one's chums to the point of perjury.

I include this here because it is referred to by Simon in the letter printed below, which he wrote to Dickie defending his republication of the gambling episode in *Boys Will Be Boys*. Ian Murray tipped Dickie off about this, and also drew his attention to Simon's code, quoted above.

3.12.63

My dear Dickie,

Please excuse type. I have been writing in longhand all day and it comes very tiring on the wrist.

I gather from what Patricia told me that it was Ian who announced the re-publication of the piece to you, indeed rang you specially to do so. Although you would almost certainly have discovered its inclusion anyway, this seems to me to have been rather officious of Ian – he might at least have waited till you'd paid 21/– for your own copy rather than quoting at you out of the one *I* gave him before publication day. Leaving all that aside, however, I think your letter is very well urged. I particularly appreciated the phrase, 'one of your regular throw-ups on loyalty'. Relevant and pungent, though in self-defence I should point out, what Ian doubtless omitted, that the passage in question makes it quite plain that while I admire loyalty etc. in theory, I have never let such virtues incommode me in practice. A disagreeable passage it no doubt was, but not, as you imply, hypocritical.

To get closer to the matter in hand. I more or less agree with your assessment of the original offence, which was partly dishonourable (I just couldn't resist it), and partly obtuse (I really didn't think it would cause *that* much trouble – after all, Aspers *et al.* are a pretty tough lot, not easily liable, one thought, to let their feelings get hurt). Still, whichever way one looks at it, the original publication was not kind: I was Aspers' guest, guaranteed by you, so it was bound to offend both of you and also imbroil you with Aspers. However, when we come to the question of *re*-publication, I think you are making much too much of a thing. This is how my mind worked.

1) Better not, I suppose.

2) Some weeks later. I am short of this kind of piece – plenty of reviews, but they're hopelessly dead now, most of them.

3) So why not this? It has interest on two levels: on a general level, as a piece of social reporting, i.e. as a scene from our time; and, for a tiny number of people, on an inside gossip level. On the first level, any merit it ever had (and it must have had some or a percipient editor wouldn't have taken it) it still has. On the second, the personal, level, *any damage it has done has been done*; it can hardly do more if published again some years later, all mixed up with a lot of other stuff, and in a form which will have not a tenth of the circulation of the original.

4) In extenuation, one might add (I told myself) that Aspers' entire set up has now changed. If he had still been running the old semi-legal private games, this might still upset him; but as it is, it speaks of a world miles removed from the Clermont Club – it has become, from his point of view and however grave the *original* betrayal, irrelevant.[11]

5) Subconscious envy and resentment. (I can't of course be sure of this but I suspect it). Why aren't I as rich as they are, it isn't fair, anyway John Derby is bloody, etc., etc.

So republished it was, and I really can't think, my dear, that it has made a hap'orth of difference to anyone, except to me, whose task in collecting the book was just perceptively eased. However, when Patricia said you were cross, I thought I would ask you both to lunch 'to make up' – being anxious to do this in any case, as I had cancelled the previous lunch we arranged. Unfortunately I was hysterically busy and harassed just then, so the invitation didn't issue as soon as I hoped – not till I sent you that p.c. in fact. So now let me try again. What about Thursday Dec.19? If that's no good, it will have to wait until after the new year, so do try.

Were it not so late, I would tell you about a rather odd party (odd in structure and atmosphere rather than in anything which occurred) which Daphne Michie gave on Sunday …. However, if I go into that, I shall miss the post, and you will then think I'm being more flippant about this than ever.

Love to Patricia,[12] and you too, you old cow,

Simon

Badinage aside it is clear that Simon thought Dickie was being rather priggish. Because he shrugged off slander himself he expected other people, particularly those in the public eye, to abide by the same conven-

[11] In 1961 the Betting and Gaming Act legalised casinos and betting shops.

[12] Dickie Muir had married Patricia Gaskell, formerly Mrs Humphrey Lyttelton, in 1956.

tion. He never budged from this position. In 1991, when Guy Nevill sued over a scabrous anecdote in *Is there anybody there? said the traveller*, Simon was most indignant. 'He ought to be too grand to bother about something like this.'

CHAPTER FOURTEEN

'Let us now praise famous men' –
    Men of little showing
For their work continueth,
And their work continueth,
Broad and deep continueth,
    Greater than their knowing!
            Kipling, *Stalky & Co*

Shortly after losing his shirt at Aspinall's Simon had to suffer Anthony Blond's Grand Remonstrance. 'I turned up as usual one morning and he said, "This is the last hand-out you get. Leave London, or leave my employ." He knew, you see, that as long as I lived in London I would wallow in extravagance. "Go at least fifty miles," he said. So that is what I did. I went to Deal, where Myles was teaching, and have based myself there or thereabouts ever since.' I bet that surprised people. – 'It did. It surprised *me*. I thought I'd miss the fleshpots, but I didn't. Or rather, I found that they were infinitely more piquant when sampled abroad. Meanwhile Deal itself grew on me. It had an insolent, old-world charm that I found most congenial. I liked the inhabitants too. They were a salty, unregenerate lot, with a taste for off-colour jokes, like the one about the famous local adulterer whose coffin turned out to be too small – "he was never happy in his own bed".'

And yet, admitted Simon, it was the presence of Myles that meant most to him about Deal: he was closer to Myles than to anyone else in the world. Those who observed them together sensed this. But since Myles rarely left Deal, except to play cricket, many of Simon's London friends were only dimly aware of his existence. Readers of this book probably feel the same way, so I had better put them in the picture.

Happy the man, Simon would say, who has something to do, knows how to do it, and does it. Myles Raven was such a man. For twenty-four years he dedicated himself, body and soul, to Tormore Preparatory School, his last hours of active life being spent in umpiring a school cricket match. Although sudden, his death in 1976 was not entirely unexpected; and while one hesitates to say that he consciously scorned to stay too long at the feast, it is undeniable that his type of schoolmaster – beery, dogmatic, misogynistic, scruffy, reactionary – did not sort well with a system in which mothers had begun to call the shots. What, one wonders, did they make of the notice he once put up on the Tormore cricket pavilion?:

NO DOGS, WOMEN OR CHILDREN BEYOND THIS POINT.

Myles was born in 1930, making him nearly three years younger than Simon. They were of similar build and appearance, with distinctive noses that ended in a snub and aggressive chins; but whereas Simon had red hair, Myles's, like Esther's, was ash-blond. The difference between their characters was equally marked. Unlike Simon, Myles was a quiet, well-behaved child 'who always kept a hold on nurse' – or, better still, Mummy. Simon recalled how, when they went to children's parties in the neighbourhood, he would see Myles sneaking off to find his coat and go home within a few minutes of their arrival.

'I would have to explain that we had to stay to tea and that there would probably be a conjuror and that we couldn't possibly leave until about six. And yet, once he got used to other children, he was a great success with them .... I don't know why he was so shy, but it may have had something to do with the fact that he had a pronounced stammer. He was also, I suspect, dyslexic. At any rate he didn't learn to read until he was seven or eight. But there was nothing wrong with his imagination. He had a whole troop of imaginary friends with rude names. "Titty's being intolerable today," he'd say.'

Although Myles missed Simon when his brother went to Cordwalles he was not at all anxious to join him there. For with Simon away he had Esther to himself for long periods, and Margaret the nanny as well. But as the years ticked by so the shades of the prison house began to close upon him, as indeed they did upon the whole country. And when, in June 1938, Esther gave birth to her daughter Robin, Myles's time was up. That autumn he accompanied Simon to Cordwalles, Lismore was sold, and nothing was ever the same again.

To his surprise, Myles passed the challenge of leaving home with flying colours. It helped, of course, that he had a powerful and protective elder brother *in situ*. But even without Simon, Myles was well-equipped to succeed in communities like Cordwalles and St Dunstan's. He was very good at games, particularly soccer and cricket, and although not as clever as Simon, able enough to follow him to Charterhouse with a scholarship. The real difference between them lay in their attitudes. Whereas Simon went his own way where possible, Myles was content to be a member of the team. He was, said John Drewett, who opened the batting with him at St Dunstan's, 'a thoroughly good egg'.

Myles joined Simon at Saunderites in September 1944, just as his brother's star was climbing towards its zenith. A year later, when it fell to earth, he was well enough launched to withstand any gravitational pull. Not that Myles ever exerted himself at Charterhouse, except perhaps when running in the school Cross Country team. Frederic Raphael described him as 'an idly elegant cricketer', while Myles's great friend Bob Arrowsmith said in the *Carthusian*,

> Myles had strong claims, and claims which he would not have denied, to be the idlest Scholar elected to Charterhouse in living recollection.

Simon said Myles's was a 'specialised' form of idleness – 'he played a lot of Chess' – but otherwise couldn't explain it. What did distress him about Myles's career at Charterhouse was Esther's obdurate refusal to have his eyes tested, which cost him his place in the Cricket XI. 'Myles was very short-sighted, but my mother simply would not acknowledge this. "Nobody in the family's ever had bad eyesight" – in fact my father's sight was none too good – "and anyway there's a war on". So poor Myles, who was very diffident about this, just put up with it, and was duly dropped after making "a pair" against Harrow. Of course once he went into the Army they insisted he wear spectacles, but the damage had been done.'

Simon subsequently wrote a radio play inspired by this 'cruel experience' which is reproduced in *Boys will be Boys*. But worse still for Myles was the flak he had to take from Esther when she became jealous of his friendship with Bob Arrowsmith. 'I recall her spitting with rage saying, "This is disgusting. I've just read another of Arrowsmith's letters to you." – "How did you find it, Mum?" – "I just happened to be going through your drawer and it fell out of its envelope." In situations like this she could be a real bitch. Crude as well. She even accused poor Bob of being a Jew because he had a hooked nose. He wasn't of course. But in any case, who the hell cared if he was?'

If Esther thought she could drive a wedge between Myles and Bob Arrowsmith she was mistaken. Their friendship continued until Myles's death, and was arguably the deepest attachment outside his family that Myles formed. From Miss Grace Arrowsmith, who kept house for her brother, I learnt that Myles's signature was in their visitors' book no less than 31 times between September 1949 and December 1950 alone – 'I think he looked on us as his second home'. For nearly 30 years he and Bob wrote to each other almost every week; sad to say, none of this correspondence has survived.

Simon insisted that although 'long and passionate', the friendship between Myles and Bob Arrowsmith was an innocent one – 'Bob was *intensely* proper'. He regretted that unlike the Victorians, people nowadays could not conceive of such relationships existing without a physical element. 'In the long run, physical goings-on spoil everything.'

Michael Webb, a colleague of Myles's at Tormore, likened Bob Arrowsmith to Miss Jean Brodie, and there is no question that Myles ordered his affairs largely in accordance with Arrowsmith's Edwardian precepts. But in contrast to Arrowsmith, whom many found pompous, Myles remained a schoolboy at heart, with a taste for gadgets, gossip and schoolboy yarns like *Pip*. For most of his life he was uninterested in the real world, although when Arthur died and he inherited a few thousand pounds' worth of stocks and shares, he did buy a pocket radio to keep abreast of the prices, and would listen, with an ear plug, when taking prep.

Myles's stammer, which he subsequently learnt to control in the classroom, ruled him out for a commission, and he spent his national service as a corporal-typist in the War Office. Then, since Arthur was too mean to pay for him to go to University and wanted him out of the house, he had to find a job, which he did at a prep school in Essex. There, not very happily, he remained for eighteen months. Then in 1952, on Bob Arrowsmith's recommendation, he joined Tormore, which in those days formed part of a thriving colony of prep schools on the East Kent coast.

Frank Turner, the Headmaster of Tormore, was a diminutive tyrant who believed, said Simon, 'in Greek, Latin and the rod'. Scholarships were what he was in business for and he ground his boys at their grammar until they were fit to drop. He got results all right – just about every other boy won an award of some kind – but as his successor, Paul Spurrier, admitted, the school was Dickensian, with harsh discipline, appalling food and grim, God-fearing Sundays when boys were expected to learn the collects and the catechism.

When Myles arrived Turner had been headmaster for over 30 years. He paid his staff a pittance[1] and ordered them about like prefects. Myles loathed him, although he did acknowledge that Turner had taught him how to keep order in class, which until then had been a problem. In fact, Myles had a lot going for him as a teacher. He was physically impressive – six foot three and built to scale; conscientious – he used to brush up his Latin and Greek with Bob Arrowsmith during the holidays; imaginative – 'he made Latin live', an ex-pupil of his told me; and, when provoked, explosive – he had a short fuse which grew shorter with the years.

But it was as a games master that Myles excelled. Cricket was his passion, closely followed by soccer; for a time he even ran the rugby as well, making up in enthusiasm and inspiration what he lacked in experience. To say he was fanatical in pursuit of success is no exaggeration: the word was used to me twice, by a colleague at Tormore, and by a master at a neighbouring school, who hinted that Myles's umpiring sometimes gave cause for concern on the circuit. However that might be, Myles's commitment to games was such that he took on many of the groundsman's duties as well. Bob Arrowsmith used to complain that even in the holidays he was loath to leave Deal for more than a day or two at a time for fear the playing fields might suffer in his absence.

[1] In 1955 Myles was paid £103 a term. By 1962 this had risen to £225, but only in the teeth of opposition by Turner, now Chairman of the Governors – 'He'll just spend it on cigarettes and beer.'

CHAPTER FOURTEEN

About a year after Myles arrived at Tormore he surprised everyone by getting engaged to the under-matron, who was called Betty. Simon and Esther were summoned to meet her, but for some reason, said Simon, she was absent. A little later they learnt that the engagement was off – 'she ordered red wine with her fish, Myles said'. Betty then left Tormore, but that was not quite that. At Myles's memorial service there was a woman unknown to Simon among the congregation. 'Who's that?' he asked an old Tormore hand. 'Betty.'

Myles never looked at a woman again. He spent the rest of his life among men and boys. Was he homosexual? Yes. Was he *active*? No – except, that is, for one lapse he admitted to his friend, Michael Strevens. 'Myles said he did once put a hand on a boy's knee, but was so nonplussed by his cool response – "And what does Mr Raven want?" – he never touched anyone again. He liked smutty talk, but that was as far as it went.'

Like most prep school masters Myles had his share of eccentricities. For instance he never wore underpants, a legacy, said Simon, of Cordwalles, where they were banned by 'faddy' Mrs Loly. He also insisted on wearing white woollen cricket socks, possibly to try and disguise the fact that his feet smelt, though they cannot have been in the same league as his farts. For what really set Myles apart was his huge appetite for beer.

> Every evening at nine o'clock [said Michael Strevens] he would leave his quarters and go next door to our local, the Admiral Keppel. There he would drink about four or five pints before closing time and then take another four pints home with him in a jug. Some nights he drank even more, but the amazing thing was he never even complained of a headache, let alone a hangover.

But consequences there were. By the time he was 35 Myles had a huge beer belly. And as Simon reported to Oscar Whitamore, he was also 'accident-prone'.

> Cricket tour a great success, except that nobody made any runs, it rained for five days out of seven in Cumberland, I have sprained my arm and can't even wank with it, and Myles pissed his bed so fiercely in Somerset that he floated out of his door in it.

The Trogs' cricket tour, a three-week affair beginning in East Kent, continuing in Somerset and Shropshire, and ending in Cumberland at a school run by Richard Ingrams' brother Peter, was Myles's favourite holiday thing. He also enjoyed golf, which he played to a handicap of four, selected race meetings like the one at Kempton Park on Boxing Day, and Canterbury Cricket week, where he could be sure to find Bob Arrowsmith in the Band of Brothers' tent. He hardly ever went abroad, partly because he hated flying and was sea-sick in the slightest swell, but also because he didn't much care for foreign food and detested foreign beer.

On the rare occasions he went to London Myles did not cut a very impressive figure. 'A big lump who smelt strongly of pubs' was how one of Simon's more polished friends summed him up. Simon was aware of this and went out of his way to shield him from any unpleasantness. 'You felt *he* was the younger brother whose job it was to look after Myles,' I was told.

But the view from Deal was very different. 'Myles,' said Michael Strevens, 'was a far tougher character than Simon. He had no Doubts. I think Simon recognised this. He would usually defer to him when they were travelling together in England.' Michael Webb, another of Myles's colleagues, agreed with Strevens, although he stressed that most of the time the brothers were of one mind.

> They were remarkably similar in all sorts of ways. They looked alike, sounded alike, and had the same obsession with their bowels and bladders. 'Well, dear, I've found the lavatory. It's over there.' Then they could settle down. Neither of them showed the slightest interest in 'kit', although Myles demanded the highest standards of turnout from the Tormore cricketers. What they sought, above all, was a supply of amusing people to talk to. What they couldn't tolerate was a break-down in arrangements.

A final point. Simon's willingness to fall in with Myles's wishes may also have arisen from guilt. For while his notoriety procured him readers, it was not an asset in the circles Myles frequented beyond the Admiral Keppel. When Myles was elected a member of Royal St George's Golf Club, he was warned not to bring Simon along as a guest.[2] And when Simon himself was put up for the Royal Cinque Ports Golf Club, he was blackballed by the property magnate, Bernard Sunley, who had been scandalised by the homosexual passages in *The English Gentleman*. All this changed when Simon wrote *The Pallisers*, but for many years he was categorised locally as a 'disreputable scribbler'.

*

Anthony Blond proposed to ease the rigours (as he supposed) of banishment with a solid financial inducement. He would pay Simon a retainer of £15 a week in cash and settle the following bills as well: dentist's, tailor's and, up to a point, wine merchant's. Knowing that Simon was a compulsive eater-out he also agreed to pay for his evening meal at the Royal Hotel,

[2] When Michael Astor, who had met Simon, heard of this, he said he would take him round regardless, but Simon declined his offer.

which with wine and brandy came to about £2. These items were set against the royalties and rights that accrued to Simon from his books.

'Ant was very generous in those early days. He became my banker, but unlike other bankers he didn't charge interest on my overdraft, which ran up to £2,000. Nor did he try and make me pay it off with the money I earned from journalism or the BBC. So what with one thing and another one had enough to live on, with a little put by for treats.'

Treats generally involved foreign travel, which thanks to a precedent set at about this time, was held to be tax-deductible if it could be proved that Simon had gone abroad 'in the proper pursuit of his trade or profession'. What happened was that the Inland Revenue tried to tax the money Blond had advanced to Simon for his four months in Greece. Simon appealed, and once it had been established that Blond had paid him 'on the strict understanding that I wrote a book', the Revenue backed down.

But treats had to be earned: Simon accepted this now. And in the next five years alone he wrote five novels, two non-fiction works, six television plays, eight radio plays, a stage play[3] and a stream of articles and reviews. He quickly established a reputation for professionalism with editors and directors. As his drama agent, Diana Baring (formerly Crawfurd) told me, 'He was the perfect client: always on time, always the right length. A *total* pleasure to represent.'

Fame and fortune did not dilute Simon's professional integrity. For instance in 1979 he was stuck in the Beverly Hills Hotel for a fortnight, working up a script for Gore Vidal's historical novel, *Burr*.[4] As he came into the home straight the studio phoned to say that they were willing to send a girl round to help type up the last scenes. 'I said, "You needn't bother. It's all in hand." And then they said, "If you ask her nicely she might go down on you." I said, "Thanks, but no thanks. I've got quite enough to attend to without that." Bloody cheek!' – *Why*? – 'Fancy assuming you needed a bribe to finish the job properly.'

Simon enjoyed working in hotel bedrooms and once he began to earn good money would spend long periods doing precisely this. A writer, says one of his characters, 'is someone who lives in passage'; if Simon did not exactly live on the wing – he was too sedentary a bird for that – he never went in for nest-building either. All he required was a 'base', in effect lodgings, with a landlady who would cook and chore. His first four years in Deal were spent at 134 Manor Road, where for £3 10s a week, rising to £5, he had a sitting room, bedroom and bathroom, cooked breakfast and

[3] *The Case of Father Brendan*, which in 1968 received a single performance by the Repertory Players. The story of a humble priest who develops stigmata, it was quite well reviewed; but Simon preferred to write for television, 'because they commissioned you, whereas theatre producers didn't'.

[4] Vidal's interest had been aroused by Simon's simile: 'Gore Vidal, as merry as a leper bell.'

high tea.[5] He then spent eight years at two different addresses in London Road, before renting half of a tiny clapboard cottage, again in Manor Road.

The few friends who were admitted to these premises were struck by how bare of Simon's possessions they were. All that was visible were some books, a cricket bat and pads (but no gaudy blazer: he always made do with a sports jacket), an ancient portable typewriter and an assortment of suitcases and grips. Francis Haskell thought this symbolised Simon's detachment.

> He's never been weighed down either by objects or relationships. If he had a book and one wanted to read it he would give it to one. That's partly his generosity, but it's also symptomatic of his attitude to things and money and people. He's incapable of deep relationships. Loyalty, yes. But fundamentally he's very, very detached. I hope Simon rather likes me, but I have no illusions about the amount of time he'd like to spend with me, or anyone else. I realised this very early on.

Simon made no bones about being 'a very selfish man'. Like Captain Detterling in *Bring Forth the Body*, he was driven by

> something inside myself .... a kind of rock-hard egotism that dictates, always and everywhere, *Detterling first*; Detterling before honour, before service, before friends, before love, before truth; Detterling before his regiment – before his sovereign, his country or his God.

And yet he was also the best of companions, as a fresh muster of impressionable young men were discovering. These were Myles's colleagues, whose average age had dropped considerably following the departure of Frank Turner. Typical of them was Michael Strevens, who taught at Tormore for a year before going up to Cambridge and returned after taking his degree 'because it was such fun'. Strevens '*adored*' Simon, whom he described as a 'maturer'.

> I really think I learnt more of value from him than anybody. He was certainly a far greater influence on me than any don. He introduced me to Trollope, turned me into a gossip and even affected the way I spoke.

This maturing process took place every evening in the Admiral Keppel. Simon would arrive there 'hot for gossip' after dinner at the Royal Hotel,

[5] 'A sneaking fondness for baked beans on toast at tea-time' was one of the reasons Simon gave for his not being upper-class.

and stay until closing time. Michael Webb, another Tormore master, was struck by Simon's 'generosity of spirit' on these occasions.

> He would make a point of putting newcomers at their ease, and would continue to be agreeable to them even after it became apparent that they didn't fit in. And another thing: he was very kind towards one of the non-Tormore regulars called Alf Taylor. Alf owned the corner shop near the pub. He was not an educated man[6] but he loved books and had a point of view. Simon lent him books and never condescended to him. He also took Alf away on holiday to give him a break from nursing his wife when she was dying of cancer. I remember when Alf himself died Simon was very upset.

When, as sometimes happened, Simon dined at the Royal with friends of his from London like Anthony Blond or Joe Ackerley, or with old Army chums like Oscar Whitamore, he would expect them to come to the Keppel afterwards. This was a real eye-opener for Diana Baring, one of the few women he ever brought along.

> I was used to seeing Simon in quite glamorous demi-mondaine circumstances, like the party Anthony Blond gave for Burgo Partridge when Burgo got married. I remember all the men kissed each other, which for someone of my respectable, middle-class background was thrilling in a spine-tingling sort of way. And now here he was in perfect harmony with his brother, who drank pint after pint of beer, wore baggy, shapeless clothes and had scurf all over his collar.

Simon's evenings at the Keppel gave him two hours of absorbing yet undemanding intimacy, during which he would add between three and five large brandies and soda to what he had already drunk, namely, a large campari and soda, most of a bottle of wine and a large liqueur brandy. Nor did it end here. For before he went to bed he would pour himself more brandy and soda, or switch to 'strong beer', and sit for an hour or two cogitating. Most of what ran through his mind was dross, but more often than not he would hit upon two or three phrases or reveries which stood the test of 'sober consideration' the following morning.

Sober consideration? Up to a point, Lord Copper. Simon believed that if writers were too clearheaded when they sat down to work their conceit went into overdrive and bulldozed aside their critical facilities. Much better to be a bit 'fuzzy' first thing, since this would promote the humility with which every artist ought to approach his task. If the right words eluded him he would simply put down whatever came into his head. Should this fail to summon the Muse he would open a volume of, e.g.,

[6] He is described by Rayner Heppenstall in his *Journals* as 'an intellectual tradesman'.

Horace or Homer, and translate out loud from the original as if he were back at school. That always did the trick.

*

In an article on European casinos written at about this time Simon reserved his highest praise for the one at Monte Carlo. Within its *Salles Privées* there still survived an air

> … of leisure, of stable currencies, of proper authority in the proper hands; even, although one is in Monaco, of long, untroubled days of cricket and soldiers in scarlet walking with housemaids in the park.

Simon had a passion for the Edwardian era and thought Grandfather Raven had shown 'great good sense' in dying when he did (January 1914). But the key clause in that passage is 'proper authority in the proper hands'. Until the Great War authority had rested with gentlemen, or, at the very least, with those who were guided by the gentleman's code. But as Simon acknowledged in his social history, *The English Gentleman*,

> Certain inevitable and on the whole desirable social developments have now rendered the gentleman a superfluous nuisance.

So what price authority now? Simon's answer, inspired by 'the gentlemanly warfare' he had conducted with dons like Patrick Wilkinson and John Raven, was the development of some form of authority between equals. But this must spring from reciprocal goodwill and mutual respect, and the greater of these was respect.

> But in the world at large there is no respect. Or rather, there is so much respect, since anything or anybody at all must now be accorded it, that the word is made meaningless. The most trivial platitudes, the most misleading and sentimental half-truths, the merest nonsense – all must be received with 'respect', lest feelings be hurt and 'justifiable resentment' aroused …. But one thing you may not respect. Excellence or merit. Because if you respect this, you stand to allow that someone is better than someone else, and that, by current reckoning, is to destroy respect.

I have dwelt on this for two reasons. First, because Simon was ahead of his time in recognising how great a problem was posed by the exercise of authority in an egalitarian society. We are no nearer to solving it now than in 1961. And secondly, because a great deal of what Simon wrote thereafter, including his novels, was in defence of excellence and merit, a very unfashionable cause to espouse in the Sixties and Seventies.

At Cambridge, I was told, Simon would put all his worst cards on the table, which allowed him to get away with just about anything: 'What can you expect from someone like me?' He employs the same technique in *The English Gentleman*, which begins with the bald statement that he is neither a gentleman nor, for that matter, a member of the upper class, 'a very different thing'. To prove his point Simon recounts various discreditable episodes from his past, including his carefully planned seduction of Alexis and how it came to grief.

> But then, for the first time since my revelation the previous summer, I made a mistake. I looked at him with a look of lust. I could not keep it out of my eyes. That this, which I had coveted for so long, should now be mine ... *mine*. But on the instant the thought came, it ceased to be true. For Alexis had seen that look .... 'No. No,' he said in a bleak, strained voice. 'I see it all now.' Miserable and ashamed, he began to pull on his clothes. 'I can't ... won't ... How could you have done this?'
>
> 'I only wanted – '
>
> ' – You wanted your way with me and you nearly cheated me into letting you have it.' And then, head hanging and eyes sorrowing, he left me.

Malcolm Muggeridge was unimpressed by this fable. '[I]n comparable heterosexual circumstances I should have been decidedly annoyed,' he wrote in the *New Statesman*. But generally speaking reviewers reacted as Simon would have wished, deploring his character while applauding his style. 'However little else Mr Raven may have in common with the angels,' said Peregrine Worsthorne in the *Sunday Telegraph*, 'he certainly writes like one.' Even Simon's old adversary, B.A. Young, weighed in with some tempered praise:

> Simon Raven can write as well as almost anyone living, and it is both our loss and his that he squanders his ability on those tiresome novels.

Most effusive of all was the *Observer*'s heavyweight, Sir Harold Nicolson.

> [This book] is an incisive attack on false values and a penetrating analysis of vulgarity. It is a manual of good manners and amusing to read. Mr Raven is a very clever young man.

Clever enough, decided the BBC, to take part in a radio discussion about

English society with Richard Hoggart and Lord Hailsham. There is no transcript of this in the BBC archives, but what happened beforehand, as told by Hoggart in *An Imagined Life*,[7] will serve to draw a line under *The English Gentleman*.

> The minister arrived, tossed his bowler hat on to a window-ledge, declared, 'I need a pee,' and was led out. Simon Raven picked up the hat, turned it over and announced: 'Thought so. Not from Lock. Cheapskate.'

*

In September 1961, just before the beginning of the Autumn term at Tormore, Esther spent a few days down at Deal with Simon and Myles. She had been suffering from varicose veins and had bandages on both legs, but the visit went off pretty well except for a small tiff with Myles over a cheque. Simon did, however, notice how much more than usual she was eating. 'Normally Mama just picked at her food. Why, one asked oneself, is she shovelling it away as if there were no tomorrow? But then she left and I thought no more of it.'

On the train back to Norfolk Esther cut her finger badly on the bolt of the lavatory door. It turned septic, so she went to have it cleaned and dressed at King's Lynn hospital. When she returned to Hunstanton she complained of a terrible headache to Mrs Bradfield, her cleaning lady, and said she was going upstairs to take an aspirin and lie down. Mrs Bradfield decided to leave without disturbing her, and it was not until tea-time, when Robin arrived home from working in Cambridge, that she was discovered curled up on the bed having suffered a massive stroke.

Myles borrowed a car from another master and he and Simon drove up to Norfolk the following day. They took their time, having ascertained that Esther would almost certainly never regain consciousness. 'She died at about one o'clock, just as Myles and I were sitting down to lunch in Essex with Dickie and Patricia Muir. My father was playing golf. He was not one for deathbed vigils either.'

Esther's Catholicism had all but withered away and her priest did not object to the family's wish that she be buried nearby in the grounds of Old Hunstanton parish church. But instead of moping about at home Simon and Myles made the mistake of visiting the local pub. 'For some reason this was considered disrespectful, although given how much my mother drank I could see no harm in it at all.'

The regulars would have been even more shocked had they known that Simon once clouted his mother, one of the few acts for which he expressed

[7] Chatto & Windus, 1992

genuine, well-attested remorse. Fielding Gray is guilty of the same offence, in circumstances which Simon allowed were 'very comparable'.

'My mother had the ability to goad people until they did or said something so unforgivable they were overwhelmed by guilt and could not wait to make it up. What would happen was that all would go well for the first few days of one's visit, and then as the time to leave grew nearer, one could almost hear the cogs revolving in her mind. "Well, they think they've done their duty by me. They won't be back for some time. Let me see .... Ah." And you go away feeling so guilty you're back much sooner than you would have been. A very disagreeable technique.'

And yet, said Simon, he did admire her 'enormously'. And fancied her too – 'though I didn't realise this at the time. She was *hugely* attractive. She remained attractive to my father long after any love had ceased between them. The trouble was that life went sour on her once she'd turned 40, as indeed it did for my father. But she at least had achieved something and I think it made her all the more miserable afterwards. She wasn't a woman of much cultivation and once we had all grown up there was nothing to occupy her. So perhaps it was a good thing that she died when she did.'

CHAPTER FIFTEEN

> Happiness is only to be had from deliberate achievement – from clearing one's own patch of jungle ... and achieving good order within it.
>
> Simon Raven, *Spectator* 9.5.69

At King's and in the Army Simon had always thought of himself as a Cavalier, guilty conscience notwithstanding. But as he made his way in the literary world he began to see that there was something to be said for the Roundheads after all. He now knew, for instance,

> that to be an artist in any medium requires more than a taste for the trappings and some unspecified 'talent', it requires moral determination and gruelling hard work. (*London Magazine*, November 1965)

The writer who in Simon's view exemplified these qualities was Conrad. And who put him on to Conrad? His old enemy, Dr Leavis, whose *The Great Tradition* he read, 'to my enormous benefit', a year or so after settling in Deal.

'Duty. This was Leavis's yardstick, as indeed it was Conrad's, which is why Leavis had such a good opinion of him. "What do we live by?" asked Conrad. "What *ought* we to do?" My first duty as a writer would always be to myself. But if I wanted to eat I must fulfil my duty to the reader as well, by turning a sound tale in good English and also trying to point up a few morals. Because by now I realised that however assiduously one might avoid things like duty oneself, it was important that someone should attend to them.'

Which brings us to *Close of Play*, Simon's fourth novel. This is the sad story of Hugo Warren, a callous young delinquent, and Baron's Lodge, the prep school he ruins in pursuit of 'the good life'. Hugo wants to be 'free' – free of anybody and anything with a claim on him. To this end he will commit virtually any crime without feeling the slightest remorse. Hired by a gentlemanly impresario of gambling and vice, he first seduces his boss's wife, then double-crosses both of them and finally murders the girl who tries to blackmail him. But what seals Hugo's fate is his betrayal of James Escome, the elderly Headmaster of Baron's Lodge who is also his guardian. As his old Cambridge Tutor points out,

'Your trouble,' said Harold, 'is that you're a second rate man with certain minor capacities which you're too proud to settle for .... You could have been a good schoolmaster, in a modest way, and a great help to James. Even now, you could give him a lot of happiness. But no, not you. You're too grand, too greedy, for such simple things ....'

Simon based Baron's Lodge on Tormore, which would have been fine had he not included some barbed asides about, e.g., patronising parents, rancorous tradespeople and spiteful bank managers – 'They're often just bitter little men bored with their safe jobs and plain wives and resentful of their social position.' Angry mutterings were heard in local Rotary circles and Simon was 'delicately' requested to stay away from the next Fathers' cricket match lest he meet a parent who was convinced ('wrongly') that he had been caricatured.

Close of Play also confirmed Simon's reputation for sexual indelicacy, a nice touch being the vulture-proof diaphragm which Hugo overlooks when he dumps his girlfriend's body in the desert near Sodom. Several reviewers commented on this, and I dare say it also caught the eye of Peter Porter, to judge from the poem about Simon he wrote soon afterwards.

'The World of Simon Raven'

Rooks are raging where great elms were felled,
Family silver's been lent for the Fete,
Nanny's facing Nigel with stained sheets,
Telegrams announce James is expelled,
Mrs Diamond from Sea View Estate
Tempts a team in training with boiled sweets.

Meanwhile sturgeon from Odessa packed
For Black's and Tan's, renowned St James's Clubs,
Laced with spanish fly, cause randy scenes
At Ascot, a Bishop's face is smacked;
Debs and guardsmen break up Chelsea pubs,
Blackmailers send snaps to dons at Queen's.

Unpaid Mess Bills get a Blue cashiered,
Boys from Balham pelt a First in Greats
With Latin Grammars, Israeli agents
Put pubic lice in Prince Muhammad's beard,
Doctor Boyce cuts off cousin Kate's
Clitoris – the favourite fails the fence.

Bookies' reminders frighten Adjutants,
Crockford's man is found with a marked deck.

Somewhere beyond Maidenhead an old
Lady rings her bank for an advance
On her pension, sends her son a cheque,
Watches with the cat as it gets cold.[1]

Simon finished *Close of Play* in June 1962. Two months later he was one of 70 delegates[2] to the Edinburgh Festival's highly-publicised International Writers' Conference. This had been organised by the avant-garde publisher, John Calder, who hoped it would advance the Anti-Censorship cause. Simon was opposed to Censorship because, he said, 'sex was (a) fun and (b) funny, so where was the harm in that?' But he parted company with everyone else over Commitment, another of the topics for debate. As John Calder recalled,

> He was the only one to raise the subject of *Money*, saying he wrote, not to further a world view or a commitment, but primarily for money. He felt the others were too coy on the subject.

This was not affectation on Simon's part. Compared with most of the other speakers he was very hard-up, harder-up than ever, in fact, following another disastrous evening's gaming.

> Simon was due to go off on a jaunt and had drawn 'funds' as he would put it [recalled Desmond Briggs].[3] The phone rang and I knew immediately that something was wrong because he sounded so flustered. 'I've been a very naughty boy, dear. I went to Aspers last night and lost a packet. You must mortify me how you will, but please let me have £100 to send to Aspinall today. It's a debt of honour, dear.' So I gave him the money and docked his stipend by £2 10s a week, which pleased him no end because he *loves* being punished!

Calamities like this reminded Simon how dependent he was on the goodwill of his publisher. Given that he would remain so for the foreseeable future, he decided to try and cement their relationship with a proposal for ten sequential novels, which would ensure 'guaranteed money and guaranteed love' for the next decade and more. But security was not the only consideration.

'I had a big canvas in mind, which it would take several books to fill. I wanted to look at the upper-middle-class scene since the war, and in

[1] Porter met Simon for the first time many years later: 'He looked at me quizzically but made no reference to the poem .... To my surprise he was affable. I'd imagined I would hardly be the sort of person he'd care for.'

[2] They included Norman Mailer and Lawrence Durrell, both of whom reminded Simon of 'fairground "punchies" '.

[3] Anthony Blond's partner and Simon's editor.

particular my generation's part in it. We had spent our early years as privileged members of a privileged class. How were we faring in the Age of the Common Man? How *ought* we to be faring? Some of us believed in duty, others in power, others were simply out for what they could get. Would the high-minded lot stoop to conquer? This was obviously going to be an important question. And what about their unscrupulous confreres? No Queensberry rules for them, so they had a flying start. But Fate has a way of bitching things up just when you least expect it. Here was another theme. The malice of time, chance and the rest of the human race.'

It was not Shakespeare but the American novelist Herman Wouk who gave Simon his overall title, *Alms for Oblivion*. 'It's the title of a novel written by the hero of *Youngblood Hawke*, Wouk's novel about a novelist. What a good title, I remember thinking. Resonant. Lapidary. At the same time modest. Because I firmly believe that very little that is written now, not least my own work, will survive, therefore "alms for oblivion". On the other hand one would hope to be read for as long as one lives, and this is more likely to happen if you write a series than a succession of one-offs, however brilliant.'

Blond was enthusiastic, sensing perhaps that in Simon he might have a potent challenger to Anthony Powell and C.P. Snow. He said he would commission the whole series and pay Simon £500 per volume on delivery (later doubled to £1,000). Blond also saw to it that when Panther Books bought the paperback rights there was a 'gentlemen's understanding (subsequently repudiated by Harper-Collins) that they would keep the series in print *sine die*, *sine anno* and, indeed, *sine saeculo*'. It only remained for Simon to go away and write volume one, which is where his troubles began.

'It was never my intention to write one long saga, like Powell's *Music of Time*, but ten independent stories with common characters and a common theme. In short, a roman-fleuve. I wanted to start in 1945, when several of these chaps were still at school, and carry on from there. I knew it would be hard to strike a balance between introducing one's characters and making the novel work on its own, but after two or three drafts had been torn up I thought I'd pulled it off.'

But Blond had changed his mind – not about the series, but about *Fielding Gray* (as the first book was called). 'He said, "I'm sick of all your fucking schools. Go and write a novel about London," meaning people like Dickie Muir who'd caught his fancy. So I said, "All right, provided you pay me for this one first," which he did. But it wasn't an auspicious start.'

Simon was soon reconciled to moving backwards and forwards in time. He thought people would be intrigued to read about someone as an adult and then read about them as a child. 'But in the end Panther wouldn't have it. They said it's got to start in 1945 with *Fielding Gray* and go on from there in the correct chronological order. This led to enormous confusion with the lists of characters when a uniform edition was published in hardback. The lists were meant as an aide-memoire, because with such a large cast you can't expect people to remember who's who. But instead of redrafting them to take account of the new order, Blond simply reproduced the old lists which were now all out of sync. So someone picking up *Fielding Gray*, volume 4 in the original sequence, had to wade through long lists of characters who belonged to subsequent volumes.'

This lack of attention to detail was typical of Blond's set-up, said Simon. 'They were all too grand to do the nitty-gritty, the corporal's job.' Not that he ever considered going elsewhere, even when he was no longer in Blond's debt. 'I detest change. In my experience it is never for the better. And leaving Blond would have meant leaving Desmond [Briggs] as well, which would have been very unwise. Desmond was, and is, the best of editors. He knows just how far one can go – not *quite* as far as I'd have wished in some instances, but like the umpire, his decision is final. He's the only person to whom I've ever dedicated a book [*The Troubadour*].'[4]

*

In January 1963 the trendy men's monthly, *Town*, invited a dozen writers in the public eye, among them Simon, to play a variant on the truth game called the Brain Game. Each player was given a profile of the human head, with the brain divided into vague phrenological bumps which they had to fill 'more or less honestly' with their thoughts. Unlike some of the others Simon entered into the spirit of the thing. His head provides a pretty accurate guide to his preoccupations, some of which I will consider here.

'Teeth, Death, Hair': Simon associated mortality with his teeth, which never really recovered from a long period of neglect in the Fifties. But he was always vain of his hair – 'my most distinguishing feature' – which retained its wavy profusion, if not its youthful auburn colouring, into late middle age.

'Legs': After *Soixante-neuf* was rejected as too lewd, Simon substituted Legs, in which, unlike the Psalmist, he delighted. But they had to be 'agreeably proportioned' and not too hairy. 'How was it?' Peter Dixon once asked Simon. 'No good. Legs like a spider's.'

'Bath': Simon rated Cleanliness far above Godliness, which was probably just as well given that he sweated profusely and was subject to bouts of chronic diarrhoea (the ulcer). But his bath, which he took every evening between six and seven, was also symbolic in that it separated work from play. Afterwards he would slap on plenty of cologne and 'dress for dinner', donning clean underclothes and a clean (usually cream) shirt, the collar of which he invariably undid without removing his tie.

'Brandy': Be it cognac, calvados, armagnac or, best of all, marc, Simon could not do without brandy, which he went on drinking ad lib long after friends of his like Dickie Muir had called it a day. His excuse was that it promoted peace of mind and helped to jolt a tired imagination, but a friend

[4] For his part Briggs represented Simon as 'Matthew Taper' in his *roman à clef*, *The Partners*, Secker 1982.

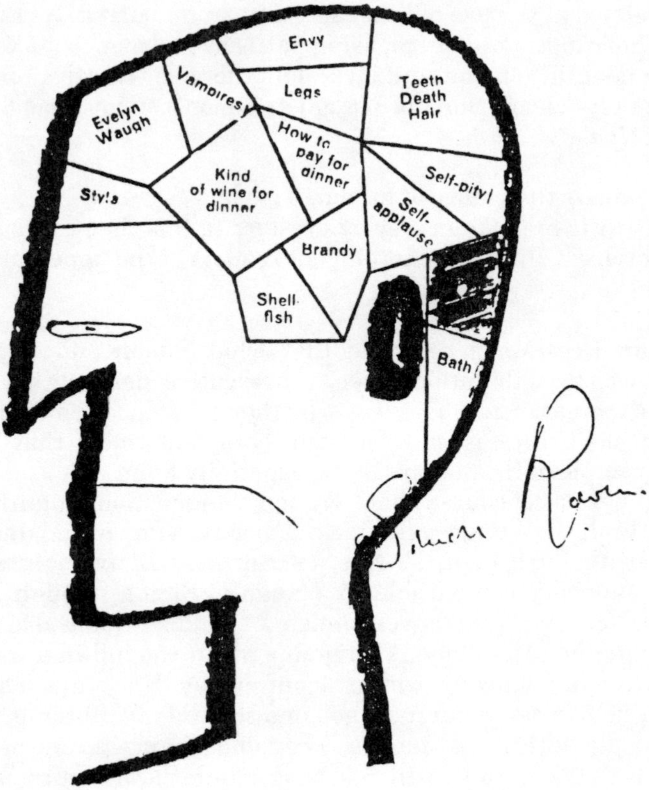

thought it had more to do with cutting a dash. 'To have given up brandy would have looked mean, the last thing Simon wanted. I remember him saying to me when he was in dire straits, "Well, dear, I'm going to be hellish mean. I'm not going to take anyone out to dinner." And I said, "What about you? Are you going to go on taking yourself out to dinner?" And he said, "Oh yes, dear. I'm not going to be *miserly*." '

'Evelyn Waugh': A big topic. Like many of Waugh's admirers Simon drew a sharp distinction between Waugh the literary stylist – 'there never was a more spare and elegant writer' – and Waugh the man – 'a knotted-up number, with knobs on'. As an old soldier he saluted Waugh's firm grasp, in his *War Trilogy*, of military custom and practice. 'And as you'd expect, he's particularly good on Class: the contrast between the middle-class, but absolutely reliable marines, and the amusing, but candidly rather shitty cavalrymen and guardsmen, is immaculately done.' But Simon could not resist adding that while he and Waugh were both unfitted for command in the field, 'I at least was never in any danger of being shot by my own men.'

Waugh said he regarded writing 'not as investigation of character, but as an exercise in the use of language.' Simon concurred. As Fielding Gray puts it: 'I arrange words in pleasing patterns in order to make money ... I try to be neat, intelligent and lucid: let others be "creative" or "inspired".' There are also clear echoes of Waugh in Simon's submission to *Contemporary Novelists*.

> My theme is the vanity of human wishes.
> My object is to make money by presenting this theme in such a way as to interest and amuse intelligent readers of the upper and middle-classes.

William Rees-Mogg reckoned that what Simon and Waugh had in common was a combination of very conservative views with a very unconservative temperament. This was why they so often failed to practise what they preached. Interestingly enough, both had voices that belied their choleric complexions, Simon's being especially light.

Simon did not of course share Waugh's unquestioning faith; it amused him to think of Waugh genuflecting before 'simpering Madonnas and semi-literate Irish priests'. Nor, as Anthony Blond pointed out, was Simon's snobbery comparable to Waugh's. 'Simon, though he wouldn't thank me for saying so, is very much a "middle-middle-class" snob. The sort of thing he can't abide is quibbling about the bill in a restaurant, or indeed any kind of awkwardness about money. He thinks it's bad behaviour. But he has never pursued, as I and some of my contemporaries have, grand people with grand names. They don't impress him at all. I know there are a few coronets in his books, but they're pure fantasy, like Wodehouse's Lord Emsworth.'

'Pure fantasy.' Blond himself connived at this when he initialled the blurb for Simon's next book, his miscellany *Boys will be Boys*, prompting one reviewer to label it the most inaccurate he had ever read. But despite the inaccuracies I doubt whether many readers felt short-changed. Because the chief interest of *Boys* lay not in the pieces themselves, however worth reprinting, but in the linking commentary and the light it shed on Simon, 'one of the most puzzling and ambivalent novelists at work today', according to George Melly in the *Sunday Times*.

Simon used to complain that because writers didn't go to an office every day, even educated persons thought they lived the life of Riley. In *Boys* he set out to refute this by describing his 'trials and machinations' since commencing man of letters five years before. To little avail. For it was clear that despite the debts and the drudgery, his was a cosy, self-indulgent, egocentric existence from which all distractions, including Adam, had been ruthlessly excluded.

> All in all, then, I am left with a pattern of life which, to a writer of my moderate aspirations, is ideal, in that it makes of me a contented

and private man, and lends me the peace and freedom necessary to the use of such talents as I possess.

So determined was Simon to impose his own agenda that for several years after settling in Deal he chose not to be on the phone ('The telephone dispenses irrelevance like a tap that won't turn off; it is also a dangerous instrument of interference and even of persecution'). Not only did he lose work by this, he also distanced himself from some of his London friends, among them Burgo Partridge.

'Burgo's trouble was that he had no esprit of his own. He relied on other people's to enliven him just as a lizard needs the sun. I think he did miss me, but it's not fair to say, as I believe his mother did, that I deserted him. He came down quite often to begin with, but stopped after he married Henrietta [Garnett]. Then he suddenly turned up a week or two before Henrietta had a baby. He got very drunk and cleaned up at chemin de fer, much to everybody's fury, because Burgo had money and most of us didn't. But the visit was a definite success.'

At one point, said Simon, Burgo had given an account of how he now spent his days. 'He said, "I really can't be bothered with writing, which I don't have to do anyway. So I usually lunch well, with a couple of gins beforehand, and then I either go home to sleep it off or spend the afternoon at a drinking club. In the evening I go out to dinner and drink a whole lot more, so that by the time I go to bed I'm absolutely pissed – so pissed, that when I wake up and want a pee I sometimes mistake one of Henrietta's cupboards for the loo and end up peeing all over her dresses."

'And I thought, "Well, you've gone a long way downhill in the past two years. God knows, you liked your food and drink then, but you didn't have two enormous meals a day, and you didn't get so drunk you couldn't find your way to the loo." I don't know why he became like this. He was happily married. Looking forward to becoming a father. I don't think he had any premonitions of death, which he did not, in any case, fear. He used to point out, very rationally, that it is an infallible prescription for happiness – or at least against unhappiness. He wasn't on the other hand suicidal: no question of breaking the rules. He was going to stay there until something hit him and very soon afterwards something did. He was talking to Blond's ex-wife Charlotte on the telephone when he had a heart-attack, and there was an end of Burgo.'

*

By November 1963, when *Boys* was published, Simon was so busy that he could take on nothing more, not even a short essay for his old comrade-in-arms, Oscar Whitamore. Oscar, now in the Parachute Regiment, was required to write 3,000 words on ' "Motivation in War", or some such subject.' Recalling what Simon had done for Rodney Haszard he proffered a bribe, which Simon turned down:

> Sorry, dear. No essay, not even for cash down. I've got one and a half plays to write by Jan 1, not to mention the novel and the usual assortment of reviews.

But Oscar persisted.

> Once [and] for all, I haven't time to write this letter, let alone an essay. Surely your journeys will excuse you; if not, say you are *ill*.

Oscar made one last appeal.

> Your offer is generous, and £50 is always handy, but I must point out, for the *last* time, that I am more in need of *time* than *money* ....

The novel Simon was writing was *The Rich Pay Late*, which with its successor, *Friends in Low Places*, provided the metropolitan basis for *Alms* that Anthony Blond required. Blond was probably right to insist on this, because it plunged readers into the world Simon had set out to explore, a world he both despised and adored.

Simon's ambivalence stemmed from his belief that the last thing the country needed was to become more dynamic, as so many of his contemporaries seemed to think. Instead, it ought to model itself on 18th-century Venice, 'carrying on in the same old way, while the rest of the world wore itself out in pursuit of the latest fads'. Reviewing Anthony Sampson's *Anatomy of Britain* he argued that although the institutions valued by most educated Englishmen were those designed to run the Empire we no longer possessed, 'the values which they promote, however limited in their scope, are morally and aesthetically far superior to anything which the new world of admass tastes and applied science can show ....'

> What it amounts to, then, is that the cure Mr Sampson proposes (more and more technical efficiency, professionalism at all levels, smart sales talk for our products) is far worse than the disease he diagnoses (complacency, nepotism, charm, the amateur spirit). But, says Mr Sampson resolutely, if we don't take the cure we shall die, i.e. we shall go broke. Myself, I am beginning to think this might be a very good thing, if only because it would mean an end of those hatchet-faced middlemen guzzling up smoked salmon in Quaglino's. What is wanted is less industry and more Horace, who points out that the surest way of being happy is to make the best of what you've got. All this talk of production and competition has gone on so long and so loudly that people have forgotten what they're competing for. The

answer is six feet of earth, and that pretty quickly; once you get that into your head, it is clear that Latin verses are every bit as relevant – or irrelevant – as money-grubbing or Sputniks, and make far less noise and smell. (*Listener*, 12.7.62)

In *The Rich Pay Late* these two schools of thought confront each other at a midsummer ball given by Donald Salinger, one of Simon's protagonists. Donald, a rich, risible booby, is trying to impress two antithetical groups of guests: the unregenerate friends of his youth, and his new 'country' acquaintances – actually city slickers whose farms are run as a tax dodge. Salvoes of increasingly derisive dialogue range back and forth across the marquee:

'... Hard money earned the hard way, I don't mind telling you. There's fifty thou, I said to Harry, fifty thou says you're on to a good thing, provided ....'

'... So there *she* was, waiting outside like someone in the corridor of a train, and at last out comes John Dorsetshire looking *green* ....'

'... A six-figure contract from the marketing board ....'

'... Pulled himself together and said, "I'm exceedingly sorry, Ma'am, but I've just been inspecting your accommodation and I fear that through some oversight it is in a deleterious condition. If you will kindly follow me ...." '

'... Irresponsible rubbish ....'

'... Cost the Warden his knighthood ....'

'... Degenerate, I'd say, all of them. Talking like that about the Royal Family. Degenerate parasites.'

'Nasty, loud-mouthed, money-grubbing toads.'

Like most of Simon's protagonists Donald Salinger is partly based on a friend, in this case Dickie Muir. 'Dickie and I never discussed his work: he was a holiday chum. But I remember that at Cambridge he used to get cross because no one would take business or commerce seriously. Whenever the subject arose – not very often – someone would make a joke, and Dickie would depart, muttering. Donald is also inclined to be snobbish, like Dickie, and at times ridiculously vain. If Dickie hired a yacht he would dress up like an Admiral and expect everyone to salute him!'

But, said Simon, Donald became less and less like Dickie as the sequence wore on. This was also true of the other characters and the people they were based on. 'I don't wish to sound pretentious, but they did begin to establish themselves in their own terms. So Gregory Stern, the publisher, who started out as a fairly recognisable version of Anthony Blond, in the end became a totally different figure. A rather noble figure, in a way, which Blond could never have become.[5] Or there was Peter Morrison, the

[5] He is eventually crucified by Levantine terrorists.

MP. When he's at school he's pretty much like James Prior was: the responsible monitor saying, "Look, if you go to bed with that boy it'll all end in tears, and we don't want that, do we?" But after a bit he diverged totally and became far more cynical than James ever was, far more calculating than James ever was, in a way far more urbane. I think James still thinks of himself as a farmer, and although Peter Morrison comes from a farm he was never a farmer.'

The other schoolfriend of Simon's to land a leading role was William Rees-Mogg, prototype of Somerset Lloyd-James, the devious Papist whose machinations run like a thread through the whole sequence. When I asked Lord Rees-Mogg about this he said he was 'flattered' that Simon should have deemed him worthy of recapsulation, 'although I think he makes me out nastier than I am. On the other hand he did remind me of one or two disagreeable things about myself I'd either forgotten, or may not even have been aware of – how greedy I was as a schoolboy, for instance. In those days a Mars bar was something that really mattered to me. He's also correct to say that I was ill a lot of the time, and looked very seedy.'

Exactly when people recognised themselves in *Alms* I cannot say, but Simon reckoned that with the exception of Hugh Thomas, 'who did complain a bit', everyone was too young and too busy to catch on to themselves while they still resembled themselves, and by the time they got older and more self-important the resemblance had passed. Anthony Blond takes up the story:

> In *The Rich Pay Late* there's a rackety young Welsh journalist called Tom Llewyllyn who gets very drunk and consorts with tarts. He's actually the most attractive character in the book, but Hugh Thomas wasn't impressed. So we sat down to talk about this and after the third bottle of hock Hugh said, 'Look, I won't sue, provided Tom Llewyllyn has a better time of it,' which he does: he writes a best-seller, makes a good marriage and becomes head of his old college. He doesn't get a peerage, like Hugh, only a knighthood. Still, amends had been made.

Perhaps. But Simon had the last word when he arranged for Tom Llewyllyn to defend Fielding Gray against charges of misrepresentation brought by a third character, Daniel Mond, whom Fielding has put in a novel:

> 'Novelists,' said Tom, 'are cannibals. Worse: they eat you *alive* for their nourishment. It's not surprising if odd things happen while they digest you.' (*The Survivors*)

Which brings us to Fielding Gray himself, the oddest specimen of all to be passed by Simon. His surname is a give-away, but I am reminded less of Oscar Wilde's novel than of Randolph Churchill as recalled by Alan Brien.

> The first time I met him he was standing under the De Lazlo portrait of himself as a golden boy. The contrast was startling – as if Dorian Gray had changed places with his picture for one day of the year. 'Yes,' he said good humouredly, 'it is hard to believe that was me, isn't it? I was a *joli garçon* in those days.'

Simon creates a similar sort of tableau when he introduces Fielding in *Friends in Low Places*.

> Fielding Gray had been, when Somerset last saw him, a lithe and beautiful boy of seventeen. From Peter Morrison's description, given four years back, Somerset gathered that he had thickened somewhat, and that drink was already beginning to show in his cheeks, but that he still retained poise and even distinction. As indeed he did now .... The only trouble was his face. It was impossible to tell now whether Peter had been right or wrong about the burst veins in the cheeks, because the cheeks, like everything else except a thin, twisted line of mouth and one red, bald, tiny eye, were coated with a mottled surface of shining pink like icing clumsily spread over a cake.

Fielding, it transpires, was wounded while serving with the Army in Cyprus. Since this happened during a truce he is a bitter man, the more so because soldiering was not his first choice of career. He wanted to become a don, 'a witty, worldly, comfortable don', and would doubtless have done so had not 'a squalid misunderstanding' robbed him of his scholarship to Lancaster College, Cambridge. This squalid misunderstanding is the subject of *Fielding Gray*, the most autobiographical novel in the sequence, and in Simon's opinion the best.

Fielding Gray opens with the thanksgiving service in chapel for victory in Europe and ends a few months later with Fielding's removal from school and his rejection by Lancaster. His crime is betrayal. His victim, Christopher Roland, a handsome but not overbright boy in the mould of Alexis. Christopher's greatest attraction for Fielding is his innocence; once he loses this, which he does in a hay-loft on the last day of term, he becomes just another appetising bundle of flesh, good for a gobble but in other respects superfluous. Christopher senses this and is destroyed by it. Hungry for love, however debased, he is arrested for soliciting outside an Army camp near his home. The next thing we know he has hanged himself.

No such tragedies attended Simon's fall from grace. But there is an echo here of an incident recorded by Robert Graves in *Goodbye to All That*. While at Charterhouse Graves had fallen chastely in love with 'Dick', a much younger boy. Despite rumours to the contrary Graves, by now serving on the Western Front, believed that Dick was pure in thought, word and deed. Then, to his horror, he learnt that his loved one had propositioned a Canadian soldier, who had reported him to the police.

> This news was nearly the end of me .... Well, with so much slaughter about, it would be easy to think of him as dead.

Simon supposed he might have borrowed from Graves, 'but whether consciously or unconsciously I couldn't say now. Too long ago.' But Fielding the character was all his own work, a portrait of the artist.

> 'I don't need you to tell me, Jules [said Fielding]. All my friends have the same [theory] ... that early frustrations and traumas have warped my nature, left me in a permanent state of retarded adolescence, and rendered me incapable of any kind of love higher than promiscuous and juvenile sexuality ....'
>
> 'Cut away the jargon, and what it comes down to is, you're just a shit. That's my theory, Fielding. Never mind early frustrations and the rest; we all had them to contend with. You're simply an old-fashioned shit who'll ride rough-shod over anything or anybody to get what he wants ... and who dissolves into floods of self-pity on the rare occasions when he doesn't get it.'

Not very flattering. – 'Agreed. Fielding Gray is a mess, but not a wholly unattractive mess, I hope. And he does manage to produce good writing. We don't say a great deal about this but it is apparent that every now and again people read what Fielding Gray writes and he gets paid a lot of money for it. Also he gets a certain amount of critical esteem. Wishful thinking, perhaps, like some of his sexual escapades, but this is as I would like things to be.'

Three other characters deserve a mention, beginning with Captain Detterling, whose preference for chaps with shit in their tanks has already been noted. Detterling (we never learn his christian name) is based on a number of Simon's friends, of indeterminate age, 'who go around making that sort of remark'. Detterling's kinsman, Lord Canteloupe, is a grandee whose feudal manner and 18th-century appetites march with a genius for entertaining the mob, who flock to his stately home. He is a great tease.

> 'Of course people can be frightening,' Canteloupe said, 'if you let them get out of hand. It's happening everywhere: students, coons, labourers, all getting out of hand because no one dares to *tell* them and put them in their place.' (*The Judas Boy*)

Finally, Angela Tuck, the only woman to share equal billing with the men. She is well equipped for this, being one of those jolly super sorts who can flay the hide off a golf ball and play off scratch in bed. 'Why can't a woman be more like a man?' Simon persisted in asking. Mrs Tuck, I think, is what he had in mind.

Simon was deeply attached to his characters and would hold conversations with them at opportune moments – 'on long drives when one's struggling to keep awake, or in the evening over a nightcap. Sometimes they say things which one can use later.' But having, as he hoped, engaged his reader's interest in these people, how best to retain it? Simon's answer was Conflict: 'You let your reader know what your characters want and then immediately give a number of sound reasons why they are unlikely to get it.'

Some of these reasons would be straightforward. 'A has a powerful rival, B has principles which get in his way, C thinks he's in love.' But although the reader must have some idea of what's in store, he must not be able to see too far ahead. 'There's nothing like a surprise, the nastier the better, to prop up drooping eyelids.'

Simon's speciality was 'concealed loose-ends – little bits left behind in the past which germinate when no one's looking.' A classic instance of this does for Somerset Lloyd-James, whose mysterious suicide is the subject of exhaustive investigation in *Bring Forth the Body*, the penultimate volume in the sequence. Only by turning back the clock twenty-seven years to his schooldays do his friends finally find what they're after, the overlooked skeleton in Somerset's cupboard which suddenly announced itself with such a terrible rattle that he slit his wrists rather than ever hear it again.

And how did the skeleton get there in the first place? Meanness on Somerset's part, 'so typical [says Detterling] that of course he didn't notice it: trying to pass off half a crown on the Boys' Maid for a job that always rated at five shillings'. Ah well, 'we are tied and bound by the chain of our sins' as another character says. Simon's laws were not Jehovah's, but the way of a transgressor could be just as hard.

*

Throughout the Sixties Simon wrote pithy articles for the *Spectator*, a recurring theme being his disdain for egalitarian dogma and, in particular, the progressive theories of education it spawned. Susan saw things differently. At one point, to Simon's horror, she had considered sending Adam to the local comprehensive, Holland Park. 'Mercifully' she relented and sent him to Bedales, 'by no means one's first choice, as you can imagine, but then the decision, quite correctly, was not mine'.

Simon did, however, pay Adam's fees at Bedales – 'they were still affordable in those days'. And now that his son was on the brink of adolescence he resolved to emulate Lord Chesterfield and offer him some good advice, hence the open 'Letter To My Son' he published in the *Spectator*. What Adam made of this (if indeed he read it) is anybody's guess, but Simon must have been gratified at the size and temper of the subsequent post-bag. Two of his suave injunctions were particularly resented:

> Sex outside marriage is an agreeable (if sometimes overrated) entertainment. If somebody fancies you and you return the compliment, then away to the hay-loft and the best of luck. I would go still further: do not, while you are still young and wholesome, neglect any tolerable opportunity which offers in this line (even if you don't feel particularly keen at the moment), or you may live to regret it too late. If I'd known then what I know now, I'd have been far less fastidious than I was (not very). This said, however, do take care lest your erotic interests preclude others more important, for this condition is as big a curse as marriage.

And:

> Religion. Church of England (if you really must). This is a quiet and decent superstition, as they go, offering a wide choice in decoration and no poisonous enthusiasms. (10.3.67)

A Bishop, a Free Church minister and the mother of a daughter 'whose virginity she wishes her to retain' were among those who registered a protest. Rather surprisingly Simon's colleague, Peter Fleming, followed up with a letter to his godson advocating chivalry, but then he may have been miffed at Simon's using *Strix*, his nom-de-plume, as the title of a business weekly that Somerset Lloyd-James suborns.

Fleming's brother Ian had a house near Deal at St Margaret's Bay, and although Simon never met him, he was fascinated by the 'gigantic genie this worldly and selfish clubman had conjured'. He was one of the reviewers to welcome *Casino Royale* – 'Ian Fleming makes his bow as a kind of supersonic John Buchan', but like everyone else could only gaze in wonderment as Bond went into orbit. So what did 007 have in his tanks? Simon gave his answer when reviewing John Pearson's *Life of Ian Fleming*.

> [Bond] is not a projection of wicked and snobbish fantasies (as the moralists have claimed), but a projection of what every spirited and normal man would like to be, particularly in a world which grows drabber and more circumscribed every day.... He is the embodiment, not of fantasy, but of sanity; he is *mens sana in corpore sano*. This, surely, is his appeal to the masses who are imprisoned by stale domestic custom, bored silly by monotonous work on worthless products in ugly surroundings, and daily lied to and frustrated by smug and flabby politicians in this sick and sorry world. (*Spectator*, 28.10.66)

Two years later Simon was hauled aboard the Bond bandwagon himself, being hired to doctor the script of *On Her Majesty's Secret Service* at a fee of '£5,000,000 a day' he told Oscar Whitamore. But no sooner had he arrived in Switzerland, where the film was being shot, than he nearly found himself on the next plane home.

'The first day I was there I was asked up to the set and invited to sit at the director, Peter Hunt's, table, a great privilege. Then one of the starlets, for whom read chorus girls, for whom in an earlier age read whores, plonked herself down beside me and said, "You're the new scriptwriter, aren't you?" And I said, "Well, I am doing the changes." Whereupon she started to scratch the inside of my thigh with her nails and said, "Will you write some nice lines for me?" And I said, "If you go on doing that I'll write all the lines in the world you want. But I don't think the director will allow you to speak them." At this point Peter Hunt, who'd been absent, reappeared. He did not like what he saw, a starlet at *his* table. He thought I'd invited her, you see, which would have been a grave breach of protocol.'

A much embellished version of Simon's enticement by the starlet is included in *Come Like Shadows*, the story of Fielding Gray's labours on a script for *The Odyssey*. Simon revered Homer, but not his hero: 'there never was a more contemptible, cowardly, incompetent and treacherous bounder than "glorious Odysseus" '. Hard though he tries Fielding is not in the same class. The best he can manage is to behave brutally towards his long-suffering mistress and put the squeeze on his employers, over whom he has a somewhat tenuous hold. They respond by having him kidnapped by an old enemy, who proposes to turn him into a junky. Luckily Canteloupe gets wind of this and gallops to the rescue:

> '[W]hoever you may be you dare not lay hands on a peer of the British Parliament and a Minister of the British Crown .... Major Gray is an Englishman and he's leaving with his English friends.'

All of which is good knockabout stuff. But the mood changes on the final page when Fielding, home to an empty house, realises that his mistress has ditched him. Now his only companion will be Conrad, the subject of his next book.

> Conrad; work; there was his consolation. Work never let a man down ... as long as he could still do it. Work suffereth long, and is kind; work vaunteth not itself, is not puffed up. Doth not behave itself unseemly .... He would sit down at Broughton and work. In loneliness? Yes, but also in tranquillity. In happiness? No, but in seemly acceptance of his lot. And there could have been many worse lots. The hours would pass quickly, he knew, the weeks would be gone almost before he noticed them, and always at his left hand the pile of written sheets would grow steadily thicker, witness and measure of his work.

As with Fielding, so with Simon, who once said he liked 'to be set in motion like a train to a distant destination'. And of course the journey was all the smoother for being undertaken alone. 'I always think there is safety in lack of numbers.'

CHAPTER SIXTEEN

There is a tide in the affairs of men,
Which, taken at the flood, leads on to fortune ...
Shakespeare, *Julius Caesar*

In December 1967 the *Spectator* asked its contributors what they wanted in 1968. Simon replied:

> Less compassion and more independence: a more *Balzacian* world, in which everyone pursues his own ends and minds his own business.

Simon could now afford to be laissez-faire. Penury was behind him, plenty lay just ahead. For this he could thank television, which was, to say the least, ironic, because neither then nor later did he ever possess a set. 'Every year someone from the TV Licence office would come snooping round and I would have to prove I wasn't hiding a set under the bed. Reactions varied from the frankly incredulous to the rather hostile. One was made to feel it was one's *duty* to have a television.'

Therein lay Simon's objection to television. 'Once it became a mass medium it was doomed, because the masses contaminate everything they are allowed to touch.' The radio audience, by comparison, was much more select; and the medium itself more satisfying to write for because it all came down to words.

But in the end it all came down to money.

'Gold won. Television made me several offers I could not refuse, and when I tried to get back into radio they didn't want to know. I dare say they thought I'd been disloyal, which was a pity, because Broadcasting House was a much more soothing place to be than Lime Grove. A television executive once said to me, "Most of them here would far sooner have a resounding inter-departmental drama than any amount of good drama on the screen." And the commercial people were even worse because they would *worry* so, mainly about what the advertisers would think.'

Simon's big break came when he was invited to dramatise Aldous Huxley's *Point Counter Point* for BBC2. Hitherto he had written original plays, which since they had to be started from scratch were a considerable drain on his energies. Now he had a ready-made cast and a ready-made plot. The challenge was to reinterpret the text as faithfully as the medium would allow. It was because she thought he could do this that Lennox

Phillips, the script editor for BBC Classic serials, chose Simon. As she explained to me in a letter,

> There was an ironic, tongue-in-cheek quality to Simon's novels and plays which suggested to me that he would catch the spirit of *Point Counter Point*.

When *Point Counter Point* was published in 1928 it was hailed as an exuberant novel of ideas. Nowadays it is more likely to be read as a contemporary satire on the Art-Smart world of the Twenties, which is how Simon chose to interpret it. He was judged to have done a good job, not just by the critics but, more importantly, by the BBC. ' "Hit them while their guard's down", I thought, so I said, "Why not do Trollope's *The Way We Live Now*?" They took that on board, so I lobbed another idea at them, Trollope's Palliser novels. They had to think twice about that, and who can blame them, but eventually I was told to prepare a story-line.'

In conversation Simon could be nonchalant about writing for television. I once heard him describe it as 'playing with words to order, like composing Latin verse'. But before he wrote a word of dialogue for *The Pallisers*, Simon had the daunting task of proposing how six quite separate stories, each almost a thousand pages long, could be bound together so neatly that their diversity would not be apparent to the viewer. His solution was to use Lady Glencora Palliser (the part played by Susan Hampshire) as a binding agent: instead of regarding her as a part, large or small, of certain stories, he would rewrite the stories so that they became parts, large or small, of Glencora.

Naturally this would require major surgery, whose scale and complexity Simon gave one brief example of in an article for the *Listener*.

> A is a boring and apparently superfluous woman: I shall delete her. But if I delete her I also delete most of the motive power behind her husband, B, who is a social climber and a minor but essential piece of mechanism. All right: let us have B motivated, not by his wife A, but by his old crony, C. A very neat suggestion – were it not that B and C have quarrelled in the second chapter and refuse to talk to each other for the next seven-eighths of the novel. Very well: delete their quarrel. I *can't*, because the quarrel is the delayed fuse which detonates the grand dénouement 700 pages later: whichever way I look at it, I cannot substitute C for A as the driving force behind B. All right: bring back A after all. But somebody has to go, indeed half of them have to go, and it is this same trouble with everyone I try to get rid of: they all keep pushing themselves back in again for seemingly ungainsayable reasons. (17.1.74)

But eventually Simon produced a scenario that was deemed acceptable and he could begin work on the 26-part script. Now he had a fresh problem: how to write dialogue which was true to Trollope yet comprehensible to viewers. He was quizzed about this by Noel Annan, who had advised him over the political background to the series:

> Did you find that the conversation written by Trollope transposed easily, or did you have entirely to re-write? His conversation has always seemed to me marvellously natural, without being naturalistic, and in fact to be an essential part of the atmosphere, e.g., when Silverbridge wants to marry and protests to the Duke that his beloved's father is a gentleman, Planty Pall replies – if my memory is right – 'So is my agent'. I think we shall find that as in the *Forsyte Saga*, and indeed in most English novels, what appears to be a love story is really all about class.

'Trollope's dialogue transposed very easily,' replied Simon,

> except that as he makes every point five times it has to be somewhat compressed. Otherwise, it is, as you say, marvellous – and great fun to try and imitate when need arises. The scene you referred to might have been made for me. In fact, Planty Pall is rebuking Lady Mary, who wants to marry a younger son from Cornwall.
>
> 'He is a gentleman, papa.'
>
> 'So is my private secretary. There is not a clerk in one of the public offices who does not consider himself to be a gentleman. The curate of the parish is a gentleman, and the medical man who comes here from Bradstock....'
>
> Splendid, splendid. But you do see what I mean about having to compress, particularly as I have to cover *The Duke's Children* in two episodes only?

Simon delivered the final draft of the final episode in August 1972 – only to be told that following the unexpected success of the *Forsyte Saga* in America it would be prudent to anticipate an American sale for *The Pallisers* by lengthening each episode to 52 minutes (par in the USA) instead of the 45 minutes commissioned. And as Simon explained in the *Listener*, 'it would not be enough just to pad on seven extra minutes to each instalment ....'

> Characters and sub-plots discarded back in 1969 would have to be brought out and dusted; each episode would have to be unstitched, and the new material cautiously inserted in such a way as not to disturb the old or set up inconsistencies with it .... Rewrites of rewrites of rewrites. Conference after conference after conference ....

Had Simon been 'difficult', as some television people alleged, now would have been the time to dig his heels in. Thanks to administrative cock-ups (see below) production was way behind schedule; consequently the first of the revised scripts were required within a few weeks. But instead of holding his employers to ransom (a national pastime in 1972), Simon accepted what was offered – £300 per episode, an additional quarter of his fee – and got on with the job.

'Simon was utterly professional,' said Lennox Phillips. 'He knew his own rights but was meticulous about keeping his side of the contract. Unlike a lot of dramatists he always delivered his scripts before the date they were due and he was very cooperative about the alterations that were sometimes necessary for technical or other reasons. He was frank about his other commitments and alert to the difficulties that might arise from them. For instance he knew that we were obliged to consult him about any changes to his scripts. But if he were going to be working abroad for a spell, as happened once or twice, he would authorise me to make any dialogue changes which might become necessary during rehearsals.'

Simon's other commitments during his researching and writing of *The Pallisers* included two novels, assorted essays, articles and reviews, and a film script – *Unman, Wittering and Zigo*, based on Giles Cooper's play. No wonder his letters and postcards to Oscar Whitamore were littered with phrases such as '*Desperately* trying to finish novel' – '*Frantic* with work' – 'Going *crazy* making up arrears of work' – 'Working like a *Nigger*' – 'Working like a *Chinaman*'.

Eventually, in March 1973, he was able to report,

> Trollope goes into production (d.v.) on May 1, and is now scheduled for transmission from January '74... a delay of nearly 18 months on the original schedule, caused by breath-taking incompetence of BBC arrangements for casting and shooting .... I have 'flu, spots, diarrhoea, impotence, piles and tooth-ache. I couldn't drink my whisky last night and have not seen my cock for a month. Nor do I want to.

But nine months later he had cheered up sufficiently to write in the *Listener* that 'despite bad patches', the time he spent with Trollope, 'an author whom I have always loved', and with his people, was rewarding in more ways than one.

> For nearly five years I have lived almost constantly with them: eaten and drunk, scoffed and prayed, gambled, cheated and intrigued with them; won and lost with them. *Trollope's* people. So I am very grateful to Trollope for their company ... and also for all the money I have earned while keeping it.

How much money? – 'Clean gone, my dear, but it can't have been far short of £100,000 *before* tax. Not all in one lump, alas, so inflation did its worst. Even so, a nice tidy sum that still pays a small divvy from time to time when they show the series in New Zealand or somewhere like that.'

Simon's television work left its mark on his novels. In the words of his editor, Desmond Briggs, 'He became less stately, dispensing with the long, sonorous passages that were a mark of his earliest novels and speeding everything up. He wrote shorter paragraphs, shorter sequences and indeed shorter chapters. And there was much more dialogue than before.'

Simon admitted that his preference for dialogue was 'partly self-indulgence because I do find it easier to compose dialogue than a strict passage of narrative prose, which is much more demanding. But I also believe, as indeed did Conrad, among others, that if you convey a thing through dialogue you're killing two birds with one stone. You're getting on with the story and at the same time helping to develop your characters .... The danger is that if you prune your narrative too much you may end up with a screenplay rather than a novel. I hope I've always managed to avoid this, but it may be that I haven't.'

*

One evening in October 1968 a policeman called at Simon's digs with the news that his father had been rushed to King's Lynn hospital with a stomach haemorrhage. The next morning he died. As Simon was committed to a series of meetings with Cubby Broccoli about *On Her Majesty's Secret Service*, he left the funeral arrangements to Myles, who saw to it that Arthur was buried next to Esther in Hunstanton churchyard.

'He missed her, took to drink and eventually it killed him. Heartsease. Heartsease. Better men than my father have died for want of that. At one point it looked as if he might remarry, to a younger woman with a very attractive thirteen-year-old son. But as I've said before, he would be master in his own house and one day she decided she'd had enough – to everyone's relief, because although we knew Papa had run through most of his inheritance, we felt entitled to what little remained.'

In the event, Arthur 'cut up for forty thou', which with the exception of one codicil was divided equally between his children. 'He left one thousand pounds to Mrs Bradfield, the daily, but for some reason the codicil wasn't signed. So the lawyer, an old golfing chum of his, put it to me that we were not *bound* to pay Mrs B her share. But I said – and I meant it – "I'd never rest easy in my bed knowing we'd cheated Mrs B." If ever a servant earned her legacy she did.'

Simon never forgave his father for 'frittering away' all the family money. The uncharitable thought occurs that it was really rather middle-class of him to complain about it so much. And in any case, would he have been more responsible? Jack Hands, for one, thought not. 'Whenever Simon brought this up, which was often enough, I'd say, "Look, if you had the money you'd fritter it away even faster." And he'd say, "It was my grandfather's money, left my father in trust to come to me." And I'd say, "Well, if you got it, how much would be left in trust for somebody else?" '

Simon's resentment was exacerbated by his belief that Arthur 'got so little pleasure out of his gold'. He determined not to make the same mistake himself. And yet in certain respects he and his father were alike. They both disliked too much formality, particularly if it involved dressing-up (Simon never wore tails in his life), and they were both rather shy (Simon was horrified when, as happened occasionally, strangers accosted him in restaurants: 'You're Simon Raven, aren't you?'). Father and son were also inordinately selfish, although to be fair to Simon he did not insist, as Arthur did, that 'other people do the things he liked as well, regardless of whether they wanted to'.

But in general Simon and Arthur were poles apart. For Arthur, what mattered was whether something was 'useful'. He had a pet term for anything that wasn't, 'rootly-toot'. A Classics degree was 'rootly-toot' because the best it could offer was a life of 'subsidised loafing' as a don. Likewise, an idea was either 'good and sensible and good' or 'bad and silly and bad'. It was 'bad and silly and bad' of the Government to send someone as 'floppy' as Simon all the way to India to train for a Commission. It would have been 'good and sensible and good' for him to have spent six months under canvas at Catterick instead.

To a man of Arthur's 'upper-suburban' outlook Simon's bisexuality was deeply shocking. If Simon's cousin John is to be believed, his uncle Arthur thought it 'despicable' that Simon should make money from writing books about 'that sort of thing'. This was news to Simon, who knew only that his father had admired *The English Gentleman* – 'otherwise no comment'.

Arthur saw little of his children following Esther's death. When they did meet, said Simon, there was invariably a row, although Myles's colleague, Michael Strevens, saw no evidence of this. 'I met Mr Raven once or twice in Deal and was struck by how very far from hostile Myles and Simon were towards him in person. It was a different story when he wasn't there.'

Fielding Gray, published a year before Arthur died, provides the last word on this subject. Half-way through the book Fielding eavesdrops on his ghastly father in bed with Angela Tuck (who is trying to wheedle money out of him). Mad with rage and lust Fielding slams the door 'on this repulsive idyll', and on returning home learns that his father has died of a heart attack while 'taking tea' with Mrs Tuck. No blame attaches to Fielding, whose part in the affair is unsuspected. And for once his conscience is clear. 'Guilt I felt none; my father had been a pestilential bully and now, by a happy accident, had been permanently removed.'

*

The improvement in Simon's fortunes was opportune. He had now entered early middle age, which as Fielding Gray observes in *The Survivors* 'is an expensive time:

> one is old enough to have taste and still young enough to have an appetite – a costly combination.'

In practice Simon lived as he had always lived, the difference being that he could now afford to do more of the things he liked, particularly travel, and, just as important, fewer of the things he disliked, e.g. chores. These he would pay almost any price to avoid. For instance when, in 1971, Anthony Blond bought a house in Corfu, Simon forked out for a huge marble refectory table 'on the absolute understanding that no form of menial labour in the house or garden would ever be required of me when staying there'.

Again, he must have spent a small fortune in laundry bills and taxi fares. He invariably went to and from the Royal Hotel every evening by cab, and Michael Webb told me that if Simon had had a hard day in London, and was 'in funds', then rather than return to Deal by train he would take a taxi all the way home instead. (By contrast he drove the same car for 20 years, a black Morris Minor Traveller with the 'arresting' number plate YOB 678. 'Isn't it time you got a new car, Simon?' – 'What for? It still goes perfectly well.')

Another expense Simon willingly incurred once the money started rolling in was what Desmond Briggs called 'State occasions'. The first of these was held at the Grill Room of the Connaught after Simon had finished dramatising *Point Counter Point*. 'There were four of us present: myself, Anthony, Diana [Crawfurd] and Simon. He'd ordered everything beforehand. All we had to do was sit there and be served. I've long since forgotten how many courses we had – too many, I suspect. There was wine in abundance and Marc de Champagne with our coffee. But for Simon the *pièce de résistance* was the enormous bill, which he took the greatest possible pleasure in paying.'

Even when there was nothing to celebrate Simon preferred to err on the side of sumptuosity. Anthony Blond, who unlike Simon did not in the least mind appearing mean, recalled an occasion when Simon was 'socking a friend lunch in Boulogne. It was nothing special. They'd gone there for the day. And it was agreed that they would order a bottle of Pouilly Fumé when Simon looked at the wine list again and said, "Wait a minute. Why don't we have two half bottles of this instead?" The point being that two half bottles cost more than a whole bottle and therefore to him were more attractive.'

In Blond's opinion Simon was not a particularly good judge of food or wine. 'As long as it was served up with a degree of style and cost enough money he was happy.' A more acute assessment of Simon's palate was offered by someone who once spent a few days with him in Paris. Simon, she said, obviously attached great importance to food and drink, and would make a point of poring over restaurant entries in both Red Michelin and Gault-Millau before deciding where to eat. 'But unless you cook yourself you're not competent to spot that a sauce contains cornflour when it shouldn't, let alone pronounce on a recherché meal.' The same lady asked Simon what wine he recommended at the duty-free shop. 'He simply said, "Go on the price, dear. The more it costs the better it will be." '

But it was on travel that Simon lavished the greatest proportion of his newly-acquired wealth. What did he understand by the term? Here is how he defined it in 1968:

> *Travel* is when you assess your money and resources and then set out, alone or with chosen friends, to make an unhurried journey to a distant and desiderated goal, repudiating official supervision, leaving only a poste restante address (if that), and giving no date for your return.
>
> Real travel, then, is independence in action, and as such is detested by the authorities .... You (and perhaps your taxes) have escaped them; their files on you rapidly become irrelevant and out of date; there is a danger that you might actually become *your own man*. (*Spectator*, 9.8.68)

In this, as in his loathing for his father, Simon was a throwback to the writers of the *entre deux guerres*. They were liberated by travel and so was he. Not that he preferred Abroad: 'I still believe what I learnt at my mother's knee, that England is the best country, and England always wins (in the end).' But it was every Englishman's right to come and go as he pleased without official hindrance. Once, at the end of a jaunt abroad, Simon turned to Michael Webb and said, 'Well, they can't take *that* away from us' – 'they' being the Government, and '*that*' being the pleasures they had just experienced.

Webb, whose background was a good deal humbler than most of Myles's colleagues, benefited 'enormously' from visiting places like Venice in Simon's company. 'He was an excellent guide, very knowledgeable but in no way pedagogic. He was particularly well informed about the lesser-known attractions of Venice, arguing that where visual stimulants are concerned, unless you get to know the third and fourth division stuff first, you don't really appreciate the top two divisions.'

When visiting a church or a gallery Simon would occasionally notice something 'curious and beautiful, or bizarre' that he could use in a novel: a tomb, perhaps, with a numinous inscription, or a suggestive painting. But this was serendipitous. As he explained in *Boys Will Be Boys*, one did not scour such places like a beachcomber:

> What does it mean, this ambiguous phrase, 'collecting material'? As far as I am concerned, it means a restful condition of mindlessness, during which impressions of places, people and atmosphere are allowed to flow in and out of consciousness without criticism or selection. One might just think, 'What a splendid setting this temple would make for a murder', but nothing more definite than that. It is later that the real work of organisation and description must be done – often when the places and people themselves are forgotten, so that one is not writing about Athens, say, or Constantinople, but about cities which are reconstructed less from what one actually saw than from personal accidents of drink or sex which occurred while one was there, from youthful preconceptions formed before one ever arrived, and from the distortions which time and longing have since imposed. For a novelist, this is a good way of working, for he is, after all, making his own world ....

Simon then described the 'series of personal reactions' he had brought back from a trip through the Near East:

> pleasure in treading the ground which Achilles and Hector trod; amusement at seeing the place where they whipped St Paul; annoyance that they have pulled down the Neon Anglias Hotel in Athens (a dotty, hospitable, unhygienic institution, now to be replaced by the inevitable office block); wonder beneath Mount Olympus and tearfulness above the gorge at Delphi; greed in the Municipal Casino at Venice; and desire in Rome. Not much, you may say, to bring back from six weeks' travel over that area the most celebrated in all the globe for reason and the arts. I agree. But I shall go back again next year (if there is money) and bring back much the same as I did this time. For it is the very stuff of novels. It is more to my purpose, as a novelist, to mourn over the debris of the Neon Anglias Hotel than to get by rote the stones of the Acropolis.

Simon generally visited places like Venice in the early spring or late autumn, thus escaping the heat and the charabancs. He also tried to be abroad at Christmas and/or New Year, his favourite thing being to organise a self-indulgent bachelor party to Dieppe or somewhere similar. They would eat and drink their fill, do a little church-crawling and play plenty of backgammon and bridge. On one of these 'Greedies' (as they came to be known) the headwaiter of their hotel asked Michael Strevens what game they were playing. '*Arrière-jambon*,' replied Strevens. The waiter chose to take this as an invitation because that night he knocked on Strevens' door and propositioned him. Strevens directed him to Simon's room. At lunch the following day Simon said, 'Did you send that queer waiter down to me?' Strevens admitted he had. 'Well here's what happened. He waddled in with his tiny French cock at high port. Came in fifteen seconds and sodded off.' Later Simon ordered Skate with Caper Sauce, whereupon Michael Webb said, 'I think we've had enough capers in the last twenty-four hours.'

Simon liked to plan trips with military precision. A large part of his correspondence with Oscar Whitamore, his longest serving travelling companion, was given over to discussion of dates, routes and costings. But his map-reading was no better than it had been in Bangalore. 'Ah!' he would exclaim to his co-driver. 'They've brought us out on the wrong road again.' And as Frances Partridge recorded, he was apt to get in a 'feminine fluster' over tickets and suchlike.

Simon feared the worst from any foreigner in uniform, including porters, and would obey regulations to the letter even when everyone else was blithely ignoring them. The only time, in Oscar Whitamore's experience, that he ever exceeded the speed limit abroad was when it looked as if they might be late checking into their hotel. 'He would insist on arriving by four-thirty at the latest, so there would be time for tea, a bath and one drink before dinner. He'd worry about this from the moment we got up from lunch.' ('Why,' I once asked Simon, 'is your watch twenty-five minutes fast?' – 'It must be a symbol of my insecurity.')

Until muggers took to the rails in the Nineties, trains were Simon's preferred mode of long-distance continental transport. 'The ferry would dock at six and dinner would be served at seven-thirty. One knew that everything would go smoothly from aperitif to digestif.' But trains are 'so boring' these days, says Gregory Stern to Fielding Gray in *The Judas Boy*. Precisely, replies Fielding.

> 'I shall have three days of complete privacy. No one, no one at all, can get at me or ring me up or dun me or make demands. I shall be sealed off in a travelling womb, without guilt or responsibility of any kind.'

In general Simon's horizons did not extend beyond the boundaries of a Classical Atlas. At one point in the early Seventies he had hoped to fly out to Singapore, where Oscar Whitamore was instructing at the Infantry Wing of the Jungle Warfare School, and drive home with him overland. But eventually pressure of work, allied to the prospect of interminable 'formaleeties' at border crossings, put the kibosh on this idea. As Simon explained to Oscar in a letter,

> The time has come for a realistic approach. Personally, I am prepared to flog shares and go to a great deal of trouble to make this drive

> home, and I know you feel the same; but I am not prepared, nor, doubtless, are you, to pay over £1000 (it will be all of that) to be relentlessly fucked about by a lot of smelly wogs ... whether in Burma (no go area), India/Pak, or Persia.

Simon did however venture 'down-under', and on a package tour at that. In early 1971 he and Dickie Muir joined a party of English cricket supporters who had the rare experience of seeing their side regain the Ashes. 'Food disastrous, on the whole,' Simon reported to Oscar;

> wine brisk, however, and people unexpectedly tolerant. Licensing laws *tormenting*, even in hotels. Tarts in Sydney rather pretty; lots of groin-look judder jobs – not for sale. Dickie now one point up at Backers – having been 35 down.

'Poor Dickie was very out of sorts to begin with, having drunk far too much gin on the flight out and seriously unsettled his liver. He soothed down a bit once we reached Adelaide, which is a very agreeable city with huge gardens and a graceful river. Neither of us cared for Melbourne. Dickie's trousers split when visiting the Roman Catholic cathedral there, and the cricket ground was like a huge gasworks. We liked everything about Sydney except its police, who were large and fat and boorish.'

Desmond Briggs had given Simon a letter of introduction to Patrick White, who had been at King's in the Thirties. He invited Simon and Dickie to dinner and insisted on cooking every course himself – 'which made for a rather long and drunken evening'. At one point there was a minor spat involving some of the other guests, one of whom had been a cook at Dickie's restaurant, *La Popote*. 'I should have known better,' said White. 'QUEENS MEANS SCENES.'

The Sydney police excepted, Simon was impressed by Australians. They were, he told readers of the *Spectator*,

> courteous, good humoured, often witty, and generous of mind as well as money. Where else in the world would a taxi driver, dropping one at a restaurant, wish one a good appetite? ('Enjoy yer supper,' he said.) Where else would a shop assistant wish one 'a safe journey home to your friends' in seven such touching words?

Australians were '*bricks*', he concluded. So why were British immigrants so rude about them and their country? His answer was characteristically provocative.

> Whereas Greeks, Italians and the rest may go to Australia because they have good reason to be dissatisfied with their own countries and

> to hope for something better, an Englishman who goes there is leaving the finest and fairest country of them all. If a man cannot be contented here, he can be contented nowhere .... What British immigrants in Australia truly hate is not so much their new country or its people as their own failure in the better world, the real world, 'at home'. (29.5.71)

Not that Simon himself was well disposed towards 'the finest and fairest country of them all'. 'There really is no point in coming back to England except to see chums,' he advised Oscar in September 1971.

> The whole place is fetid with whining workers who cannot get it into their cretinous heads that if none of them produces anything there will be nothing for any of them to buy, even if they are issued with a Million Welfare Notes each.

Two months later he wrote,

> No one in this country can get a simple order for ten cigarettes straight any more; the plebs are all buying bigger and tinnier and smellier motor cars; and cinema usherettes give themselves the airs of princesses. 'Oh that the mob had one single throat, that I might slit it' (Nero). For the rest, there is unceasing news of murder in Belfast ... while TV and the Press do nothing but whine about the maltreatment dished out to IRA suspects. As though we were bound to put them all in luxury hotels.

It was about now that I myself met Simon for the first time. I had recently been fired from my job as an advertising copywriter and thought I might try to get into publishing, which sounded more congenial. A friend suggested that by way of credentials I ought to submit a long interview with a writer like Simon whose work I knew well. I thought this was a good idea but doubted whether I could pull it off. Why should a writer of Simon's stature consent to be grilled by a wannabe literary journalist (which was how I represented myself)? Then I remembered that years before I had entered a competition run by Blond for the best amateur review of *Friends in Low Places*. I hadn't won, but perhaps Simon would see some merit in my entry – *if* I still had a copy. Luckily I did, and it must have found favour, because one afternoon in September 1971 a taxi drew up outside my grotty Chelsea flat and Captain Raven, as I then thought of him, emerged.

He was bigger than I'd imagined, pinker than I'd imagined (a good advertisement for 'succulent middle-age'), and softer-spoken than I'd imagined, with a light, cultivated accent I thought slightly affected. I'd half expected him to sport a bowler and a brolly, as Evelyn Waugh does in

Osbert Lancaster's brilliant caricature,[1] but in other respects his turn-out was *comme il faut*: amply cut grey-green tweed suit, cream silk shirt worn with a discreet foulard tie and lapis lazuli cuff links, clip-on braces, black brogues. Nor were there any concessions to trendiness in the length of his curly, lightly oiled hair, which ended abruptly at the top of the ear with not the slightest suspicion of a sideburn (remember, this was 1971). Throughout the interview he smoked Camels, methodically extracting them with broad, freckled hands from a crumpled pack.

I had sent Simon a detailed list of questions beforehand. Even so I was unprepared for the ease with which he dealt with them – and on top of a heavy lunch, too. It emerged that we had one person in common, a contemporary of mine at prep school called Andrew McCall, who Simon said was now living with Anthony Blond. Although I had not seen Andrew since we were both thirteen I was not altogether surprised at this news; he had, I recalled, been a very fetching Gwendolen in *The Importance of Being Earnest*. Andrew will soon come into this story, which is why I have introduced him here.

I never found a berth in publishing, but the following May my interview was published in *Books and Bookmen* and I began to scrape a living on the fringes of the literary world. From time to time I interviewed Simon and on each occasion found him as courteous and forthcoming as when first we met. He was, I discovered, a far more complex character than I had previously assumed, with a rich crop of contradictions. The rules he lived by were different from most people's, but they had served him well. When he departed from them, as he did in the Eighties, he paid a high price.

[1] 'Evelyn Waugh confronting the Age of the Common Man'.

CHAPTER SEVENTEEN

'Love is a disease. A weakness. It interferes with one's work. I want none of it.'

Oscar Wilde, *The Picture of Dorian Gray*

For several years after leaving the Army Simon was too busy to play more than an occasional game of cricket. When he did take the field his lack of practice was very apparent. Alan Ross, who twice played in a Fathers' Match with him, said he performed as if he had never held a bat in his life before, 'which surprised me, because I'd heard from Peter May how good he'd been at school'. But in 1966 Simon began to play regularly again, for Worth, a small village near Sandwich, and for the Trogs.

The Trogs were very much to Simon's taste, being largely composed of bachelor schoolmasters like Myles who were free to devote three weeks of their hols to playing cricket and getting drunk. How rare such licence had now become was brought home to Simon when he inquired why so many of the Trogs' opponents were under 20 or over 40.

> Only when a man has reached middle age (I was told) is he sufficiently strong-minded or sufficiently desperate to tell his wife to go to hell and take his bat out of the junk-cupboard. This is less true, for reasons I will not go into, of club cricketers of the upper or middle classes; but even among these there are pallid faces and strained, jocular references to the ill temper which is waiting at home as the cost of the afternoon's cricket. (*Spectator*, 2.10.71)

Simon could not have chosen a more inauspicious moment to pad up again. It was now, in the wake of England's winning the World Cup at Wembley, that soccer replaced cricket as the so-called national sport. Furthermore by 1966 it was clear that one-day first-class cricket was here to stay, to the dismay of traditionalists like Simon who argued that cricket, like the Englishman in the song, needed *time* – 'and what good is this in swinging England, where the hourly orgasm is god?'

Not that Simon had anything against a bit of dash. When batting he was loath to hang about himself. But the answer did not lie in the 'cheap thrills and quick runs' that one-day cricket provided. What was needed was players with 'character and colour and style, like Hammond or Compton.' Simon explored some of these themes in *Panther Larkin*, his radio play about a highly promising young batsman who forfeits his chance of an England cap when an envious colleague exploits a row he has with his pregnant wife:

> 'So you'd leave me alone for six months, while I'm carrying your first child, to go ramping after fame?'

Alas, Homer nodded, for the play opens with young Larkin hooking Lance Gibbs, the wily off-spinner, off his nose *while the ball is still rising* (my italics). But then, as Dickie Muir told me, he and Simon did not spend their days at Lord's or Canterbury 'choosing the next team to go to Australia or anything like that'. They went there to reminisce, to gossip, and to enjoy 'the whole atmosphere of the thing – the Germans would call it *Stimmung*'. When, in the Sixties, Kent got rid of the band that used to play on Ladies' Day during Canterbury Cricket Week, Simon was furious. 'Bloody professionals said it put them off their game. It never put Frank Woolley off his game. Players today have a shop steward's mentality – niggardly, put-upon, always searching for a grievance.'

Cricket inspired some of Simon's most lyrical passages, notably this one from *Close of Play*:

> And now it was for James as if all the years had fallen away and he was back on the Canterbury green in the full pride of his youth and skill. There was no more fumbling and snatching, no more dithering and backing away. Now that he had played his square cut everything was come right. Each stroke was as sure as the one before, neat, essential and precise. Most of them, to be sure, were strokes which scored behind the wicket or not at all (for where should an old man find strength to drive and force?), but they were crisp and firm, models of seemliness and grace. He cut square, he cut late; he glanced the ball to leg off the back foot and off the front; he played back in defence with the calculated suavity of a matador; when he hooked, it was with a feather-light touch, a mere deflection, by which he stole for his own end the bowler's power. It was a captain's innings in time of need; he batted from a quarter past twelve to half past one; and when he came back to the marquee, having declared the Baron's Lodge innings closed for 401 runs of which he himself had made sixty-five, the spectators rose to greet him with a great shout of triumph, many of them turning away to hide the tears which were running down their cheeks.

But this 'most beautiful, thrilling and intricate of games' was also the peg on which Simon hung, albeit precariously, *Shadows on the Grass*, a memoir containing more than its fair share of foul play. It was in *Shadows* that Simon recalled 'Colonel K' and the obliging NAAFI girls; and it was here too that he told tales out of school about the great and the good. In the same subversive spirit Simon arranged for a review copy to be sent to his distant acquaintance (and near-neighbour), E.W. Swanton. Soon afterwards they met at Canterbury, where Swanton announced that *Shadows* was 'the filthiest book on cricket' he'd ever read. 'Can I quote you on that, Jim?', said Simon, whose ambition it was to display his book, with Swanton's encomium, in the members' pavilion.

Simon's cricketing career was cut short by injury in August 1975 at St Margaret's Bay. Turning for a second run 'that probably wasn't there', he tore his Achilles tendon. 'Served me right for being greedy, my excuse being that having bought a pair of glasses I could now see the ball properly, which had not been the case for some while.' This injury made him even less inclined to walk very far. Once, on a visit to Dieppe, Michael Webb was staggered by Simon's suggestion that they 'go for a blow' on the cliffs. 'But it turned out to be a stroll of at most fifty yards, since all but a short stretch of the cliffs were "*interdit aux promeneurs*".'

In Deal, Simon was now leasing part of a tiny clapboard cottage across the road from the Admiral Keppel. His quarters consisted of a kitchen downstairs and a bathroom and bedsitting room above, the latter so cluttered with books and empty suitcases that there was barely room for Simon at all. The art dealer David Carritt, who owned the much larger cottage next door, described where Simon lived as a 'kennel'. He thought he must have had to 'crawl' upstairs.

Very occasionally Simon tried his hand at cooking. Michael Webb recalled 'some brave attempts at devilled chicken and even a "prawn bisque" which stank the house out for days'. But by and large he continued to dine at the Royal.

> 'It's absurdly expensive for the rubbish they dish up,' said Gray, in a voice audible to the hovering Head Waiter, 'but they know me, and I get some sort of service. Anyway, I've no patience for cooking my own food at home.'
>
> Detterling and Percival ordered their meal. Gray took the wine list from Detterling and closed it firmly. 'You'd better have what they keep for me,' he said. And to the Head Waiter, 'A bottle of Les Pucelles, Charles, and one of Cent Vignes. I'll have coffee and brandy here, while these gentlemen eat.'
>
> 'Yes, Major Gray,' said the Head Waiter, whose tone and manner (Detterling thought) showed the kind of wary affection that a zoo-keeper might bestow on a man-eating animal which had been many years in his charge and was now, supposedly, tamed. 'The Hine as usual, sir?'
>
> 'The Hine,' said Gray. 'My measure.' (*Bring Forth the Body*)

In fact Simon was a good deal more considerate towards the staff than this implies. When Norman Routledge, visiting from Eton, embarked on some risqué anecdotes over lunch, Simon whispered, 'Do be careful what you say, dear. Mustn't offend the waiters.' And when the Head Waitress went into hospital for a hysterectomy Simon sent her flowers, receiving in return the 'very generous' gift of a cut-glass brandy glass which from then on graced 'the Captain's table'.

*

Reviewing *The Rich Pay Late* in 1964 Christopher Ricks could not 'help wondering if the author has enough malice, squalor and perversion in reserve' for the remainder of the sequence. In 1976, with the publication of *The Survivors*, it was apparent that Simon had. 'The whole [sequence] contains enough phosphorescent bourgeois decadence to win the Order of Lenin', declared Maurice Richardson in the *Observer*. And the heading above Tom Rosenthal's long and appreciative review in *The Times* prepared readers for 'A grim world where every man is vile.'

But could 'so ambitious a fictional project be sustained without a really *nice* character?' Anthony Burgess had asked this back in 1964. The answer I think is Yes, not least because nice guys finish last and *Alms* is about winning. Re-reading the sequence I was reminded of something Harold Laski said:

> The gentlemen of England always play the game, but reserve the right to change the rules in the middle if they find they are losing.

This is the code of the Old Gang. They draw the line at blowing up the stadium; otherwise anything goes. So the prizes they carry off are not glittering, but tarnished by cynicism and bad faith. We see this most clearly at the conclusion of *The Survivors*, when Peter Morrison arrives in Venice on Government business. Morrison is what passes for an honourable man. He is certainly a civilised man. But he is also Minister of Commerce, and determined to remain so – even if this means conniving at the destruction of Venice by industrial pollution from Mestre.

> 'We need this contract from Mestre to go to a British firm [said Morrison] .... Venice is a beautiful city, Canteloupe;[1] but I think the tide of progress may be allowed to claim a few of her outlying churches in the popular interest. The people – both British and Italian – want a certain kind of wealth, and Venice is one of the things that stands in the way of their getting it.' ...
>
> 'But Peter ... *you* can't sympathise with such attitudes?'

[1] Formerly Detterling. He inherits his cousin's Marquisate at the beginning of *The Survivors*.

'If I don't, someone else will. And that someone else,' said Peter Morrison, 'would very soon be Minister of Commerce.'

To Anthony Blond's annoyance Simon disdained personal publicity. He thought it was 'shaming' to promote his own books. This may explain why there is so little about him on the dust jackets of the sequence ('Ant getting his own back'). But Simon made an exception in the case of *The Survivors*, receiving 'a good chitty' from Caroline Moorehead in *The Times* – 'considerably nicer than his characters', and 'film-star treatment' from Godfrey Smith in the *Sunday Times Colour Magazine* (for whom Susan worked as well). Smith said Simon was on 'good terms' with Susan, which was true when he wrote it. But by the time the piece appeared relations had soured following some 'spiteful' editing of a television interview Simon did with Ludovic Kennedy.

'Ludovic was perfectly agreeable until we got on to the subject of my bookmaking debts. He wanted me to admit that I'd been warned off the Turf,[2] which I was not prepared to do because this was not one of the topics we had previously agreed to discuss. I said the debts were being taken care of and left it at that. But Ludovic wanted his pound of flesh, and he got it by splicing together two quite separate answers I'd given about marriage. I'd explained how I came to marry Susan and my reasons for not living with her. Later, Ludovic asked me whether I would ever marry again. I said No, I was too fond of my own company to want to share it with anyone else: "What could be worse than years and years of the same dreary face hanging over the breakfast?" This was not intended as a slur on Susan, but that was how it appeared after Ludovic had got to work in the cutting room.'

Simon was still nursing this 'low blow' when Fate caught him flush on the chin. 'I'm afraid all arrangements must be deferred,' he told Oscar Whitamore on July 2nd,

> Myles is horribly ill of a stroke, not likely to live – or not in any way worth living. I'll be in touch when the matter is resolved. No condolences, my dear: they only upset me.

Myles died on July 4th. He was 45. Although the official cause of death was cerebral haemorrhage, it would be truer to say that he died of self-neglect. Three years before he had been diagnosed as diabetic, a condition he regarded as both 'a hideous inconvenience' and 'a contamination'. He was willing to take the pills prescribed for him but refused to inject insulin. Nor would he limit his intake of ale. When the landlord of the Keppel heard about Myles's diabetes he ordered a supply of lager with

[2] When, in the early Eighties, Simon successfully applied to resume racegoing, it transpired that the only firm to have laid a complaint against him had long since ceased to trade.

a low sugar content. Myles persevered with this 'gnat's piss' for an evening or two and then went back to bitter.

Could Simon have persuaded Myles to take better care of himself? Almost certainly not. And in any case, what would have been the point? For as Bob Arrowsmith said, all Myles had to look forward to was increasing infirmity, which given his horror of imposing on anyone, would have been a fate worse than death.

In fact, as Bob Arrowsmith also pointed out, Myles died just as the shadows had begun to lengthen across the playing fields that were his pride and joy. When he joined Tormore in 1952 it was one of eight such schools in the neighbourhood. By 1976 all but two had closed, my own among them, casualties of the long retreat from imperial glory which began when Simon was shipped home from India in 1947.

'Bob was retired now, but he knew which way the wind was blowing in private education, and how disagreeable it would have proved for someone like Myles. Already Tormore had had to accept day-boys, and one or two girls had even slunk in from somewhere, to Myles's great dismay.' But numbers continued to fall and in 1980 the Governors shut up shop. The playing fields became a building site and the staff and pupils removed to nearby Betteshanger School, which was renamed Northbourne Park.

Tormore adjoined St Leonard's, the 12th-century parish church of Deal, and it was here that Myles's funeral was held. The vicar ('ex-RAF, but a gentleman') gave him a good send-off. Myles, he declared in his address, 'was not a man of faith but a faithful man'. Afterwards Michael Webb accompanied Simon to the Municipal Cemetery. 'He was obviously very distressed, but putting a brave face on it. "What's keeping me going, dear, is trying to work out how much he was worth." '[3]

Believing that this was what his brother would have wanted Simon insisted on 'business as usual.' Within a few days of Myles's death he kept a dinner date with Francis Haskell and his wife at the Stafford Hotel in London. 'We got a letter the day before saying Myles has died but the dinner will go on and we won't talk about it at all. This was very characteristic of his idea of stoicism. Of course we were all very conscious of *not* talking about Myles, but it was a very jolly meal in the circumstances.'

But it was no good behaving like this in Deal. Simon had either to bite the bullet or spend as much time as possible somewhere else. By chance his next novel, commissioned a few months before, was tailor-made for 'tax-free travel in Europe', being a romantic yarn about the search for some legendary rubies – 'The Roses of Picardie' – whose whereabouts could be anywhere from Calais to Constantinople.

Simon had a very good run at the Exchequer's expense. During the three years he took to complete the novel he 'reconnoitred' the Adriatic Coast, the Peloponnese, Corfu, Venice, South-West France, the Riviera

[3] About £8,000, all of which he left to Simon.

and Dieppe. But Deal remained his base so it was lucky that he had plenty of television work to distract him. Myles's colleagues, particularly Michael Webb, were also very supportive. But the person whose company he increasingly sought was Andrew McCall, the 'violet-eyed Antinous' (Peter Green's description) with whom he had been 'mildly infatuated' for several years.

Slim, broad-shouldered and with a dash of Maori blood on his mother's side, Andrew was 34, the author of two novels, a natural linguist and an accomplished cook. During his last year at Cambridge he had got to know Robin Raven, who was working as a waitress in the town. On learning that Andrew was hoping to rent somewhere in Greece for the summer, Robin had suggested, with Simon's blessing, that he contact Anthony Blond, whose house on Ithaca was to let. Andrew met Blond, and soon afterwards moved in with him at Blond's house in Chester Row. They lived together for fourteen years, finally separating in 1977. Simon spent long periods in their company, and could almost be said to have been one of the family. So when, in the Spring of 1976, Andrew had to find somewhere to live while Blond paid an extended visit to Israel and Chester Row was let, it was quite natural that he should take a cottage at Walmer, close to Simon's digs. What nobody could have foreseen was that he should be within reach when Simon, for perhaps the first time in his life, was really vulnerable.

Kindness is sometimes open to misinterpretation, and it may be that because Andrew was so considerate towards Simon in the wake of Myles's death – cooking meals for him, accompanying him on short expeditions, *being there* – he inadvertently gave Simon the wrong message. On the other hand, as Simon himself noted on more than one occasion, even the Gods themselves were not proof against Infatuation, *Até*, 'she that blindeth all'. So what chance had he?

But enough of conjecture. What is certain is that as usual Simon spent several weeks of the winter on Corfu with Andrew and Anthony Blond, his presence much appreciated by Andrew who found 'Anthony's increasingly difficult behaviour – he'd become a born-again Jew – easier to bear with someone else there as well.' The following Spring Andrew left Blond for good, following which he was 'slightly horrified' to receive an emotional letter from Simon saying they were meant for each other and must link up. 'I thought, "He's going to regret that." ' – Why? – 'Because it was so uncharacteristic. Simon didn't believe in letting his feelings show. It was not what a gentleman did.'

For reasons which seemed persuasive at the time Andrew decided to ignore Simon's letter and try to carry on as before. 'I showed it to one other person and then tore it up. I thought, "He's been under a lot of strain and was probably drunk when he wrote that. Best not to mention it." You must remember that we'd known each other for years and had a lot of fun together. He was a marvellous companion, much more restful than Anthony, who was so impulsive.'

What did Simon want? Not a Ganymede. He fancied Andrew, but had sufficient sense of the ridiculous to put aside any thoughts of their sharing a bed. A soulmate then? Yes. Simon considered himself 'a great Platonist'.[4] He really did believe in 'all that business of searching for the soul'. To what extent his desire for such a union was triggered by Myles's death I cannot say. Andrew certainly felt he was 'helping to fill the gap left by Myles', but this was not why he went down to Deal again after parting from Blond.

'I was way behind on a book I was writing about the medieval underworld.[5] I knew I'd never finish it if I stayed in London, which would have been too expensive anyway. And I thought, "It worked pretty well before, finding somewhere near Simon. Why not do it again?" So I rented a cottage at Kingsdown, owned by some friends of friends, and we had the same arrangement as before whereby I cooked the evening meal and Simon bought the wine. He wasn't there all the time, but when he was he couldn't have been nicer. I'd never have finished the book without him. He was a wonderful line editor, reading through it chapter by chapter and making constructive suggestions.'

One of the things Simon liked about Deal was its comparative remoteness. Although only 80 miles from London it took two hours to get there by train and not much less by car. And since it was on the road to nowhere, 'people didn't suddenly drop in on you, thank God!' Andrew, whose parents lived nearby, at one point thought of settling there permanently too, but opted instead for Brighton because most of his friends were that side of London. This was in 1980, by which time Simon had begun to suspect that he and Andrew were not so well suited after all.

'But it was still only a suspicion, nothing more. And as I've always been inclined, like Trollope, to "let the thing go on", I made my dispositions accordingly. I retained my lodgings in Deal and at Andrew's suggestion took a pied à terre in Hove in the next square to his. After a bit he urged me to buy a flat, as he had done, but I couldn't be bothered. If you're spending half your time abroad, as I was, property is a liability.'

One of Simon's arguments against co-habitation was 'constant physical proximity, the notion of which appals me'. This was why (except perhaps when flown with wine) he never seriously contemplated living with Andrew. But twice during the next two years they did spend longish periods together under the same roof, at Tony Richardson's house in the south of France and in 1982 at Cortona, where Dickie Muir's old fiancée, Lyndall Paserini, had a house. On the first occasion they were joined by Joe Ackerley's half-sister, Diana Petre, who hoped, mistakenly, that with their assistance she could overcome her writer's block.

Simon's was a biddable Muse, whom he summoned at ten and dismissed

[4] Frances Partridge recalled a conversation about Plato's *Symposium*, and how she could tell from Simon's face that that attitude was a key thing with him.
[5] *The Medieval Underworld*, Hamish Hamilton 1981.

at five. He had scant sympathy with those who could not command the same docility, particularly if they expected him to commiserate in off-duty hours. You did not talk shop in the Mess. The day's work done, you gave yourself over to pleasure, which in Simon's case meant a large amount to eat and drink followed by backgammon or piquet and gossip. Miss Petre, who considered such behaviour 'un-writerly', felt so let down she never spoke of those four months again without a shudder.

The following year, chez Paserini at Cortona, Simon made what for him was the grandest of gestures: he did the washing-up. But Andrew was discontented. For a month he and Simon were left on their own by their hostess and by the end it was clear to him that he was 'completely leading Simon's life' and that this was not what he wanted. 'I told Dickie Muir I loved Simon but I couldn't live his life – or anybody else's. I was writing books just for the sake of it. I didn't enjoy writing. It was a dreadful sweat. And although I didn't realise it at the time, Simon had become rather overbearing. For instance if someone was coming to dinner in Hove and they were a bit late, he'd look at his watch and say, "That's it. They're late. We'll bloody well have dinner now." And it was *my* flat!'

Had Simon and Andrew spent much longer together in the same house then no doubt they would have separated sooner rather than later. But both moved around a good deal independently of each other in the next two years and it was not until May 1984 that Simon gave up his flat in Hove. By then Andrew had begun to interest himself in mysticism, a tendency Simon ridiculed; and when he took himself off to India the breach between them was complete.

Simon believed that you should accept your fate with classical detachment, but when Andrew broke with him he failed to live up to this ideal. His anger and resentment festered away like a chancre for years, poisoning other relationships in the process, for of course people took sides. What made him so bitter? His own folly, for a start. He knew very well what risks he ran involving himself with Andrew, yet he went ahead. *Mea culpa* ....

But Simon also felt he had been wronged, for reasons which are summarised here in a passage from his novel, *Before the Cock Crow*. Fielding Gray has just been dumped by his protégé, Jeremy Morrison, the son of his old school chum, Peter Morrison. Peter has a low opinion of his son, 'all wind and piss ....'

> 'So if I were you, I'd now be thankful he's given you your cards.'
>
> 'Only I can't be, Peter. I adored him, you see.'
>
> 'The more fool you. You were always adoring someone or other that didn't suit.'
>
> 'I knew I had faults that bored or irritated him, we all do. So I tried to get rid of them – and I tried very hard, and successfully on the whole, to bear with *his*. He didn't seem to think it possible that he had any, Peter: Jeremy simply was not aware that it was even

possible for him to be just as tiresome or *maladroit* or repetitious or spiteful as anyone else. But I bore with him, as I say, because I thought that one *did* bear with one's friends, that that was one of the obligations of friendship, that one did one's level best to keep things pleasant, that one overlooked their clumsiness or malice or parsimony if one possibly could. The trouble was that, latterly at least, he has not extended the same courtesy to me. The minute *I* committed some *sottise* he was on to me like a nest of vipers. So unforgiving, so cruel, so *violent*.'

It is a measure of how toxic Simon's animosity remained that five years later he was even more explicit about Andrew's shortcomings in his memoir, *Is there anybody there? said the traveller*. But the story behind that belongs to a later stage in his life and I shall deal with it where appropriate. My next task is to illustrate how Simon's career waxed and waned following the completion of *Alms for Oblivion*.

CHAPTER EIGHTEEN

> [H]e wrote everything and anything – would probably have consented, as Spike Milligan observed, to dramatise the telephone directory had the price been right …
>
> Simon Raven, *My Obituary*

As a reward for being 'such a good boy' over the rewriting of *The Pallisers*, Simon was commissioned to dramatise Iris Murdoch's *An Unofficial Rose*. He assumed there would be more of the same, but in 1977 time and chance removed his two most powerful patrons at the BBC, Martin Lisemore and Lennox Phillips. Lisemore, the producer of *The Pallisers*, was tragically killed in a car crash. Then Lennox Phillips retired and her successor, Betty Whittingale, did not like the cut of Simon's jib. Luckily there was someone at Thames Television who did. This was Andrew Brown, with whom Simon had worked some years before on two adaptations of Somerset Maugham stories.

'Andrew asked if I would like to dramatise Frances Donaldson's version of the abdication of Edward VIII, and I said, "Yes, very much." I had my own memories of the Windsors, you see, from that time I was in Biarritz. We were once in the same restaurant together, where they insisted on dining behind a screen. This struck me as a very shoddy act, all too typical of the Duke in particular. How could he have been so foolish? one asked oneself. How could he have been so weak? To say, as people did, that he was seriously under-hung and that she was the only woman who could cope with this does not seem to me to be an adequate excuse for dereliction of duty. You don't throw away a kingdom, do you, just for a girl who makes you come?'

There was another reason why Simon was so willing to tackle the abdication: Frances Donaldson had done the donkey work. 'She saved me months of drudgery, which I was no keener on at 50 than as a tyro at Cambridge. All the reading of bad books, all the absorption of horrible clichés. What a nightmare that would have been!'

Simon repaid Lady Donaldson by turning out a cracking script which won over television critics like Michael Ratcliffe and Sylvia Clayton, both of whom thought he had taken far too many liberties with Trollope in *The Pallisers*. '[He] is at ease in the world of Thelma Furness and Sybil Colefax as he was not in that of Planty Pall,' wrote Ratcliffe in *The Times*; while in the *Daily Telegraph* Sylvia Clayton praised Simon's 'discreet dialogue, which has made the personages sound as if they knew themselves to be taking part in a semi-public performance and has eschewed all psychological speculation or imaginative invention'.

Simon was well aware that his cast did not talk like this in real life. 'Like everybody else they talked in dots and dashes and ums and ers and discontinued clauses. But the story demanded that they sound like princes and royal duchesses and American divorcees hoping to become Queen. So for Princess Margaret to complain, as I believe she did to Gore Vidal, that her family did not talk remotely as I had scripted them is missing the point.'

Some years later, while staying with his friend Sir Ralph Anstruther, Simon attended a luncheon party for the Queen Mother, who as Duchess of York had some very trenchant lines in Simon's script. 'Very nerve-racking. She must have been told who one was, but she didn't let on. I was worried stiff I'd spill something and say "Fuck". "Off with his head." And I had prostate trouble too. What was the drill? "Permission to piddle, Ma'am?" This is why I have never had the slightest desire to hob-nob with Royalty – or anyone else in whose company you cannot relax.'

No sooner had Simon finished *Edward and Mrs Simpson* than Thames came up with another plum, an eight-part adaptation of Nancy Mitford's *The Pursuit of Love* and *Love in a Cold Climate*. The Mitford milieu was not one Simon knew at first hand, but for once he did not begrudge some research because it encompassed writers he enjoyed like Evelyn Waugh, Harold Acton and Lord Berners. Also involved in the production was Julian Slade, whom Simon had not seen since leaving Cambridge.

Slade was arranging the music which meant, among other things, that he had to pay close attention to the scripts. He admired the way Simon had stitched the two books together – 'it must have been fiendishly difficult' – and was relieved to find that after thirty years they understood each other perfectly. 'We talked the same language and I very much appreciated the fact that he never took umbrage or suggested that I was de trop at script conferences.'

But two things about Simon did surprise Slade. 'His curious relish for the old boy set-up, which seemed at odds with his urbanity, and his professional detachment. All that interested him was the script. When I told him that I went to rehearsals he said, "I don't know why you bother, dear." '

Success had not mitigated Simon's disdain for television. He refused to do more than was absolutely consistent with earning his fee and preferred, where possible, to keep everyone else involved at arm's length. Nothing irritated him more than having to go to London for 'discussions'; even the promise of an expensive lunch could not compensate for such an upheaval, which could cost him up to two days' work if he had to spend the night in town.

So long as Simon delivered the goods nobody complained. But when problems arose, as they did soon afterwards with *Clemmie*, his whole attitude was called into question.

Clemmie was to be a series about Clementine Churchill based on the biography by her daughter, Mary Soames. Lady Soames was at pains to show that however loyal to Sir Winston her mother had been, she was always her own woman, with robustly independent views that sometimes ran contrary to her husband's. This was precisely what the producer, Stella Richman, was determined to bring out. She wanted Vanessa Redgrave playing Clemmie, in Simon's view a classic case of putting the cart before the horse.

'You don't write a series like this around a star, at least not in my experience. It distorts everything. Stella seemed to think that Clemmie would have had her name in lights without Churchill. I disagreed. With the wind behind her, she might have become headmistress of a fairly decent girls' school. Otherwise she was unremarkable except as Churchill's wife, at which, it must be said, she excelled. I was particularly keen to examine her role as political pimp for him during the Great War. It was after the Dardanelles fiasco and he was at the front in France, desperate to get back into office and relying on her to look out for him. But Stella wasn't interested in the world's game. She wanted domestic scenes: Clemmie moving house, that sort of thing. I said I suppose you're going to offer the scripts to *Homes and Gardens*. She wasn't amused and we parted company soon afterwards.'

With hindsight Simon seems a rather bizarre choice for *Clemmie*, and in fact Stella Richman had had qualms almost from the start. Accustomed to establishing a close personal rapport with dramatists, she found Simon 'painfully shy. He never opened up about himself at all.' She tried to draw him out about casting. 'He didn't want to know. Gradually it dawned on me that all he wanted was to be left alone to write the scripts. At one point I offered to lend him all Clemmie's letters, which Mary Soames had entrusted to me before she went to Rhodesia.[1] He said No thanks, he preferred to rely on Mary Soames's biography.'

After several weeks Stella Richman still didn't know how Simon really felt about Clemmie as a person. On the flight out to Salisbury, where they were to spend a few days in conference with Mary Soames, she challenged him. Simon came straight to the point. 'I can't stand the woman.' – 'Then why are you doing this?' – 'Money, dear.'

In Salisbury, said Mrs Richman, Simon got on well with Christopher Soames and his team, chatting to them about cricket. But he didn't hit it off with Mary Soames. 'I think she got the message that Simon didn't care for assertive women. He must have felt outnumbered with me, Mary Soames and Clemmie ranged against him!'

Stella Richman was right. Simon didn't like women who were 'bossy

[1] Her husband, Christopher (Lord) Soames, was in 1979 made Governor of Southern Rhodesia.

and interfering' (what he understood by 'assertive'). But it was on women who were jealous of male institutions that he trained his biggest guns. This passage from *Close of Play* is exemplary. Hugo Warren, having bumped into a boyhood acquaintance and his wife at Delphi, has been invited to 'drift home' in their company. 'Why,' he asks a few weeks later, 'did you suggest that I came with you?'

> 'Largely for my sake,' said Nigel.
>
> 'You see,' said Nancy, 'Nigel, like all Englishmen, enjoys the company of men. It is sometimes said that Englishmen dislike women, but this is simply not true. They like women well enough – but their upbringing places so much emphasis on male institutions and loyalties that the need for both lasts a lifetime. A sympathetic wife will see this need fulfilled.'
>
> 'You are very generous,' Hugo said: 'most women are jealous even of their husband's clubs.'
>
> 'They are the greedy ones,' said Nancy. 'They want that part of a man that is not rightly theirs.'
>
> 'They would say they had a right to every part.'
>
> 'Which is why I call them greedy.'

It is a nice irony that when Hugo betrays his old school, Nancy devises his quietus.

Simon's attitude to women was characteristically ambivalent. With old bachelor cronies like Oscar Whitamore he was uncompromisingly misogynistic. 'Many thanks for the splendid birds', he wrote one January in the mid-Sixties,

> in return for which I send you six lines from Propertius (II, iv), together with a crude and hasty translation, to amuse you on your journey ....
>
> Let love of girls my enemy destroy,
> But let my friend take pleasure in a boy.
> Upon safe waters then his boat will glide,
> For who can drown in such a gentle tide?
> A word may win whichever lad you choose:
> Women will drain your heart's blood – then refuse.
>
> Propertius knew little about boys and is therefore unduly optimistic in that quarter; but he knew a lot about women, so his warning about them is to be remembered.

Simon preferred the company of men and thought the male shape was 'aesthetically superior' to that of the female. But unlike Myles (and Captain Grimes) he did not regard women as an enigma. He had many women friends and at least one lover of 30 years' standing whom he would see at carefully regulated intervals 'so that custom shall not stale our intercourse'. He thought women novelists were superior to men in all departments except action ('Better at lying, for a start!'). And the nicest and noblest character in *Alms for Oblivion* is female – poor, brave Hetta Frith, who lays down her life for the East Window of Lancaster College Chapel.

*

One of the things about Simon that surprised old friends of his like Conrad Dehn was his middle-aged flirtation with the occult. Dehn first became aware of this when he and Simon and Dehn's teenage daughter Kate were strolling along the beach at Deal.

> Kate was telling us about a French exchange holiday she'd been on and how she and some French children had played with an ouija board. And then Simon said, in a very portentous voice, 'If I were you I would never do that again.' There was a pause, and Kate said, 'Why?' And Simon said, with great finality, 'You might raise Beelzebub.' And I imagine Kate has never played with an ouija board since.

Simon told me he was kidding. Nevertheless as he grew older he was more and more inclined to give the Devil his due. This was why he was fascinated by the Cathars, at least one branch of which believed that Satan, far from being subordinate to God, was in fact His equal – 'so you had nothing to lose by serving him'.

The Cathars feature in the gaudy tapestry Simon wove for his avowedly Gothic 'romance', *The Roses of Picardie*. One definition of romance is 'a tale with scenes and incidents remote from everyday life'. Just how remote is apparent from the opening pages, in which a 900-year-old curse is invoked to explain the brutal, and apparently motiveless, murder of a decrepit French Count. What follows is a bizarre treasure hunt for a priceless necklace of rubies which first went astray following the botched circumcision of a boyfriend of Alexander the Great (To snip, or not to snip, is a question never quite resolved in Simon's novels). The cast includes vampires and revenants, dons and spies, and a species of necrophiliac rats who literally threaten the foundations of Christendom. There is enough black magic to warrant an exorcism and enough gourmandising to excuse consequences like this:

> Marigold tottered out of the gate and then crossed the road with long, desperate strides, calculating that speed was now even more important than constriction. As Jacquiz followed her into the café, she squawked at a man behind the bar, then plunged through a tiny door by a juke box. Jacquiz started to order coffee and cognac for two,

hoping that the preparation of this refection would distract the man from the celebratory noises which issued from behind the narrow door.

After quite a short while Marigold came out and said:

'Only a pair of feet. No paper. I had to use four pages of the Green *Michelin*. Unsuitable texture.'

While acknowledging that the story was preposterous, reviewers were won over by Simon's 'outrageously fertile imagination' and his elegant way with words. As Bernard Levin put it in the *Sunday Times*:

> ... however strong the feeling that the thing is absurd, impossible, worthless and in general a disgrace to belles-lettres, the pleasure and entertainment never falter.

Neither *The Roses of Picardie* nor its even more Gothic successor, *September Castle*, were written as part of a grand design. But the fact that some of the characters had had minor roles in *Alms*, while others would reappear in his second sequence, *The First Born of Egypt*, is evidence of Simon's growing admiration for Balzac and his methods. As an undergraduate he had identified with Rastignac; now what impressed him was Balzac's determination to create 'an entire world of his own, not just little pockets of one. He got a tremendous amount of mileage out of his characters. They're constantly coming and going, sometimes in major roles, sometimes in minor roles, sometimes in supernatural roles – Balzac could be very silly when he tried, or when he didn't – whichever way you want to put it – but basically it's the same gang time after time.'

Of course Simon's range was far, far narrower than Balzac's, and his characters were, to put it mildly, dated – and determined to remain so. 'Unrepentantly of the Thirties, Forties and Fifties. Or the Nineties even. Like me they hanker after the Pax Britannica, Lord Salisbury, the world of Wilde and Saki and *Belchamber*.' So when it was suggested to him that he might write a sequel to *Alms*, his first task was to reinvigorate these dodos and create a world in which they would not seem too out of place.

' "Rather a long order", as Trollope would say. For a start some of them were dead and others were clearly going potty. And the world was even less to my liking in the Eighties than it had been in the Sixties, so it was going to be difficult to adopt a sufficiently modern, "caring" attitude to the issues of the day like one-parent families and race relations. Still, one was being paid a lot of money to deliver the goods – proportionately far more than for *Alms* – so deliver them one must. And the only solution I could see was to try and focus on the survivors' children.' – But weren't most of them imbeciles? – 'Yes. And of course quite a few of the old gang were either sterile or queer. (Not that being queer stops you getting offspring.

Far from it.) But not all the children were wrong 'uns. And there were nephews and nieces and adopted children as well. So in the end one had a quorum.' In any case, added Simon, he never felt *bound* by synopses. They were simply a way of getting you into the starting stalls. Once the tape went up you ran your own race.

The trouble was that Simon began with a bigger handicap than he could carry, the absence of his old friend and editor, Desmond Briggs. In 1979 Briggs had left publishing to write novels himself, and there was no one else from whom Simon would accept either advice or admonishment. Consequently, as he himself admitted, both *The Roses of Picardie* and, in particular, *September Castle* had more than their fair share of longueurs.

'Desmond was very good at detecting self-indulgence and silliness. Blond, it must be said, recognised this. Once it became apparent that part one of *Morning Star* had gone badly wrong and would need rewriting, he said we must get Desmond back on board. Fortunately Harlech Television, who were underwriting Blond at this point, agreed. So Desmond became my editor on a freelance basis and remained at his post even after Harlech had bailed out.'

An update is needed here. Like many before him Anthony Blond had discovered that the way to make a small fortune in publishing was to start out with a large one (his came courtesy of Emu Wool, the family business). He had flair, energy and panache, but was useless with money and lacked thoroughness. This didn't matter so much while Desmond Briggs was his partner because Desmond, as Blond admitted, enjoyed the sort of things he didn't, 'like getting up in the morning, sussing out the Australian market and keeping an eye on the cashflow'. But following Briggs' departure in 1979 Blond lurched from one crisis to another until in 1982 he managed to effect a merger with the firm of Frederick Muller, which had recently been bought by Harlech Television.

Simon was the major beneficiary of this merger. His stock was riding high following the success of *Shadows* and his agent, Felicity Bryan, was able to obtain very favourable terms for *The First Born of Egypt*: £8,000 down, plus a guaranteed advance on delivery of £6,000 per novel, making £50,000 in all. This is not much in blockbuster terms, but it represents a considerable investment in a writer whose appeal was limited, and who admitted to being lukewarm about the idea anyway. 'I think Ant sensed this, but his new partner, Anthony White, was very bullish and so were Harlech. They wanted to televise *Alms* and paid me £5,000 to do two breakdowns. Nothing came of it because no one would put up the hundred grand per episode needed, but for a short while there was a lot of optimism about.'

Simon was wrestling with the rewrite of *Morning Star* when he learnt that Harlech had had second thoughts about involving themselves in publishing and were pulling out. 'Whooppee! I thought. Now I shan't have to write these novels after all. I can pocket wads of cash[2] and start work on another memoir, which was what I'd wanted to do all along.' But to Simon's astonishment Blond was not yet willing to call it a day, and he managed to find enough money from somewhere to stay afloat until 1987. By then the authors' ledger showed a figure of minus £28,000 in royalties against Simon's name, so it was certainly an act of 'faith, hope and charity' on Century Hutchinson's part to guarantee publication of the remaining four volumes in the series.

Although the money came in very handy, Simon found the contract as much of a millstone as did his publishers. 'One would wake up in the morning and think, "How can I go on with this? Please God, let me win a football pool and disappear out of this appalling world and this appalling undertaking for ever and ever, Amen." But of course the cheque does not arrive from Littlewoods, and so in the end one plods on .... Not that there isn't something to be said for boredom when you're writing. If you're too excited you're liable to balls the whole thing up. Whereas sheer boredom, sheer desire to amuse oneself out of being bored and get something worthwhile on paper is probably as good a discipline as any I know.'

Simon declared that *First Born* would examine 'the purposes, beliefs and ways of life of the growing young, as observed, deplored or encouraged by their elders'. Later he amended this, saying it was really about the struggle between 'basic good and basic evil, the prize being somebody's soul'. That somebody is blond, green-eyed Marius Stern, 'the most scrumptious and exciting person I ever saw' according to a breathless schoolchum of his sister.

Marius has such winning ways that he is singled out for special attention by a sinister and manipulative Classics master at his public school. This is Raisley Conyngham, who has modelled himself on Vautrin, Balzac's arch-crook. But whereas Vautrin's speciality was picking potential champions and grooming them for success, Conyngham trains up Jokers – in other words, 'perfect and unsuspected agents of subversion – unsuspected even by themselves'. Actually Marius does realise that something is amiss, but so powerful is Conyngham's hold over him, and so eager is he for réclame, that he will willingly root around in the dirt for the sake of the truffles hidden there. 'But you can't like the dirt,' says Fielding Gray.

> 'The dirt is a necessary condition of what I have learned to call "the world's game". The most amusing and exciting game of them all, Fielding.'

Not that Marius needs much tutoring in the ways of the world. Although it would be stretching a point to say that he is 'as knowledgeable and articulate as Sir Isaiah Berlin' – the complaint Simon made about the

[2] Simon 'hoped' he might walk away with 'about £30,000'.

adolescents in Angus Wilson's *No Laughing Matter* – he comes across as preposterously mature for his years, handling his affairs (in every sense) with the same skill which he brings to Latin verse and Eton fives. In fact all Simon's 'growing young' are old before their time. In thought, word and deed they are virtually indistinguishable from their elders. It is as if British society since 1945 had not changed a bit.

Of course Simon would much rather it hadn't changed. And in *First Born* he deliberately set out to create a world in which, e.g., cricketers, whether Gentlemen or Players, still wore *real* white flannels and the Durbar was not yet done. Fair enough. But no amount of diabolism, grand guignol and other lurid theatricals can conceal the fact that this is too cosy a set-up for real conflict of the sort which characterised *Alms*. In *Alms* Simon showed us a group of unscrupulous young thrusters making their way in a hostile world. Their methods weren't pretty but they were compelling. How tame by comparison are the cast of *First Born*. The young are smugly aware that, come what may, the ball will remain at their feet and the old have long since hung up their boots. Thank God, then, for Raisley Conyngham, who would tilt the world on its axis rather than concede a goal. There is a *point* to Raisley, whereas Marius, for all his pert menace, is just a glove puppet.

But, as always with Simon, there is the consolation of style, a beguiling blend of the classical and the coarse in which formal, not to say archaic, constructions are juxtaposed with spicy slang. In a curious way it is reminiscent of a ball at Versailles: all that pomp and glitter and finery while the chamber pots overflow in every corner. Another comparison was volunteered by Simon's contemporary at King's, Christopher Moorsom:

> I always think of Simon as such a curious mixture. A combination of Henty and Huysmans. You have the public school ethos, play the game and so on...and at the same time really decadent tastes, which come across more and more in the later novels. Reading these is like eating your way through a cake which is made of chestnuts, and covered with layers of cream and treacle. When I put this to Anthony Blond, he said, 'Yes, *and* covered with shit, my dear.'

I shall conclude with two one-liners from the sequence which only Simon could have written:

> 'Darling Mummy. Please may I be circumcised?'

And this 'irresistible request':

> 'Please, sir, may I bugger you, sir?'

Truly, manners makyth man.

*

When Simon began writing he nursed the vague hope that if all went well he might eventually have accumulated enough capital to retire and live off the income. By the Seventies this did not seem quite so far-fetched, and had he been a more prudent man he might, by 1980, have had more to show for his labours than a few life policies. In that year and in the previous one he earned 'between 70 and 80 thousand pounds'. The next few years also brought in significant five-figure sums, yet by June 1985 he was, he told Oscar Whitamore,

> seriously, horribly broke until the end of Blond's accounting period, when American notes are due. If you have 500 or even one thousand sovs. lying idle, please send them to poor Ermyntrude.[3]

Where did it go, all that money? A large slice went on living and working in the style Simon thought proper for an established writer, his favourite thing being to go to either South-West France or Provence, find a hotel which offered 'good food and solid comfort', stay there for about five days and then move on – 'for as long as possible. Nobody knows where you are. You can get on with your work entirely undisturbed. Varying scenes, varying climate, varying food. Every now and then you end up near a Casino, so that takes care of the evenings, otherwise I would walk in the town for a little and then read.'

If Simon wanted to stay put abroad he would either park himself on a chum 'for as long as he'd have me', or book himself into one of two hotels – La Présidence at Dieppe or, if he was feeling really extravagant, the Carlton at Cannes. Dieppe he liked for its Wildean associations and its 'crumbling charm', but he went to Cannes for 'nasty Somerset Maugham reasons'. Nasty?

> 'Nasty' is ironic [he explained on a postcard]. The reasons are the aroma of wealth and worldliness, the Casino (only elegant one left), luxurious hotels (with hotel tarts), and admirable restaurants. *Also* (nice) great natural beauty of bay and islands; and (a final *nasty*) CLASS.

The sight of a hotel tart 'discreetly showing off her suspenders in a Public Salon' suggested to Simon that it was still not quite closing time in the pleasure gardens of the West. But the price of admission had soared. As he told me in 1983, 'Nowadays a satisfactory hotel room with a proper

[3] Simon usually signed off to Oscar using a female Edwardian *nom de plume*, e.g. Letitia, Mirabelle, Hyacinth, Cora, Myrtle etc.

desk to work at will set you back £20 a day without food and drink – and I am a greedy man.' Throw in the cost of a hire car and periodic indulgences like the hotel tart and the Casino – 'Please God, let it be 33!' – and by the end of the week you had 'precious little change out of a thousand quid'.

But it was no longer the case that only when abroad, or when dining in London, did Simon spend like a sailor. On learning from Tattersalls that he was free to go racing again he did so in abundance, but with no more success than before. And finding that time hung heavy on his hands in Hove when Andrew was away he conquered his distaste for legalised gaming in Britain and patronised the Brighton Casino, to their benefit, not his. Then there was the cost of keeping two addresses, even when abroad. And demands for back tax, which were always more than he and his accountant had budgeted for. 'So where did it all go? It went. Spent.'

A coda needs to be entered here. Simon was, as I have said, a lavish host, and during the years of plenty he picked up some very substantial tabs, not just for meals, but for holidays as well. He was particularly generous towards the Trogs, whose tours he continued to go on even after he gave up playing. Peter Budden, who took over the side after Peter Ingrams' death in 1975, recalled how ' "The Author" ', as Simon was known, 'would always buy the first, middle and last drink.'

> He paid for the fixture cards, many of the balls we used and at least two slap-up meals each season. But there was more to it than money. He was an immensely exciting person to be around. The younger players were fascinated by him. All they had to remember was never to call him 'Mr Raven'.[4] He could not bear that. Otherwise, for someone who could be pretty scathing about young people, he was incredibly kind, tolerant and correct.

Simon also gave away money, notably to his sister Robin and her two sons. Because her childhood had been overshadowed by war and austerity Robin always felt she had missed out. For several years after leaving school she led a rather 'iffish' life as a waitress and artist's model, during which time she would apply to Simon for hand-outs. Although at this period he was often short himself, he generally obliged. Then in 1971 Robin married Tom Espley, a well-to-do artist. Simon paid for their honeymoon and offered up a prayer that the marriage would last. It didn't, and by the early Eighties he had resumed his role as benefactor.

Two months after Simon had appealed to Oscar for a loan, he had a lucky break. An old BBC acquaintance, now in films, hired him to go to Vienna and do a treatment for *The Fourth Man*, a sequel to *The Third*

[4] Envelopes addressed to 'Mr Simon Raven' were his very worst thing. ' "Simon Raven, Esq." is correct. "Simon Raven" will do. But "Mr" will not. "Mr" is the boiler man.'

Man, which an Austrian company was proposing to make. It was, said Simon, 'typical of their ineptitude' that he had to write the thing virtually from scratch. 'All they were agreed upon was the climax, which would involve a chase down the corridors which link the top floors of houses in some Viennese streets.'

Simon did two treatments but the project was aborted, like everything else he had done in that line since *Love in a Cold Climate*. 'Curious really. In the Seventies, when the country was rapidly going to pot, there seemed to be plenty of money to spare for major series. Then along came Mrs Thatcher to drag us out of the mire and suddenly it all dried up. Nobody would move an *inch* without back-up money. It was very depressing, particularly when one worked on something really worthwhile, like *The Memoirs of George Sherston*. They even commissioned a swish new edition of the book[5] to tie-in with that, all to no avail.'

Simon was paid enough for *The Fourth Man* to alleviate the most pressing of his debts, and on his return home he was put in the clear by a job which was far more to his taste, dramatising *An Ice Cream War*, Will Boyd's subversive 'yarn' about East Africa in the Great War. Here was something he could get his teeth into and nine years later he still sounded most aggrieved that this too had come to naught. 'I think the money was there but not the necessary goodwill from countries like Kenya, which did not like to be reminded of their colonial past. I dare say they could have filmed it in South Africa, but that would have been unacceptable to the Unions – or at any rate to the Union bosses. I don't think the clapper boys minded where they were as long as they were in work.'

It will surprise no one to be told that Simon resented the power of the Unions and rejoiced at their drubbing in the Eighties. He was equally predictable in his opposition to sanctions, whether economic or sporting, against South Africa. But unlike some, he was honest enough to say why he thought the South African cricketers ought to be allowed to play here in 1970.

> It is all, in the last resort, a question of *pleasure*. By all means let the idealists, the students, the revolutionaries feel as passionately as they must, write as much as they choose, shout as loud as they please, and carry banners as wide as they will: *but for God's sake let them not spoil other people's pleasure*. If I go to watch the South Africans, it is on my conscience, not theirs, and they must let me be its keeper. (*Spectator*, 25.4.69)

Myself, I think Simon was wrong on this issue. But in general I applaud his stand against 'interference', whether by shrill minorities, officious vested interests or the nanny state. Apropos, he would quote Macaulay,

[5] *Siegfried's Long Journey*, edited by Paul Fussell (Faber 1983).

who said people could get by under a debauchee or even a tyrant, 'but to be ruled by a busybody was more than human nature could bear'. At the same time he approved of rules and regulations, if only because he enjoyed the challenge of finding ways to evade them. He was definitely not a Thatcherite, describing Mrs Thatcher as 'a perfectly dreadful woman whom one would go out of one's way *not* to dine with .... It's true she pulled the country round, but her manner and her methods were so inelegant. There had been a certain elegance about politics at one stage, but Thatcherism really is the antithesis of any sort of elegance. Philistine too. So although one's grateful for what she did, one can quite see why people like James [Prior] fell out with her.'

CHAPTER NINETEEN

Years foll'wing years, steal something ev'ry day,
At last they steal us from ourselves away;
In one our Frolicks, one Amusements end,
In one a Mistress drops, in one a Friend:
This subtle Thief of Life, this Paltry Time,
What will it leave me, if it snatch my Rhime?
Alexander Pope, *Imitations of Horace*, Ep. II ii

Simon had now been based at 109 Manor Road for almost twelve years, a record stay. So he was rather put out when, in February 1984, he was given notice to quit by his landlady who said she wanted to move. He contemplated defying her – 'after all, one was a sitting tenant' – but his solicitor, Paul Spurrier's son, Julian, advised against. 'He said, "You'll only have her sitting next door sticking pins in your image!" Then she said, "It's customary when leaving lodgings after so many years to have the place done up." I left it to Julian to explain to her that far from being obliged to do the place up, I was very kindly *not* insisting on having some two or three thousand pounds out of her as the price for surrendering the roof over my head.'

Simon then went to live at the Glen Hotel, a small private hotel nearby where for £30 a week he had a comfortable serviced room. 'A lovely set-up, the next best thing to chambers such as Mr Pickwick had. They'd send your brekker up, tidy the room, take care of the laundry and so on. When I went away the rent was only £30 a month. But I'd been warned that the owner wanted to retire and two years later she did. The place became a nursing home for handicapped old ladies and I came here.'

'Here' was a modest post-war semi in Walmer owned by Simon's friend Peter Budden, the Head of Classics at Wellesley House school, Broadstairs. 'Peter had recently acquired this house, which came to him via his mother. But because he lived at Wellesley during the term it suited him to have me around to keep an eye on the place. I have my own room, which is all I've ever needed, and there's a lady down the street who comes in to clean. It's only a few minutes from the station, which means one doesn't have to hang around for a taxi after getting back from London.'

For many years after settling in Deal Simon could count on Anthony Blond for a bed whenever he went to London. But always in the back of his mind had been the thought that, money permitting, 'one ought to have a

Club'. By 1976 he was well able to afford this, and at Conrad Dehn's instigation joined the Reform. 'I liked the look of the place, the atrium in particular. It had a good library, the staff were attentive and it cost a lot less to stay there than a decent hotel. Of course the food wasn't up to much – it never is in Clubs – but not far away was the Stafford Hotel, where I've eaten some of the best meals of my life.'

The Reform had one other advantage, too, which Alan Watkins may have overlooked when in *Brief Lives*[1] he described it as 'a surprisingly staid choice for someone of his adventurous tastes'. For many of the years Simon was a member he had only to cross Pall Mall to reach a massage parlour, 'where you got a good housemaid's wank'. – A *what*? – 'First two fingers and thumb, as opposed to a full palm job. Ever read Brian Aldiss's book, *A Hand Reared Boy*? Well, there's this very arousing bit about a non-quite-pubertal boy tossing himself off when he's interrupted by the maid, who takes over, using this method .... In my experience,' pursued Simon, 'some women have kind hands, and some don't. It's a bit like green fingers, though a love of penises helps. The woman in the massage parlour had kind hands, which is why one enjoyed going there. And of course in those days they only charged you a couple of quid. Now, I gather, they won't do it for less than thirty.'

At fifty-plus, having 'kissed the boys good-bye', Simon preferred massage parlours to whores. For a start he could no longer manage a reliable erection (there is a graphic description of Fielding Gray's efforts to 'get his thing what the French call *dur*' in *Morning Star*). Then there was the ritual – the disrobing, the shower, the oiling and so on. Finally, there was no hypocrisy about the act itself, no question but that what was going on in your head was of more consequence than what was being done down there, however skilfully contrived. 'One lay back and thought of England, as it were.'

Or, as it might be, 'Small boys and elder women .... Homosexual affairs between fifteen-year-old boys.....Nice juicy pubescent girls' – to name some of the erotic fantasies he unveiled for the *Sunday Telegraph's* Dave Sexton in his sixtieth year. Simon fleshed out these fantasies in his books, although latterly there was often a whiff of decay coming off the page as well. 'Boys will be boys indeed; but not for long.'

That same year, 1987, Simon agreed to talk to Peter Parker, who was writing the biography of Joe Ackerley. Here are Parker's impressions of their meeting.

> In Ravenesque manner, he had been very difficult to track down. The first letter I sent eventually returned undelivered, having gone half way round the world via assorted postes restantes. I tried again and got an answer scrawled on my own letter, which gave me his address

[1] Hamish Hamilton, 1982.

and telephone number in Deal and added the warning: 'Neither address nor number are to be given to anybody else'. He originally said that he never came to London and that I might therefore visit him in Deal, but when I telephoned he said that he was coming up to town for an afternoon at Lord's. He proposed that I should meet him at the Tate in front of John Martin's apocalyptic canvases. He told me that his most distinguishing feature was his 'auburn hair', but I knew, of course, what he looked like, and had no difficulty finding him. He was very red in the face and coughed alarmingly throughout our interview. He glanced round the gallery, noting its hushed atmosphere, and said: 'It's a bit difficult here, but I don't think we need use *stentorian* tones.' He then proceeded to talk, not quite sufficiently sotto voce, about whether or not people with red hair smelled of fish at the point of orgasm. I asked him about the odours purportedly given off by Ivor Novello, and he said: 'Where did you hear that?' I replied that he had said as much in *Shadows on the Grass*. 'Oh dear, did I? I fear that was probably an embellishment. The trouble is that one's made up so much over the years that it is difficult now to remember what's true and what's not. He had a teenie-weenie pee-wee, of course, and I think he might have suffered from the same thing as Joe – both of them coming before they'd really started. I don't like to think of poor old Joe ejaculating all over the tiled walls of public lavatories,' he continued, as heads turned ....

Simon's preoccupation with 'filth', with what went on behind the pavilion rather than at the wicket, was why, said Anthony Blond, he could never hope to be selected for the First XI. 'Someone once said to me – it may have been Marguerite Yourcenar, at any rate somebody like her – "He is flawed by salacity." Very true. You cannot conceive of the battles Desmond and I had with him over certain passages. He'd fight like a cat to keep them in.'

And why not? These were often the bits which gave him 'real pleasure and excitement to write'. They were what readers expected of him, too. On the other hand, I think that because, at bottom, Simon regarded sex as essentially comic, ridiculous even, he writes best about it in his essays and reviews. He is at his pithiest here reviewing *The Latin Sexual Vocabulary*[2] in the *Observer*:

> Chapter One is devoted to the male *mentula*, a word perversely feminine in gender. *Mentula* has synonyms which range from the comprehensive *res* ('thing'), through *caulis* ('stalk') and the rather confusing *filix* ('fern'), and on to the delightful nonsense word *xurikilla*, which may, however, be a spurious reading for *Auricilla*.

[2] Edited by J.N. Adams (Duckworth, 1982).

Its public and rigid representation was not only tolerated but absolutely required for such respectable purposes as warding off evil spirits (it made them helpless with lust or laughter) and ritually encouraging fertility in fields or females. Whereas in England these days the image of an active *mentula* is the banner of hard pornography, in ancient Rome such a *res* was unremarkable, except insofar as copious dimension might rouse 'fear, admiration and pride'.

The second chapter is concerned with the female *cunnus*, a word perversely masculine in gender. This excited altogether less affection (in terms of nomenclature, that is), and tends to have synonyms that are either boring ('ditch', 'door', 'bag') or downright nasty ('bladder', 'swine' – this latter a nursery name). However, *pinnacula* ('little wings') is visually effective, while *navis* ('ship'), which at first seems quite incomprehensible in this context, is perceived to be brilliantly apt when one drives one's car on to, or rather into, a Channel ferry.

Female chauvinists, and indeed all women, may be annoyed to learn that the *cunnus* has many rather gritty synonyms in common with the adjacent *culus*, which is the subject of the next chapter. After a brisk digression on the *culus* in the windy role of *podex*, Mr Adams considers metaphors such as 'little ring', 'vegetable garden' and the forceful medical expression *inferior guttur* or 'lower throat'. The male *culus*, it appears (more bad news for the fair sex), is superior in quality, as any experienced *pedicator* will affirm, to the female one; for while the former has the ripe texture of a prime Chian fig, the latter resembles that most wretched of fruits, the flabby and overblown *marisca*.

In Chapter Four Mr Adams discusses what one actually does with all this apparatus. The most common appetite is for *fututio*. *Pedicatio*, of which we have already said something, is also a popular taste. The verb *irrumo* is of particular interest to me personally, as for the past 35 years I have thought it meant the same as *fello*, the sense in which Beardsley used it in 'Under the Hill', which I read when an undergraduate. In fact it now turns out to mean precisely the opposite: what a vile unscholarly fellow Beardsley was. Heaven knows how many other young lives have been blighted by this howler. Legitimate alternatives to *fello* are *sugo*, *lambo* and *lingo*, though the last two are subtly different, and *lingo* at least is usually and more elegantly applied elsewhere.

For those to whom none of these *deliciae* is available, the pastimes of *glubendum*, *palpandum*, *tractatio*, *terendum* or the Petronian *mascarpio* may be of solace. As a final resort, they can always retire for a good *cacaturio* …. (5.12.82)

One thing puzzled Simon about this Vocabulary: 'There is no mention here of any kind of venereal disease .... Something beastly there must have been, lurking (as it always has been down the ages) under the bed.'

Although he never suffered from anything worse than crabs, Simon was fascinated by clap and its consequences, returning to it again and again in his work. Two of the Old Gang, Tom Llewyllyn and the gambler, Max de Freville, are eventually undone by it, and another character, Carmilla Salinger, is writing a book about it. As for AIDS (to which none of his cast succumb – though not for want of trying), this simply proved that God always had something up his sleeve, 'but it would be small-minded to blame him'. – So AIDS is not retributive? – 'No. It's God pissing on us rather than punishing us.'

By 'God', Simon meant 'a kind of brooding, malignant Fate who allows one occasional treats'. As a Classicist he sometimes invoked the Pagan gods, but never underestimated their capacity for divine malice. He often quoted these two lines from *Lear*:

> As flies to wanton boys, are we to the gods;
> They kill us for their sport.

The death of Mark Boxer was a typical instance of divine malice. 'I never saw much of Mark after leaving Cambridge, but most years Dickie and I could count on meeting him at Lord's. We'd all have dinner together and play bridge. And on the last occasion he told me how well things were going for him – how happily married he was, how much money he was making (he was too, thanks to a friend of Dickie's who invested it for him) and how he'd just been given this second editorship. "It's all going so well," he said, "that I think something nasty's going to happen." And so, a few months later, it did.'

Mark Boxer died in July 1988. In August Simon went to stay with Dickie in Essex. 'He and Patricia were in the throes of moving house, but Dickie and I managed to watch some cricket at Colchester. I think we talked a bit about his daughter Darcy, who was causing him some concern. Otherwise it was the mixture as before: dry jokes, gossip and badinage – we used to call each other by our surnames, as if we were still at school – interspersed with companionable silences .... And that, I'm afraid, was that. I never saw him again.'

Dickie, it transpired, had cancer of the colon. ('How typical of God to wrong-foot him. He always blamed his liver when he wasn't feeling well.') He was operated on the following summer, but the strain was too much for his heart: it conked out, said Simon, just as he sat down to watch some cricket on the television. 'So there was an end of Dickie, my very favourite companion whenever pleasure beckoned.'

As it happened, pleasure was the last thing on Simon's mind in the summer of 1989. That spring he had begun to have difficulty in urinating. At first he thought it was a recurrence of the periodic discomfort he'd suffered since contracting cystitis 20 years before. 'Then it suddenly got much worse. One was busting for a pee but not a drop appeared. Oh God, that was dreadful. Real *agony*.'

It turned out to be prostatitis. He went into hospital in Dover and had the operation, but found immediately afterwards that he still had considerable difficulty and pain when peeing. 'At this point they suddenly became *very* polite. They'd been quite kind and considerate before but now, I noticed, they became positively *slavish*. And the reason was that they'd botched it. They'd left a bit inside. So one had to go under the knife and, what was worse, under the anaesthetic for the second time in a few days.'

Simon was in hospital for over a month. Towards the end he had 'crucifying constipation' which no laxative would shift. Eventually the ward sister had to don a rubber glove and tackle the blockage digitally. 'Some people pay to have this done,' Simon told her. 'Why, I can't imagine.'

In view of all he'd been through I wondered whether Simon had considered suing for medical negligence. Not a bit of it. 'Doctors are human. They are bound to make mistakes. Indeed one could wish they made more, so the country wasn't cluttered with people whose lives have been artificially prolonged at enormous public expense. How very glad I am for Myles's sake – and for mine – that there was nothing they could do for him.'

And in any case, continued Simon, he had always been contemptuous of people who went 'whining off to the Courts', whether because they thought they'd been libelled, or, 'as is the fashion now', because the surgeon's knife had slipped. 'It is a nasty, greedy, American and, in this country, lower-middle-class trait.'

What Simon resented far more than the surgeon's 'making a fuck-up of my op.' was his behaviour a month later when he went back as an out-patient for a final check-up. 'I was met by this nurse – she was about 40, quite good-looking – and told to undress, put on a sort of shift, and lie on the bed. "I'll tell Mr So-and-So you're here," she said, and went next door to his office. So I lay there and then this rather muffled giggling started. A little later it was clear from the crescendo of moans why I was being kept waiting. Eventually the chap came in, not exactly buttoning his flies, but with that slightly sweaty look people get after a climax. And I thought to myself, "That's rubbing it in and no mistake." Because if you were pretty well impotent anyway, as I was, losing your prostate is not going to improve matters.'

In fact Simon was not totally *hors de combat* after all. In the right hands he could still achieve the sort of dry 'juddering' orgasms granted to him at Cordwalles. But taken in conjunction with the death of Dickie Muir, which hit him hard, his two operations propelled him downhill rather faster than a man of 61 might have wished. Even before he went into hospital he had begun to find long distance driving too taxing for comfort; now he would only take the wheel with the greatest reluctance. At the same time the limp he had had since tearing his Achilles tendon became more pronounced, as indeed did the stammer he was prone to when talking on the telephone (an instrument he never wholly came to terms with).

Hospital also had the effect of modifying his régime. Irritated at having to haul himself out of bed and shuffle down the corridor to a squalid day room if he wanted a fag, he simply gave up smoking altogether. And on returning home he discovered that he had lost his appetite for whisky and water after supper, 'though thankfully I still enjoyed plenty of wine with my meal and a large glass of brandy or calvados to round things off'.

One consequence of Simon's reluctance to drive was that he saw more of his son Adam, who would chauffeur him to race meetings and cricket matches, and who was also good at coping with traffic abroad. Adam has barely featured in this story for the simple reason that he came low down Simon's list of priorities. No doubt this was tough on the boy, but it was also consistent with his father's views on parenthood, views he had held from an early age. 'I knew about "the pram in the hall" long before I came across it in Connolly.'

Luckily for Adam, Susan was a most devoted mother; indeed she never really abandoned this role and continues to provide a home for him even now. In his twenties he was diagnosed as being schizophrenic, although Simon blamed his fecklessness on smoking too much pot. What is certain is that he had difficulty in holding down a job, a problem for which Simon could see only one solution. In May 1977 he appealed for help to Oscar Whitamore, who had left the Army and was working for a trading company in Qatar.

> I have decided it is time to sort out Adam. Can you employ him in your store? Or find a job for him in Qatar? Or anywhere which is so far from England that he won't be able to come home without saving up for a year?
>
> I am quite serious. He is stupid (or rather slow), but he is also biddable and presentable, polite, keen to please, and now anxious to get on in the world. Just the sort of boy who would have been sent to the Colonies in the old days, so why not to the Persian Gulf now? He is good, incidentally, at putting up with wogs.

Oscar said he would ask around, encouraging another testimonial from Simon. 'Adam will do *anything* to earn money and save it,' he wrote on 3 June.

> At the moment he is doing a physical job, but I think he wd prefer a clerical one. He would also make an *excellent* servant, valet or housekeeper.

Despite Simon's offer of 'a monkey if you can fix this for me', Oscar found nothing he could safely recommend. Eventually Adam took up oil painting, his rather childlike urban landscapes enjoying a modest success. Simon was relieved that 'the boy had an occupation at last', and loyally distributed post-cards of Adam's paintings. But there is no use pretending that his affection for his son could compare with the love he bore his books. 'My books are my babes,' he would say.

*

Graham Greene is supposed to have said of Ford Madox Ford's anecdotes that although unreliable, they not only entertained, but also 'enshrined a finer truth than dull factuality'. This was the spirit in which Simon wrote memoirs like *Shadows on the Grass* and *Bird of Ill-Omen*, and Gore Vidal for one approved. Commenting on 'Isherwood Gored', which contains Simon's account of the supper Vidal gave in October 1979 for him, Christopher Isherwood and Isherwood's pal, Don Bachardy, at a Mexican restaurant in Los Angeles, Vidal said,

> His description of the evening with Isherwood and me contains not one accurate quotation, and yet every word is true!

A more cautionary assessment of Simon as memoirist was given by Lord Annan, who compared him to Thomas Mann's Felix Krull. 'His autobiographical stuff is tremendously tuppence-coloured and stems from his romantic view of places like Charterhouse and King's. King's wasn't really as he describes it. He's playing a sort of obligato on his past.'

Places and their associations were very important to Simon, who tried 'constantly' to remind himself in his writing of what had happened where, and with whom. But any writer who canters over the same ground again and again risks boring both himself and his readers, hence the refinements and embellishments Simon added when, as sometimes happened, he told the same story more than once. He was also prone to poetic amnesia, as witness this exchange that occurs in his autobiographical study, *The Old School*.

At Bangalore, writes Simon, a fellow officer cadet, a Catholic, threatened to report him to their Company Commander for unjustly bawling out the bearer they shared.

> 'Report me?' I said. 'You mean *sneak* on me, Giles?'
>
> 'I do not understand the word "sneak".'
>
> 'It means to tell tales,' I said, 'to inform or delate, which is behaviour regarded with contempt by any gentleman who has been to a public school.'
>
> 'Not if he went to *my* public school,' said Giles. 'We were taught

that it is our duty under God to report wrong doing and corruption.'

'You mean some fucking priest got at you,' I said.

'If you like to put it coarsely, yes.'

'But what sort of a place was Ampleforth,' I said, 'if everyone was running round denouncing each other? ….'

The answer, as Simon seems to have forgotten, is that Ampleforth was very like Saunderites ('We don't use the word sneaking … we talk about "showing up" ').

Simon liked to weave a plot into his memoirs, to accommodate which he had sometimes to 'rearrange things' in a manner that would have been unacceptable in an autobiography. He got away with this because although he did, on occasions, wound people, they responded more in sorrow than in anger. Consequently the accuracy of what he had written was never formally challenged. But his luck ran out in 1991 with the publication of his atrabilious memoir, *Is there anybody there? said the traveller*.

Simon called *The traveller* 'a study in nastiness', which just about sums it up. Reading it, I was reminded of a scene in *The Survivors* when Fielding Gray tells his fellow diners at a Venetian palazzo what a scabby lot they are.

> 'There's something badly wrong, physical or mental, with every single one of us at this table. I myself have a hideously deformed face, a self-pitying disposition and a near-absolute addiction to drink. Max is pathologically obsessed with a dead woman, whom he couldn't fuck when she was living; Lykiadopoulos hopes to make money by preying, in the meanest and nastiest way, on the most contemptible failing of his fellow creatures; Daniel talks, or rather croaks, like a sick frog; Canteloupe is callous, cowardly, corrupt and viciously smug; Tom could only ever copulate with his wife when she put on an act like a kitchen maid in heat for the butcher's boy (quick, quick, we can do it under the stairs); and Baby is a greedy and conceited little bitch. So why, in this company,' he said to Piero, 'it should worry you or anybody else that you happen to smile like a seventy-year-old street walker I cannot begin to imagine.'

In *The traveller* Simon drew up an equally candid inventory of friends' and acquaintances' misdeeds and shortcomings, defending himself on the same grounds as Fielding: however unflattering, it was the truth. Most reviewers doubted this, but Simon's attitude to reviews was, 'Don't read them. *Measure* them,' and by this computation *The traveller* was one of his most successful books. For three weeks sales were brisk and then the Marquess of Abergavenny's nephew and heir, Guy Nevill, issued a writ, whereupon all unsold copies had to be withdrawn.

Nevill, who subsequently died of AIDS, strongly objected to Simon's version of how, at Blond's villa on Corfu, Lord and Lady Glenconner came to be served with a dish containing semen. ('A vital fluid,' said Simon. 'Never done me any harm.') Nevill's action disconcerted Simon's publisher, Century Hutchinson, who had been assured by the author that there were no grounds for libel in his book. Naturally he could substantiate what he had written? Well, no, he couldn't. It had not happened *quite* like that, although the story was true 'in essence'.

At this, Century Hutchinson caved in. *The traveller* was pulped and the case settled out of court, with Nevill receiving £15,000. Meanwhile Anthony Blond and Andrew McCall, both of whom Simon had cloaked in the flimsiest of disguises, noted this precedent and, late in the day, issued writs of their own. In due course they too received damages for the 'distress' and 'disgust' they said Simon had caused them, this despite Blond's having reviewed the book in the *Spectator*, an unusual preliminary on the part of a prospective plaintiff.

Readers have been told of Simon's lingering animus against Andrew McCall, whose portrait is etched in vitriol; but nothing has been said of his falling out with Anthony Blond, whom he depicts as a pretentious clown. There was no single issue that caused the breach (which has since been healed), rather an accumulation of grievances on Simon's part for which *The traveller* provided some means of redress. He hadn't, he told me, deliberately set out to vilify Andrew and Anthony, 'but late middle-age is a time of bitterness and spleen, of envy, resentment and sulk. And looking back all I could remember was a series of disputes, at work and at play, in which I invariably came off worse. So I'm afraid it was paying off old scores time.'

Authors, as Blond himself noted in *The Publishing Game*,[3] 'work alone … and they are prone to all the neuroses of lonely people'. Hitherto Simon had seemed resistant to these neuroses ('I can honestly say of myself, *Nunquam minus solus quam cum solus* – Never less lonely than when alone'); but *The traveller*, its critics said, was the product of a deranged mind. Could that double dose of anaesthetic have been to blame?

Guy Nevill's old girlfriend, Philippa Pullar, thought so. Although furious at what Simon had written about her – 'It's true I drank the bath essence by mistake, but I have never, ever, sucked my thumb' – she was disposed to be charitable, having had a bad experience with anaesthetics herself. 'Like Simon I was a very heavy drinker. Then I had a long operation, following which my memory was poor and I was apt to confuse fact with fantasy. I'm sure that was Simon's problem when he wrote that dreadful book.'

I consulted two anaesthetists about this. One, met casually at a party, said Ms Pullar was entitled to her opinion, if only because medical science

[3] Jonathan Cape, 1971.

was unable to determine what effect, if any, anaesthetics had on the brain. But, he added, 'we do know that alcohol destroys brain cells!' His colleague, Dr David Saunders of the Association of Anaesthetists, agreed that you couldn't entirely exclude the possibility of after-effects, and indeed people were apt to say, 'Granny hasn't been the same since her anaesthetic.' But he knew of no evidence to support claims that heavy drinkers were more vulnerable to a general anaesthetic than anyone else.

Although he was not personally liable for any damages, Simon was sore at the demise of *The traveller* and astonished at how much offence it had caused. 'How very self-important people become as they get older. Self-important, priggish, unctuous and puritanical. They start to worry about what posterity will make of them. As if that mattered! But in any case, virtue stands a better chance of being remembered if it is preceded by vice. The whore who becomes a Duchess, or even an Empress, like Justinian's wife Theodosia. So perhaps I've done them a favour after all.'

I myself think that if *The traveller* and its consequences prove anything, it is not how 'cruelly insensitive' Simon could be, but how naive. 'I don't care what people write about me, so long as I have the reciprocal right,' he would say, as if that settled everything. But there was a funny side to his naiveté. I particularly like the story of how he was invited to submit an 'appropriate' article to the *Tatler*, so he wrote a piece about what a tiresome instrument the telephone was and how women would yack away on it all day long. It was only 'on reflection' that he realised why they rejected it.

*

Simon had other worries besides libel writs. Once again he was deeply in the red, having run up large debts on each of the four credit cards he carried. He also owed his bank a five-figure sum, this being a consequence of the generous overdraft facility to which holders of Gold Amex cards were automatically entitled at Lloyds.

Simon accused Amex and Lloyds of sharp practice. 'They dangle money before you, so naturally you grab what you can.' But as Julian Spurrier reminded him, only irresponsible proles were supposed to succumb to such blandishments. 'He conceded this. It was the sort of ironic reproof he relished. And when I insisted he hand over all his credit cards, he did so without a murmur. "You must always pay for your pleasures," he said.'

Thanks to Spurrier's skill and diplomacy Simon steered clear of Carey Street. But he had to resign from both his clubs,[4] and he had also to cash in two insurance policies at considerably below their maturity value. Had he been relying on novels and memoirs for his bread and butter – let alone

[4] Simon was a member of Brooks's as well as the Reform; he and Dickie Muir used to play backgammon there.

the jam which he had come to take for granted – the outlook would have been bleak.

> 'I've got nothing left to say,' Fielding said. 'I haven't had for years. But one learns a lot of tricks as one grows old in the profession, so one can go on for a long time dolling up the same old thing to look fresh and attractive. Beef dressed as veal (like all veal these days). But sooner or later one gets rumbled, and anyway I've lost patience.' (*The Troubadour*)

Fielding is rescued by a legacy. But the only way Simon could hope to put money in his purse was by writing for television. That well, at least, had not run dry.

CHAPTER TWENTY

An impure mind is a perpetual feast.
Logan Pearsall Smith

So bloody good luck to you, mate,
That you weren't born too late
For at least a chance of happiness,
Before unchangeable crappiness
Spreads over all the land ....
Kingsley Amis, *Ode to Me*

One of Simon's neighbours at Walmer was the author and critic, Julian Symons. They had first met through Nina Bawden, whose sons had been taught at Tormore by Myles. Symons had been dismissive about *Alms* in the *New Statesman*, but Simon did not hold this against him, particularly since Symons had acknowledged his talent for 'melodrama' and 'wild lubricious comedy', the very qualities he demonstrated when dramatising Symons' Victorian whodunit, *The Blackheath Poisonings*.

'Julian had no say in commissioning me, but we went to a screening together and I think he was pleased with the result. It was nothing like as subtle as the book, of course, because the makers wanted as big an audience as possible,[1] and in any case television simply cannot convey the nuances and ambiguities that were Julian's hallmark. What you need on television is a mini-crisis every five minutes otherwise the viewers get bored. It's a very superficial medium which is probably why, in the opinion of people like Julian, I am well fitted to write for it!'

Readers may recall that Simon's opening scene, a very noisy bonk, earned Central Television a rap over the knuckles from the Broadcasting Standards Council. Strange to relate he was at first a little reluctant to ladle on the sauce. Perhaps he had been unnerved by what people said about *The traveller*; at any rate Anne-Marie Casey, the young script editor, said she had to ask for 'more skirts up', the first and only time Simon can have received such a request.

Anne-Marie was 'vastly entertained by Simon's politically incorrect comments and his uninhibited, almost 18th-century approach to life'. She remembered the 'deathly hush' that fell over a busy tea room in Deal as

[1] They got 11 million.

Simon described how he was 'unblocked' in hospital and what happened when he went for his final check-up afterwards. 'He was frank about needing money too. He'd phone up and say, "I've just had the Electricity bill, dear, so how about a bit on account? You can send the cheque directly to me. Sebastian [Born: Simon's agent] has okayed it." '

Simon made an equally vivid impression on Anne-Marie's friend, Nickie Lund, the script editor on his next assignment, a black comedy inspired by the De Stempel case[2] called *Mummy Knows Best*. Nickie had done her homework; even so she was quite unprepared either for Simon or the set-up she found at Walmer.

'I knew there were some nice old town houses in Deal,' said Nickie, 'and from what I'd heard about Simon I assumed my taxi would take me to one of them. Instead we arrived at a close that was straight out of *Brookside*. What made it even more incongruous was that instead of milk bottles on the doorstep I found a case of wine.'

Once inside Nickie was struck by how masculine the atmosphere was, 'What I'd call "a den". The walls were covered with prints of cricket matches and colleges and schools, and the mantelpiece was full of school calendars and fixture cards. There were a couple of very deep armchairs and a rather battered sofa in the middle of the living room, with a round dining table at one end and a large partner's desk, which we worked at, at the other. Simon led me to believe that both the desk and the table were priceless antiques, "So do be careful with your coffee, dear." (That was another surprise: absolutely basic instant out of a jar beside the kettle. No wonder he always added a little something to it!) He was very houseproud, always rinsing the cups straight afterwards. But I got the feeling that this was because it was somebody else's house, and that otherwise he might not have been so meticulous.'

Apart from a scattering of books, most of them marked with postcards, a painting by Adam and a drawing of Esther on the stairs ('She's looking at me still!' he would say), very little of what visitors saw downstairs belonged to Simon. He was more in evidence upstairs, particularly in the loo, where Nickie once counted eleven different bottles of mouthwash. Peeping into his bedroom, which was where he usually worked, she noticed 'a lot more stuff from the chemist's – pills, potions, ointments and so on, plus bottles of cologne and hair tonic. But it was a rather impersonal room, I thought, almost cell-like. The only splash of colour came from his books.'

(Simon's books were piled higgledy-piggledy on three deep bookshelves which ran the length of one wall. The ones you noticed first were the red and green Loeb editions of the Classics, most of them well thumbed, because it was Simon's habit to spend a half hour or so each day reading

[2] Baroness De Stempel, her ex-husband and their two children were in 1990 sent to prison for stealing money and property worth £500,000 from her rich, elderly and senile aunt.

aloud from a Classical text. Other old favourites were Dante, Milton and the Victorian triumvirate of Tennyson, Browning and Arnold.)

Like many before her Nickie Lund was pleasantly surprised to discover that Simon was not nearly so snobbish in person as he sometimes appeared in print. 'A bit of an intellectual snob perhaps, but otherwise I got the distinct impression that if he despised anyone it was the chattering classes. He told me about a cricket match he'd helped arrange[3] in which Harold Pinter played, and how appalled he'd been at the manner of Pinter and Lady Antonia, who behaved, he said, "as if they expected half Fleet Street to be there, and were rather annoyed that they weren't".

'Anything that smacked of literary pretension riled him. He said he knew of writers "so self-regarding" that they entered into "carefully-crafted" correspondence with other, equally self-regarding writers, each letter being written with an eye to eventual publication. "People should always remember," he said, "that novelists are professional liars." '

There were three things about working with Simon that really struck Nickie. 'First, how "un-ageist" he was. All the other older writers I'd worked with had been very condescending. Simon treated me as an equal. "What do *you* think she'd say at this point?" And if he liked my suggestion, in it would go.' (Conversely he was, said Anne-Marie, 'very irritated by script conferences at which "everyone including the wardrobe mistress" had their say. "Could somebody *please* tell me what's been decided?" ')

'Secondly, I remember how careful he was to keep me informed of his movements. If he was going away, even for a day or two, he'd send me a postcard to say where he would be, and for how long. And thirdly, his scripts! Not the dialogue, which was brilliant, but the lay-out. His old typewriter simply couldn't cope, and consequently I'm afraid he was not the most popular writer we employed with our secretaries.'

Sadly, Channel 4 decided against proceeding with *Mummy Knows Best*. 'They said they were afraid of libel, but I'm sure there was more to it than that because at a very early stage we'd decided not to try and reconstruct the De Stempel case but simply to give Simon a free hand. I think that was the problem. He cooked up too rich a stew even for Channel 4's strong stomach. The opening scene had me in fits. Two old lesbians in a Morris Minor Traveller who become so excited by the gear stick that they drive over a cliff!'

Simon was convinced that most of what he wrote latterly had little appeal for the young, but the very positive response of Nickie and Anne-Marie suggests otherwise. He would have enjoyed hearing the gurgle of pleasure in Anne-Marie's voice as she told me of her last conversation with him, in which reference was made to the holiday she and Nickie had taken together. ' "Yes," ' said Simon, in a voice at once wistful and suggestive, ' "I often think about you and Nickie on holiday." '

[3] It was the Trogs against an XI raised by Dickie Muir, for a side stake of £250.

*

In 1994 Simon's macabre Venetian novella, *The Islands of Sorrow*, appeared. Since he was grateful to the publishers, The Winged Lion, for commissioning him at a time when he was persona non grata everywhere else, Simon agreed to do a little publicity, in the course of which he reaffirmed his commitment to 'order':

> I really do like order. I would happily settle for not much happening, even a degree of boredom, if it would avoid disorder.

By 'disorder' Simon understood any unexpected interruption to his routine, even if this promised to be pleasurable. Charles Sprawson, a former pupil of Myles, was by no means the only old friend to be turned away because Simon was not prepared to 'down tools' at short notice.

When Simon first moved in with Peter Budden, Peter's nephew Simon was living there as well. Then Simon Budden left to get married, which meant that most of the time Simon had the house to himself. He generally rose at about 8.15, breakfasted off grapefruit, toast and, as often as not, a large glass of milk, and then, the *Daily Telegraph* having arrived, turned to the racing pages and ticked off his selections for the day. By 10 at the latest these would have been phoned over and he would sit down to work, 'not raising my head, except for a pee, until 1.30.'

After a light lunch with at most a half pint of lager or what remained of last night's wine, he would either doze off over a book or, if a horse of his was running or a Test match was on, watch (Peter's) television. Weather permitting he would venture out between 3 and 4, to post a letter and do some shopping at the local corner shop ('the Indiana'). Sometimes he would take a turn in the graveyard of St Mary's, the nearby Norman church where the Duke of Wellington worshipped when Warden of the Cinque Ports.

At about 6.30 Simon would go upstairs for his bath, following which he would have something like a large vodka and orange or a Campari and soda. On Tuesdays he generally dined out with Michael Webb and it was rare for him not to have at least one other dinner engagement during the week – 'after all, one's lived down here for half one's life'. If Peter was about he could count on some 'good, plain home cooking'; otherwise, like thousands of other single persons, he had come to 'bless the name of Marks and Spencer'.

If there was a high profile Classic serial on television like *Middlemarch* or *Pride and Prejudice* Simon would generally watch it, although he always insisted that you'd be better off reading the book. 'I want you to make it plain,' he said to me, 'that while I am not ashamed of what I have written for television, I would far, far prefer to be remembered, if at all, for my novels.' He would allow that you saw good documentaries on television and enjoyed programmes like *Newsnight*. 'But think of what television has to answer for: Esther Rantzen, *Stars on Sunday*, the dissemination of ugly accents and even uglier behaviour. How glad I am to have grown up before it arrived.'

Simon was very conscious of belonging, albeit by the skin of his teeth, to 'Our Age', that generation nominated by Sir Maurice Bowra and codified by Noel Annan in his eponymous history.[4] After reading this, Simon sent his old friend a congratulatory post-card:

> One does yearn for this kind of thing in our NEW AGE of imbecility, unction and cant. I find Greek and Latin lit. a very helpful antidote. Thank God (& King's) for a Classical education.

'A Classical education': not a day passed but Simon gave thanks for this. It overrode any other loyalty he acknowledged; and loyalty, in Noel Annan's opinion 'the supreme asset of a public school education', was Simon's strongest suit. What did he think he had learnt from Greek and Latin literature? Civilised values. And what were these values? At the very beginning of his literary career he summarised them in the *TLS*. I think it is worth quoting the last paragraph and the sentence that precedes it since together they constitute Simon's credo.

> [For] a person who believes wholeheartedly in the teaching of the Ancients will believe not only in pleasure but in the proper and delicate ordering of pleasure.
>
> He will believe in tolerance – which is to say he will not believe, like the Churches on the one hand or the Communists on the other, that he possesses a monopoly of truth. He will believe in the use of reason and practical method, being disinclined, like some MP's, to countenance a foolish course of action because it sorts well with the complacency or bigotry of his neighbours. He will see the good in democracy, its freedom and its hope, but he will also realise that democracy gives a loud voice to fools (an unpopular and neglected truth) and be prepared accordingly. He will despise superstitions, except insofar as they are merely amusing or decorative (the gods, after all, were a great literary convenience); and he will reject both enthusiasms and faiths, if only because of the ridiculous postures, whether mental or physical, which they require. He will admire courage, and will not be so foolish as to decry bodily or athletic excellence. He will be curious and will travel. He will not despise men for their colour, taking diversity to be one of the world's greatest gifts, nor will he forbid a man his creed – provided only that no attempt is

[4] *Our Age* (Weidenfeld & Nicolson, 1990).

made to force that creed upon himself. Above all he will not fear death, knowing that it is preferable to senility, and that it will either resemble sleep or will else reveal some new facet of existence which, as a man of curiosity, he will be delighted to examine. Such men are few; but few as they are, they play a civilising part in the affairs of the nation out of all proportion to their modest numbers, and they had their knowledge from the letters of Greece and Rome. (7.8.59)

The nearest Simon came to 'playing a civilising part in the affairs of the nation' was in writing articles like this and books like *The English Gentleman*. Nor did he always adhere to the values he so admired (for a rational man he was surprisingly superstitious, forever touching wood). But without reference to what he understood by a Classical education you cannot hope to see the point of him. He is, in the words of the distinguished Latinist, Professor Jasper Griffin, 'a Classicist's Classicist'.

*

Simon's New Year resolution for 1992 was 'Never to come to London again in my life (except to watch cricket at Lord's).' Entry to the pavilion at Lord's, that last bastion of the Forsytes, was one privilege he was not prepared to forgo in the interests of economy – 'though each year the shades become more oppressive'. Otherwise he endorsed Gibbon's objections to the metropolis,

> ... the noisy and expensive scene of crowds without company and dissipation without pleasure.

Even as a young man Simon never really had the measure of London. There is a story that in the days when he was lodging with Ian Murray he picked up a tart at a West End club and went home with her. Emerging some hours later he hailed a cab and asked to be taken to 71 Cromwell Road.

'Sure that's where you want, guv?'

'Of course I'm sure.'

'Well, I think you ought to know you're standing outside number 70.'

'Exile from Rome' was only briefly a hardship, indeed Simon soon came to think of it as an escape. But was 'a boarding house in Deal' the answer? Peter Dixon thought not. And he was by no means alone in arguing that Simon had spent too much of his writing life cut off from society – 'or at any rate what most of us understand by the term. If you are going to live on your own, with only prep school masters for company, then unless you're Balzac it's no use writing about the ways of the world.'

Dixon's point is valid, I think, when you look at Simon's later fiction. By then the rich vein of material he had accumulated as a young man was exhausted, and all he could do was recycle the end product. But I don't believe it made the slightest difference to his television work, since all that required was technique, which he had in abundance. There is also the matter of Simon's 'daemon', that recalcitrant imp he blamed for his youthful excesses. In London and, as we have heard, in Brighton, it could still get up to mischief; in Deal it was tamed.

*

One of the few arguments for marriage that Simon would allow was 'having someone to keep an eye on you as you get old'. Who was going to keep an eye on him? Not Peter Budden, kind as he was. And not his sister Robin either, 'because although she has been a good mother, I do not see her in the role of responsible housekeeper, still less, if it came to it – which God forbid – of nurse'.

What about a Roman solution? 'You mean suicide? Only with a foolproof pill. I haven't the guts to slit my wrists like Somerset Lloyd-James. Think what would happen if you botched it, or the pill didn't work.'

Simon had begun seriously to consider his future after his prostate operation, but it was a chance meeting in 1990 with an exact contemporary of his at school, Lt.Col. Ian MacDonald, that directed his course. MacDonald was, and is, Bursar of Sutton's Hospital,[5] an alms house for impoverished old gentlemen that occupies what remains of the London Charterhouse in Charterhouse Square. Simon was impoverished. And although in his own estimation no gentleman, he could point to the original constitution which said preference would be given to, among others, 'decrepit or old Captaynes either at Sea or Land' and 'Souldiers maymed or ympotent'.

Colonel MacDonald thought Simon had a good case. But he pointed out that although 'ympotent', Simon was neither very old nor particularly decrepit. Consequently were he to be accepted he would have to wait his turn – which might not be for some years yet. So it proved. Simon was not admitted until December 12th, 1995, shortly before his 68th birthday.

As one of Sutton's Pensioners, Brother Raven (to give him his new title) is guaranteed 'a full library and a full stomach and peace and quiet in which to enjoy them both'. For although a stone's throw from Smithfield, the London Charterhouse is as tranquil and secluded as the University colleges it so closely resembles – much more tranquil in fact, since tourists are rare and there are no undergraduates. Meanwhile Lord's and the House of Lords, at both of which he will find friendly faces, are not twenty minutes in a taxi.

At the time of writing Simon is engaged on a 'Plain Man's Guide to

[5] After Sir Thomas Sutton (1532-1611), who also founded Charterhouse School.

Dante', for which he has yet to find a publisher. He still does occasional treatments for television, but says he would now far rather read than write – 'except as a hobby: I still enjoy translating Greek and Latin verse'. I believe he has more than earned his retirement and I pray that he has joy of it. But given his fear of infirmity and his approval of those who scorn to stay too long at the feast, I hope he will not take offence if I sign off with the last two lines of Kingsley Amis's *Ode to Me*, quoted above:

> So here's wishing you many more years,
> But not all that many. Cheers!

BOOKS BY SIMON RAVEN

Novels
The Feathers of Death, 1959
Brother Cain, 1959
Doctors Wear Scarlet, 1960
Close of Play, 1962
The Roses of Picardie, 1980
An Inch of Fortune, 1980
September Castle, 1983
The Islands of Sorrow, 1994

Alms for Oblivion sequence
Fielding Gray, 1967
Sound the Retreat, 1971
The Sabre Squadron, 1966
The Rich Pay Late, 1964
Friends in Low Places, 1965
The Judas Boy, 1968
Places Where They Sing, 1970
Come Like Shadows, 1972
Bring Forth the Body, 1974
The Survivors, 1976

The First Born of Egypt sequence
Morning Star, 1984
The Face of the Waters, 1985
Before the Cock Crow, 1986
New Seed For Old, 1988
Blood of My Bone, 1989
In the Image of God, 1990
The Troubadour, 1992

Belles Lettres
The English Gentleman, 1961
Boys Will Be Boys, 1963
The Fortunes of Fingel, 1976
The Old School, 1986

Plays
Royal Foundation and Other
Plays, 1965

Memoirs
Shadows on the Grass, 1982
The Old Gang, 1988
Bird of Ill Omen, 1989
Is There Anybody There? Said
The Traveller, 1991

Index

Simon Raven's activities have been indexed under the people, places, institutions and themes to which they relate, i.e. not in a series of subheadings under Raven, Simon. His name, wherever appropriate, is indicated by the initials SR. Page numbers in italic indicate that information is in a footnote.